COACHING & MENTORING RESEARCH

Sara Miller McCune founded SAGE Publishing in 1965 to support the dissemination of usable knowledge and educate a global community. SAGE publishes more than 1000 journals and over 800 new books each year, spanning a wide range of subject areas. Our growing selection of library products includes archives, data, case studies and video. SAGE remains majority owned by our founder and after her lifetime will become owned by a charitable trust that secures the company's continued independence.

Los Angeles | London | New Delhi | Singapore | Washington DC | Melbourne

LINDSAY G. OADES
CHRISTINE L. SIOKOU
GAVIN R. SLEMP

COACHING & MENTORING RESEARCH

A PRACTICAL GUIDE

Los Angeles | London | New Delhi
Singapore | Washington DC | Melbourne

Los Angeles | London | New Delhi
Singapore | Washington DC | Melbourne

SAGE Publications Ltd
1 Oliver's Yard
55 City Road
London EC1Y 1SP

SAGE Publications Inc.
2455 Teller Road
Thousand Oaks, California 91320

SAGE Publications India Pvt Ltd
B 1/I 1 Mohan Cooperative Industrial Area
Mathura Road
New Delhi 110 044

SAGE Publications Asia-Pacific Pte Ltd
3 Church Street
#10-04 Samsung Hub
Singapore 049483

Editor: Susannah Trefgarne
Assistant editor: Talulah Hall
Production editor: Rachel Burrows
Copyeditor: Diana Chambers
Proofreader: Brian McDowell
Indexer: Gary Kirby
Marketing manager: Samantha Glorioso
Cover design: Wendy Scott
Typeset by: C&M Digitals (P) Ltd, Chennai, India
Printed in the UK

Library of Congress Control Number: 2018964718

British Library Cataloguing in Publication data

A catalogue record for this book is available from
the British Library

ISBN 978-1-4739-1296-0
ISBN 978-1-4739-1297-7 (pbk)

At SAGE we take sustainability seriously. Most of our products are printed in the UK using responsibly sourced
papers and boards. When we print overseas we ensure sustainable papers are used as measured by the PREPS
grading system. We undertake an annual audit to monitor our sustainability.

This book is dedicated to its second author, Dr Christine L. Siokou, a vivacious and intelligent young person, who died suddenly in late April 2017. Despite this loss, we completed the book in her honour, as Christine would wish for you to get out there and make a difference, particularly for the disadvantaged. In honour of Christine Siokou, Lindsay G. Oades penned the poem below.

The most gracious of gifts

Bouncy breazy but brash be nay

Frolicsome yet fierce

Jousting for justice

The most ardent of allies

… with lampoonery corralled only for self

The most gracious of gifts

Boundless be yours

CONTENTS

ABOUT THE AUTHORS

Lindsay G. Oades PhD is Professor of Positive Psychology and Director of the Centre for Positive Psychology at the University of Melbourne, Australia, which pioneers new approaches in applied positive psychology including coaching. He has taught, supervised and mentored numerous research students in psychology, mental health, business and education, including multiple coaching projects involving 15 completed doctoral students. Lindsay oversaw the first ever randomised controlled trial of life coaching and served for five years on the Scientific Advisory Council at the Institute of Coaching affiliated with Harvard University. Lindsay combines a background in philosophy with research methodology in psychology, including qualitative and quantitative methods, to assist the journey of new researchers in applied contexts.

Christine L. Siokou PhD was Research Fellow at the Centre for Positive Psychology at the University of Melbourne, Australia. Christine had an undergraduate degree in Sociology and Politics from the University of Melbourne and a PhD in Public Health from Curtin University. She had expertise in systems thinking and methods, public health including applications in harm reduction, with a focus on qualitative methodology. She was instrumental in leading the development of systems thinking linked to positive psychology and well-being at the Centre for Positive Psychology. Previously she was a post-doctoral research fellow in the Systems Science and Implementation Capacity at The Australian Prevention Partnership Centre.

Dr. Gavin R. Slemp (Psy.D, BA, Hons) is a registered organisational psychologist (AHPRA), a research psychologist, and a senior lecturer in the Centre for Positive Psychology at the University of Melbourne, Australia. Gavin's research interests include the predictors of autonomous work motivation and employee well-being, including job crafting, leader autonomy support, personality, and health interventions, including coaching and mindfulness. Gavin has expertise primarily in quantitative research methods and, since March 2017, he has been serving as co-editor of the *International Journal of Wellbeing*. In addition to his research activity, Gavin is the Director of Undergraduate Teaching at the Centre for Positive Psychology, and Program Coordinator of undergraduate offerings in the Melbourne Graduate School of Education, University of Melbourne. In these roles, he manages and leads subjects that have been voted as amongst the best at the University of Melbourne.

PREFACE

People know what they do; they frequently know why they do what they do; but what they don't know is what what they do does.

(Foucault, cited in Dreyfus & Rainbow 1983)

Our aim for this book is to enable you to understand the role of research in coaching and mentoring contexts, the several phases of the research process, and an overview of commonly used quantitative and qualitative methods used in the coaching and mentoring contexts. We use a reflexive approach; from a mentoring perspective, the author team has significant experience in research in general, research on coaching, the practice of coaching, the practice of mentoring, and also teaching and being students of postgraduate education. From a coaching perspective, our key message is *use the methods and processes of coaching to learn and do research*. We believe the research process involves a series of important decisions that impact each other in a non-linear fashion. We address these decisions as a sequence in Chapter 6. To assist with these decisions, each chapter is structured around the well-known GROW structure from coaching sessions. To refresh, GROW stands for Goal, Reality, Options and What next? Each chapter starts with the Goal, a clear statement of the learning outcome for the chapter. The Reality is examined in general relating to the topic, and then for you personally. The Options are chosen from our experience as research supervisors, i.e., what the key decisions are that researchers make when planning and doing their research. As we are coaches and mentors, we believe in the magic of the question, the socratic questioning style. Hence, every chapter is subtitled with a question, and the personal learning activities in each chapter use questions addressed directly to you.

Each chapter requires you to do activities, just as a coach may do during a session. The What next (or Wrap-up) leaves you with things to do, relevant to your situation and includes a Further reading and resources section.

There are so many good resources on how to do research. The role of this book is specific to coaching and mentoring research, but by using a coaching method itself, it guides you through the process and refers you where to go, rather than trying to include every detail in this introductory research book. This is also aided by shorter chapters for you to dip in and out of as needed and not necessarily read from beginning to end, but also to go back and forward following your personal journey.

Part I of the book introduces coaching and mentoring research. The book commences with the important question of 'Why do research on coaching and mentoring?' While some readers may answer that they do so as it is a course requirement, we encourage you to think more deeply and longer term about the important role of research for the growing area of coaching and mentoring. For intervention-based research, we introduce the distinction between process, outcome and implementation/fidelity. The Appendix illustrates this difference and is referred to in several locations across the book.

We deliberately ask you to think early about the 'big issues' of conducting research – that is, why bother doing your project and what are your assumptions about knowledge with reference to 'ologies' and 'isms'. We encourage you to think intentionally about building a research team and avoiding common pitfalls made by new researchers.

Part II is an important section of the book, providing a road map from conception to conclusion of the research endeavour. While there are numerous methods, designs and analyses, it makes sense to commence with your viewpoint, enabling you to locate your current challenge in the phases of the research process. The aim is then to help you locate which aspects of methods in Part III and Part IV of the book are most relevant to you for your current purpose.

Part III examines introductory quantitative methodology, methods, designs and analyses. Rather than commence with the standard and exhaustive, and sometimes exhausting, research methodology and statistics, this section helps you to understand the most commonly and appropriately used quantitative methods in coaching research and mentoring. You will be challenged directly with the question, 'Why quantitative methods?' – a core skill in selecting methodology, rather than just using methods. Following on from Part I, you will also be encouraged to reflect upon approaches to knowledge – i.e., epistemology – when considering methodology. This requires you to loop back to Chapter 5.

Part IV brings you to the important area of qualitative methods. In addition to exploring qualitative methods commonly used in coaching and mentoring, there is also a chapter that directly addresses programme evaluation and action research, which is often used by coaching and mentoring practitioners. The final chapter addresses the important and increasing use of mixed methods and how this approach may be beneficial for the coach or mentor researcher.

This book can be considered a companion to your research process, to which the student can return to map your journey. We wish you well with your research, learning and doing.

Professor Lindsay G. Oades, Dr Christine L. Siokou and Dr Gavin R. Slemp

PART I

BECOMING A RESEARCHER IN COACHING AND MENTORING

BENEFITS OF RESEARCH

1

WHY DO RESEARCH ON COACHING AND MENTORING?

LEARNING OUTCOMES

In completing this chapter and related exercises, you will be able to:

1. define types of coaching and mentoring research;

2. describe the current status of coaching and mentoring research;

3. state the benefits of conducting research into coaching and mentoring;

4. describe what other areas of research (theory and evidence) may be beneficial to assisting the development of coaching and mentoring research.

WHAT IS THE CURRENT REALITY IN COACHING AND MENTORING RESEARCH?

Research and acquiring knowledge go hand in hand. The OECD and UNESCO in 2001 defined research as comprising 'creative work undertaken on a systematic basis in order to increase the stock of knowledge, including knowledge of humans, culture and society, and the use of this stock of knowledge to devise new applications'. Research uses systematic processes and tools to establish or confirm facts, reaffirm the results of previous work, solve new or existing problems, confirm or disconfirm propositions, or to develop new theories.

Research allows us to build on existing work in order to generate new concepts, methodologies or understandings that advance human knowledge.

Why does knowledge advancement matter for coaching and mentoring? Well, without this, there would be no way of really knowing what 'works' and what doesn't with respect to coaching and mentoring, or what outcomes we can expect from particular programmes. There would be no way of understanding the extent to which people change as a result of coaching or mentoring, or how to improve existing coaching and mentoring practices. We would have no understanding of whether current practices contain any unhelpful or harmful side-effects, or whether different people respond differently to different types of programmes, or whether different policies support or inhibit coaching or mentoring practices. Importantly, there would be no way of understanding the changes that take place during the coaching or mentoring process, and how these changes explain observed outcomes to result from the coaching or mentoring experience. Ultimately, without research, there would be no reliable or valid knowledge that we can use to build theory and, in turn, inform practice. Hence, this book is about empowering you with the tools and skills of a researcher, so that you can go about conducting your own coaching and/or mentoring research.

While we clearly recognize that coaching and mentoring are indeed different, from a research perspective they are very similar in the challenges they face. For this reason, they are discussed within this volume side-by-side. Coaching and mentoring may occur in many contexts (e.g., think of the adjective often placed before coaching, such as 'life', 'health', 'executive', 'performance'), and we remain relatively silent on how coaching and mentoring might differ depending on idiosyncrasies between these different areas. While all represent different domains in which coaching or mentoring could take place, the essential concepts, methodologies and methods we cover will apply across these different contexts. With that in mind, let's start with some fundamental definitions of coaching and mentoring before moving to research.

Definitions of Coaching and Mentoring

Coaching can be defined as an action-oriented, collaborative process that seeks to facilitate goal-attainment, self-directed learning, and/or enhance performance in the coachee's personal or professional life (Spence and Grant, 2007). It is a way of thinking, managing, treating people, and a way of being that can lead to transformation in people's lives.

Mentoring is a process for the informal transmission of knowledge, social capital and the psychosocial support perceived by the recipient as relevant to work, career or professional development; mentoring entails informal communication, usually face-to-face and during a sustained period of time, between a person who is perceived to have greater relevant knowledge, wisdom or experience (the mentor) and a person who is perceived to have less (the protégé) (Bozeman and Feeney, 2007).

To help map out the different types of coaching and mentoring research, we propose the four-part schema summarized in Table 1.1. This can be used to locate four different types of coaching and mentoring research, with the first three types assuming that research is examining an active coaching or mentoring intervention – that is, a coaching or mentoring intervention is actively occurring and participants are currently participating in this programme, either as a coach/mentor or a coachee/protégé.

Table 1.1   Different types of coaching and mentoring research

Types of research

1. **Process research:** Examining the process of coaching/mentoring, which may include the relationship between coach and coachee/mentor and mentee or the personal experiences over time of the coach/mentor or coachee/mentee. An example of a process study may be videoing the interaction of the relationship between coach and coachee and looking for 'turning points' in coaching. Process research often adopts qualitative methodology, but it is also a focus of quantitative methodology.

2. **Outcome research:** Examines what outcomes are achieved by a coaching/mentoring intervention, or what predicts desired or undesired coaching/mentoring outcomes. An example of an outcome study is a randomized controlled trial that shows that a coaching or mentoring intervention has had an effect. Outcome research often, but not necessarily, adopts quantitative methodologies. Outcome research may be further classified in terms of whether it focuses on coach/mentor factors, relationship factors or coachee/mentee factors, each of which may predict better outcomes.

3. **Implementation, quality and fidelity research:** Examines how coaching interventions or practices may be implemented by individuals, teams or organizations. Fidelity refers to how well/closely an intervention matches what is meant to be delivered. An example of an implementation study may examine the best way to implement coaching across a whole department. For example, there may be factors that make coaching/mentoring relationships more or less effective, such as frequency of meetings, length of meetings, communication mechanisms between meetings, and so forth.

4. **Non-intervention research:** Other research that does not assume an intervention – for example, professional research that explores who is using coaching or mentoring: the coaching market place or industry regulation.

Because the fields of mentoring research and, in particular, coaching research are developing endeavours, it is useful and possibly necessary to borrow theories and evidence from other areas in order to inform the research process. This does not mean that coaching and mentoring are not their own areas of investigation, but rather it suggests that each may be informed by existing and related fields. Science is ultimately a cumulative exercise and it is necessary to use knowledge that is developed from related fields to inform the research process. The following box provides an example of this for coaching research.

CHALLENGES IN COACHING RESEARCH

Coaching is not yet a mature field of study and care should be taken not to overstate what is known from the existing literature. If validation of your research or practice is important and cannot be gained from the existing knowledge base, the Self-Determination Theory literature may be useful to draw upon. There have been relatively few attempts to provide a detailed theoretical account of what happens in coaching or to build our understanding about why coaching works in certain contexts (Spence and Grant, 2012). It is our hope that researchers and practitioners will build on and continue to develop new hypotheses and research studies against the backdrop of the well-established and relevant theories of well-being and human functioning.

Nonetheless, while both coaching and mentoring are developing fields, they are growing and neither can now be considered 'new' because consistent research efforts have been pursued in each field for a decade or more. For example, in recent years, comprehensive reviews that synthesize the existing available research are emerging on both coaching (e.g., Theeboom, Beersmam & Fidell, 2014) and mentoring (e.g., Eby et al., 2008, 2013) in the workplace context. This is generally a sign that research is beginning to mature because integrative reviews, such as these, require available research studies to use as inputs. We touch on these later in Chapter 9 as we explore literature review as a research method.

 Activity

What is your current reality related to coaching and mentoring research?

To learn more about coaching and mentoring research, it is useful to explore the current reality: in this case, what you already know about coaching and mentoring research.

On a blank page, please answer the following questions.

1. Why is coaching/mentoring important?
2. Why is coaching/mentoring *research* important – that is, why do we need it?
3. In addition to obvious things such as course requirements, what are you trying to achieve by doing coaching or mentoring research?

What are your options in conducting coaching and mentoring research?

Before leaping into a study, it will be useful to know 'what type' of coaching or mentoring research you intend to conduct. This can be done before choosing an exact topic, sample or method, and it can also be done after these stages as well. Table 1.2 builds upon Table 1.1, and is designed to prompt you to identify for yourself different possible advantages and disadvantages of the different types of research. This activity will also be useful in helping you to establish your current level of knowledge across each of these types of research.

Using the four options from Table 1.2, list a one-sentence advantage and a one-sentence disadvantage of each one, explaining why you personally think it would be valuable to do research in that area. For further examples of these types of research, see the Appendix.

Table 1.2   Possible advantages and disadvantages of the different types of coaching and mentoring research

	Advantages	Disadvantages
Process research		
Outcome research		
Implementation, quality and fidelity research		
Non-intervention research		

WHAT NEXT?

Reflect on your answers regarding advantages and disadvantages from the above exercise. Explore the Appendix. Then, ask yourself: do I wish to/are you able to do intervention or non-intervention research? If you are deciding on intervention research, consider process or implementation research also – it does not necessarily mean that you need to do outcome research. While the coaching and mentoring research area needs more outcome research, your time frame and resources may mean that this is not the best approach for you at this stage of your research development.

Read Theeboom, Beersma and van Vianen (2014) for a more detailed insight into the current state of play regarding coaching in organizations. See if you can locate for yourself similar review articles and meta-analyses in the area of coaching or mentoring. If you are not yet familiar with what a 'meta-analysis' is, skip forward to Chapter 9.

CONCLUSION

This chapter commenced with some of the defining features for coaching and mentoring research, including what may distinguish it from other areas of research. By exploring the important question regarding why do research in this area, this chapter goes beyond the answer of 'because it is part of my course'. This chapter highlighted the important scientific, professional, ethical and practical benefits of conducting research in coaching, and locates the answer in the current situation for the coaching industry, internationally.

Further reading and resources

The Appendix provides an extended annotated section for further reading to ensure that you have an entry point into the three areas of intervention research in coaching and mentoring – i.e., process research, outcome research and implementation, quality and fidelity research. This is meant to provide you with a sample of each area rather than an exhaustive review of the literature. Conducting your own literature review is discussed in Chapter 9.

Eby, L. T., Allen, T. D., Hoffman, B. J., Baranik, L. E., Sauer, J. B., Baldwin, S., ... & Evans, S. C. (2013). An interdisciplinary meta-analysis of the potential antecedents, correlates and consequences of protégé perceptions of mentoring. *Psychological Bulletin, 139*(2), 441.

Grant, A. M. (2016). What constitutes evidence-based coaching?: A two-by-two framework for distinguishing strong from weak evidence for coaching. *International Journal of Evidence Based Coaching and Mentoring, 14*(1), 74.

Passmore, J., & Theeboom, T. (2016). Coaching psychology research: a journey of development in research. In L. E. van Zyl, et al. (Eds.), *Meta-theoretical perspectives and applications for multicultural contexts of coaching and psychology.* Switzerland: Springer International Publishing.

Theeboom, T., Beersma, B., & van Vianen, A.E. (2014). Does coaching work? A meta-analysis on the effects of coaching on individual level outcomes in an organizational context. *The Journal of Positive Psychology, 9*(1), 1–18.

IMPACTFUL RESEARCH

2

HOW DO I MAKE MY RESEARCH INNOVATIVE, SIGNIFICANT AND BENEFICIAL?

LEARNING OUTCOMES

In completing this chapter and related exercises, you will be able to:

1. define key terms related to impact;
2. assess the perceived significance of your planned research;
3. assess the perceived innovativeness of your planned research;
4. generate simple ways to answer the questions 'Why is your research important?' and 'Who benefits from your research?'

WHAT IS THE CURRENT REALITY IN TERMS OF IMPACTFUL RESEARCH IN COACHING AND MENTORING?

In the words of Albert Einstein: 'If we knew what it was we were doing, it would not be called research, would it?' Nevertheless, research is the foundation for knowledge that makes possible so much of the innovation, impact and application that provides wider benefit. It can be challenging to assess the perceived significance and innovation of one's planned research and we need to acknowledge that for every successful research project, there are many projects that will not succeed in the same way. However, they all contribute to our knowledge base and can be the basis of new ideas, methods, techniques and innovation across a range of multidisciplinary areas.

This chapter addresses directly the important issue of research impact. In different contexts there are different meanings to the word 'impact'. In organizational contexts, it may mean that the research is useful, in that it leads to a change of practice. In education, it might mean that we are able to shape policy that allows coaching and mentoring to be pursued more easily. In another context, our impact might be different entirely. In this chapter, we explore the issue of research impact, its significance and innovation, and it includes a critical discussion of issues in quantifying impact.

WHAT IS RESEARCH IMPACT?

Like most things in knowledge production and dissemination, the issue of impact is not simple, nor is it devoid of politics. Governments wishing to seek more funding from industry have a stake in greater industry research and hence, to reduce costs have a stake in valuing research instrumentally in terms of how it has 'applications in the real world' that voters see as driving economic outputs. Likewise, in an organizational context, managers may only be interested in research that leads to tangible and immediate gains for the organization, and metrics such as Return on Investment become relevant (De Meuse, Dai, & Lee, 2009). See Pragmatism in Chapter 5 and Programme evaluation and action research in Chapter 22).

While there are different perspectives on what constitutes impact, a useful definition that demonstrates this instrumental and pragmatic position is provided by the Australian Research Council (ARC, 2017):

> **Research impact** is the **demonstrable contribution** that research makes to the **economy, society, environment, or culture** beyond the contribution to academic research.

In this definition, research is seen as instrumental and must have demonstrable benefit in an economic, societal, environmental or cultural sense. Note that this is the position the ARC takes in deciding what *is* and what *is not* worthy of receiving research funding. Moreover, the ARC also offers guiding principles about how researchers can plan for, report on, evaluate and maximize their impact, which are covered in Table 2.1. Note that we have adjusted the wording in the table to make it more accessible.

As you will see in the table, these are quite lofty heights for researchers to aspire towards. For beginning researchers, some may present a challenge to the extent that they become unfeasible. We stress that this definition and the associated principles are designed for research teams who receive considerable government funding to complete their project. However, they do offer useful guidance about what to consider in determining what impact

Table 2.1 ARC guiding principles about planning, reporting, evaluating and maximizing research impact

Planning for impact	• Early on, establish clear expectations on targets for research impact against which you will monitor progress.
	• Develop your capability to effectively collect data and undertake impact monitoring and evaluation. What skills and resources will be needed?
	• Identify appropriate data elements or metrics that you can use to assess research impact.
	• Identify important stakeholders or interested parties to whom you will communicate the results of your research.
Reporting impact	• Set up reporting requirements that are appropriate to what has been invested in the research.
	• Accommodate multidisciplinary and collaborative research through flexibly designed impact reporting appropriate for its intended outcomes.
Evaluating impact	• Use planned data elements and metrics to monitor and evaluate research impact.
	• Consider any learnings from other studies, evaluations and reviews. How did they evaluate their impact?
Maximizing impact	• Appreciate and value both intended and serendipitous research outcomes.
	• Regularly communicate research impact to stakeholders and other interested parties.
	• Be aware of government agendas – for example, Open Access and Open Data can facilitate impact.

is and how your work will have an impact. It will also be useful for you to consider how you go about reporting or evaluating your impact, which are steps that are often omitted entirely. Several terms that are closely related to impact are introduced below.

RELATED TERMS THAT FALL UNDER THE UMBRELLA OF 'IMPACT'

Significance

The **significance** of a project is why the research is worth doing. Significance answers the question 'So what?' by placing the study/research within the context of past research and highlighting why it is needed. This is where you demonstrate the importance of your ideas and establish to the audience why they should be interested in your study. The significance of a project will persuasively tell how your study is going to make a substantive contribution to the field. Capturing the significance of your project will also be key in terms of harnessing support for your project, which is important if you need funding.

Implications

Closely related to significance are the implications of research, which refers to how a study has advanced theory or practice, or methods, or provided much-needed new data. Hence, implications differ from significance in that they are generally written retrospectively, after the conclusion of the project and after we know what we have discovered through our research. Significance, in contrast, is more prospective. Implications (as well as significance) are typically divided into different types: practical, theoretical, methodological or empirical. **Practical implications** are how the results of the research might influence practice in some sense. **Theoretical implications** are how the results of the project has advanced our theoretical understanding of the area. Research can also have **methodological implications** if your study advances research methods, so that others can then use those methods to do better research. Research can also have **empirical implications**, where it will yield much-needed new data. An example of this might be a study that evaluates the efficacy of an intervention in an unexplored population where previously not much was known. Commonly, but not always, a research project will focus more on its practical *or* theoretical *or* methodological *or* empirical implications, though there are some instances where a study may contribute across more than one area. The word 'implication' is often used synonymously with 'contribution'. Thus, in some studies you may see 'practical contribution' or 'theoretical contribution' etc. instead of implications.

Innovation

Related to significance and implications is innovation. A research project is innovative if it uses a *novel combination of ideas that meets a research need*. Innovation may be seen as yielding **a novel perspective** if the idea is new, different or offers a fresh angle to enhance our understanding of phenomena. In doing so, it will **synthesize, analyse and translate** ideas by weaving together different strands of research on a topic. And this will also be done to **fill a gap** in knowledge**.** A gap is something yet to be done or learned in an area of research. Not only must every project address a gap in knowledge in some way, but that gap needs to be of practical or theoretical or methodological **significance** (as above).

Pragmatism

A research project is said to be **pragmatic**, or practical, to the extent that it has the potential for application. If your coaching and mentoring study will actually shift how people practise in these fields, then your study is likely to have pragmatic merit. The pragmatist position is essentially that knowledge generated by research is for acting (or doing), in that it must be used in some real-world sense and is not just for descriptive purposes. We touch on pragmatism again in Chapter 5 when we discuss research epistemology. Note that just because a study is practical, it does mean that it is significant, innovative or beneficial. We coin the term **'fatuous pragmatism'** to refer to a pragmatic stance that is hollow (fatuous) because it is all about action (doing) and is lacking in the groundwork that gives a project substance or significance. A fatuous pragmatist will tend to turn ideas into direct applications without thinking things through and carefully examining the significance or value of their work. Similarly, a fatuous pragmatist will tend to dismiss the role of theory as the terrain of people who are not concerned with the 'real-world'. Instead, it is all about the application. Consider an example of someone who has developed what they believe is a great idea for a coaching intervention and uses that approach while ignoring or avoiding accountability to broader theory and evidence, claiming that 'it is not practical'. While a project might be promising in terms of its practical viability, it does not mean that it has significance because it may not address an important need. To be pragmatic and significant, the project must lead to some applied benefit that addresses a worthwhile need.

 Activity

What is your current reality in terms of making your research innovative and impactful?

Research impact is typically forecast in advance (i.e., it is envisaged *a priori*) and it may not be entirely clear how to determine the impact of a project before it has been completed. Notwithstanding the difficulties in how to measure research impact before the research takes place, it is worth attempting to understand its potential impact and implications at the beginning of the research process. The following personal learning activity is designed to navigate you through this process. As you begin to write your research proposal (this is covered in more depth in Chapter 10), put the big picture squarely in your sights and aim to answer the questions below. Write short paragraph responses to the following question,

* Who benefits from your research? Really?

What are your key options to make your research innovative and impactful?

There are ten questions you may want to consider when writing about the significance of your proposed research project. They include the following.

1. Why is this work important?
2. What are the implications of doing it (think about practical and/or theoretical implications)?
3. How does it contribute to other knowledge and the broader context?

(Continued)

(Continued)

4. What are the practical benefits to those in the context where data is collected/generated?
5. What new perspective will you bring to the topic?
6. How does it stand to inform policy making?
7. How might you evaluate your impact?
8. Who might you decide to share your findings with once the project is complete?
9. What use might your research have for others in this field or for the general public?
10. What steps can you take to maximize the reach of your work and its impact?

Now reflect on your answers and examine what type of significance you are trying to have in your work. Assign a percentage contribution to each of the following areas to ascertain what type of contribution you are trying to make through your coaching and mentoring research project when it is completed.

- **Theoretical significance:** e.g., your study will advance theoretical understanding on a particular perspective related to coaching or mentoring.
- **Methodological significance:** e.g., you will develop a novel method that will enhance the coaching or mentoring research process.
- **Empirical significance:** e.g., your study will contribute *needed* data that has not been collected with a population before (e.g., children, senior leaders, etc.). Note the emphasis – it can't just be any population that has not been examined. There needs to be an *important* reason you plan to investigate a particular group of people.
- **Practical significance:** e.g., research that has an impact on the practice of coaching or mentoring in an organization.

IMPACT IN SCHOLARSHIP

So far, we have discussed impact in a general sense, but you might also consider your options about how you can maximize your impact when you publish your work. Providing an indication of the 'impact' of your research is now a standard activity in academia and is done in several ways in scholarly research. When it comes to publishing research, a researcher writes up their study and results in a manuscript, and then submits the manuscript to a journal. The manuscript will be reviewed by two or more peers (i.e., it undergoes peer-review), as well as a journal editor, who evaluate the manuscript on factors such as impact, credibility, limitations and acceptability for publication. If the manuscript survives the peer-review process (normally requiring several rounds of revision), it will then be published and made available to others. Other scholars can then find the published article and 'cite' it in their own work – that is, they reference your work to inform their own work. Thus, one indicator of research impact is the citation count that a study receives after it has been published. High-impact research tends to be cited more than low-impact research.

Citations matter, because they are one of the best ways that a researcher can quantify the impact of their work in the scholarly context (Moosa, 2018). While a full review of how you can increase your publishing impact is beyond the scope of this book, there are a number of ways we will introduce you to here, which you may want to explore further if you plan to publish your work in an academic journal.

TRY TO PUBLISH IN HIGH-IMPACT JOURNALS

Journals come with metrics that quantify their impact, in terms of citations. These might be, for example, the impact factor, which is the measure of the frequency with which the average article is cited from that journal in a particular year. It might also be the h-index, which is the set of a journal's most cited papers. An index of h requires that a journal has published h articles which have each been cited h times. For example, if a journal has an h-index of 100, it means that it has at least 100 articles that have each been cited 100 times or more. At the time of writing this book, some coaching and mentoring journals include the following.

- *Coaching: An International Journal of Theory, Research and Practice.*
- *International Journal of Evidence Based Coaching and Mentoring.*
- *International Coaching Psychology Review.*
- *International Journal of Mentoring and Coaching in Education.*
- *Mentoring & Tutoring: Partnership in Learning.*

Unfortunately, while there are some well-cited and recognized studies in these journals, none of those listed above are considered high impact in terms of their impact factor or h-index. Thus, to increase the visibility of your work, you might consider publishing in more generalist high-impact alternatives in your discipline. For example, if you are interested in coaching or mentoring in the organizational behaviour and/or human resource management context, you might try top-listed journals on the SCImago Journal and Country Rank (SJR indicator: www.scimagojr.com/journalrank.php?category=1407) system.

While publishing in high-impact journals will increase the visibility and impact of your work, it can be very competitive and onerous to do so. We recommend Clark, Wright, & Ketchen (2016), which is an excellent resource for strategies to help you along this somewhat daunting path. While the focus is on management research, the tips and strategies will be useful across all scholarly contexts.

CONSIDER RESEARCH THAT GETS MORE RECOGNIZED

There are some types of studies that tend to be more highly cited than others. For example, literature review and meta-analysis (see Chapter 9) tend to be more highly cited than other areas of research (Clark et al., 2016). Thus, if it is relevant and possible for your area of interest and your own research questions, you might consider such techniques as research methods.

CONSIDER ALTMETRICS

Altmetrics keep track of how much attention your published work gets in the news/ media, blogs, as well as on platforms such as Twitter, Facebook, LinkedIn and Wikipedia, among others. Altmetrics are valuable because they show practical impact of scholarship and tend to be more immediate, just after publication, rather than citations, which can take many years to accumulate. When you publish, consider how you can get more visibility for your work by actively publicizing your work in these domains, which will increase its altmetric score.

WHAT NEXT?

As mentioned, it is not always easy to know beforehand the impact of your project. It is, however, easier to say why your project involves some novel ideas, fills a gap, meets a need or something similar. Beware of comparing your small project to a multi-site, multimillion dollar- or pound-funded project done by a major research team, over several years. While these projects tend to have high impact, research that is smaller in scope can still have an impact, too. While your study does have to be unique and it does have to address a need, it alone does not need to have huge impact to be worthwhile. But impact, and how you can maximize your impact, is worth considering from the outset because it makes the research more worthwhile.

While we ask you to do this activity now, we suggest that you continue to do this 'What next' activity throughout your research career.

- Continue to ask and answer the questions: Why is this research important? Who benefits from this research?

CONCLUSION

This chapter has introduced you to the issue of research impact and closely related concepts of quality, innovation and significance. The metrics for high-quality research used in academic contexts was also explored, and we provided you with several tips to help you both consider and maximize the impact of your work. We emphasize that this is not as simple as it may first appear, and that knowing impact before the research is not always possible. We suggest that you continue to work with our exercises in this chapter, which provide a series of iterative questions that you may ask at different stages of the research process to maximize your impact.

 **Further reading and resources**

Australian Research Council (2017). *Engagement and impact assessment pilot 2017: report*. www.arc. gov.au/policies-strategies/strategy/research-impact-principles-framework

Clark, T., Wright, M., & Ketchen, D. J. (Eds.). (2016). *How to get published in the best management journals*. Cheltenham: Edward Elgar Publishing.

SCImago Journal and Country Rank (SJR, for organizational behaviour and human resource management research: www.scimagojr.com/journalrank.php?category=1407).

RESEARCH TEAMS

WHO WILL BE A PART
OF MY RESEARCH TEAM?

3

LEARNING OUTCOMES

In completing this chapter and related exercises, you will be able to:

1. describe the importance of building a team to support both your personal and technical needs to complete research;

2. create a plan to build a team to support your personal needs during the research process;

3. create a plan to build a team to support your technical needs during the research process;

4. understand the importance of ongoing feedback during the research process.

WHAT IS THE CURRENT REALITY OF RESEARCH TEAMS FOR COACHING AND MENTORING?

By 'research team' we mean anyone who is explicitly trying to help you complete the research project. We do not necessarily mean a formal team of collaborating researchers. In an academic context, your supervisor or adviser is considered part of the research team.

Universities require someone who has done a PhD to be involved in supervising a PhD candidate. Hence, at the essence of formal research training, there is a mentoring model. Therefore, for those in doctoral-level research, the quality of the relationship with a supervisor and the expertise of the supervisor become central to the research process. In this chapter, we encourage you to think about building a 'research team'. This does not just involve solely relying on one or two individuals as your conduit to the research world, but instead refers to allowing you to become part of a wider researcher community.

Many early-career researchers, such as student researchers, describe research as being a lonely process. It can be lonely if you decide to do everything yourself – and this often seems like the most natural path for a student in a doctoral research programme. However, research does not have to be lonely, and it can instead create opportunities to network with others and to meet people with similar interests or complementary skills to those of your own. When thinking about research teams, people often think of *formal* teams. Formal teams might be, for example, formal arrangements between two or more people, including a PhD student and his or her research supervisor/s. Another example might be a formal arrangement between team-members listed on a research funding application. However, research teams can also be *informal*, which is another way to think about conducting collaborative research. Informal team-members work together on a common goal, but don't do so under any formal governing arrangement. For example, given the technical requirements of different parts of the research process, a student might consult with an expert with a particular set of skills (e.g., statistics) or seek feedback on his or her research project to optimize it prior to publication. This could happen at any stage throughout the research project, and does not require any bureaucratic paperwork to allow it to happen.

Both formal and informal relationships are a great way to build connections with others in your research field. Teams can be formed at any stage from the outset of the research process, be it deciding on the scope and questions (Chapters 7 and 8), or the more technical aspects of design and methods (Chapters 15–24), or writing up your paper for maximal impact (Chapter 2). It is important to address both your technical and personal needs when considering who could form your research team. We consider it to be essential to have a wider set of experts to provide you with feedback and to support you through your research journey. Not only will it make your research outputs better, but it will likely make the process of doing research immensely more enjoyable and rewarding. While technical feedback on methods, theory, analysis and writing are commonly addressed under formal arrangements with an academic supervisor, these aspects can also be improved under informal arrangements, including experts in your field, other students or peers, journal editors and referees, and other professionals in your area. To build your informal network, it may be useful to join in on public lectures, seminars or interest groups, either in person or online.

Cooksey and McDonald (2011) have identified some characteristics of a 'good' research team. These will be useful for you to consider when building a research team. They include the following.

- **Complementary skill sets of members.** The research team composition should include an array of knowledge, skills and abilities that lead to different perspectives. Diversity in knowledge, skills and abilities can help groups to solve complex problems that arise during the research process. Diversity will also allow you to learn from each other and to build upon or refine each other's ideas.
- An **open-mindedness** to other team members' perspectives, epistemologies, research methodologies and methods.
- **Open and honest communication** between yourself and the other team members. This requires being upfront about intra-team roles, including the preferred nature of team-meetings, preferred communication channels and the support you can expect.

- **Establishing internal expectations.** Early in your research journey it will be important to clarify the expectations of your research team. Cooksey and McDonald (2011) outline some important expectations on which you may want to reach consensus. We include some of them here.

    o **Expectations of each other.** It will be important to communicate these early on, outlining your needs and preferences, including what each of you will contribute to the collaborative effort.

    o **Expectations about the nature of your research.** Team members may differ in their expertise, epistemologies, preferred methodologies and methods, and experience. Some may be strong in certain areas and weak in other areas. It is important to consider how this may shape your research project.

    o **Expectations about communication.** Face-to-face meetings with your research team are just one mode of communication. It is important to also consider preferences for other modes of communication, particularly if you are collaborating across countries, time-zones or different locations.

    o **Expectations about meetings.** These are fairly mechanistic, but nonetheless it will be important to set expectations for meetings. These might include the preferred locations, times, frequency, length, formats (virtual vs. in person) and so on.

    o **Expectations about publishing and ownership of ideas.** It is very important to pin down expectations about publishing from your research. Will you be publishing as you go? How many publications do you have planned and what is the nature of each one? Will each member of your research team be co-authors on publications and, if so, in what order? What will each team member contribute?

- **Interpersonal dynamics** allow for all team members to have a voice in the discussions of your research project, without dominating the conversation. Consider how you will ensure each team-member's perspective is considered.

 **Activity**

What is your current reality as a researcher? What do you need from your team?

To help you to identify how you could contribute in the best possible way to a research team, complete the following personal learning activity. Imagine you are coaching yourself and answer the following questions.

- What are your personal strengths that would contribute to a research team?
- What areas have been difficult for you in any past research you've done?
- What are your personal qualities that may (a) help make your project of high quality; (b) sustain you or others during what can be a difficult process?
- What are the technical skills where you are strongest and areas in which you need improvement?

(Continued)

(Continued)

- Are there people you know of who could help compensate for some areas in which you need improvement? How will you sell your project to them (i.e., what will they get out of it?).
- What is your current work and personal-life situation, and might you have to make adjustments to accommodate these areas?

What are your key options in terms of developing a research team?

To help you identify your options in terms of developing a research team, we recommend working through the following three tasks before starting your research.

- **Identify potential members of your research team.** Identify people who could potentially support your personal and professional needs during your research journey, which can be onerous and daunting. Pay particular attention to choosing a supervisor/adviser if you are in an academic context. What skills, attributes or qualities would you ideally need in your adviser to a) support your own preferences in a working relationship (e.g., punctuality, responsiveness, emotional support, etc.), b) accommodate some of your deficiencies in skills or expertise and c) help you to learn as much as possible?
- **Identify ways to receive feedback.** Feedback is crucial and will almost certainly help make your research more enjoyable and also improve the quality of your outputs. Consider including people who are going to help you think critically about your topic and who will challenge you to think about your idea from a different angle or perspective (see Confirmation bias, Chapter 4).
- **Be clear about your needs.** We suggest that you are clear about what you need from those in your research team. People are very willing to help when you come with a structured plan, and are prepared and upfront about your needs. This step should be clearer after answering the questions above.
- **Have a plan to 'sell' your work.** We don't mean 'selling' as in a traditional sales sense, but if you need to seek the assistance of an expert to assist with your project, they are likely to be very busy and will not necessarily want to get involved for reasons involving kindness alone (although that would be nice). Try to identify ways that others could potentially benefit from being involved in your work, so that it becomes a more attractive proposition. For example, is there scope to include the expert as an author on a high-impact journal publication (see Chapters 2 and 14)?

WHAT NEXT?

Start thinking about who you could invite to be on your research team. Also think about the current stage you are in your research journey. For example, you may already have a formal supervisor or you may not. While formal team members could include formal supervisors and so forth, informal teams could be made up of consultations, friends, coffee buddies, people who hold a particular expertise, people who provide feedback or whatever else you need. Be clear about whether you are seeking more technical support or emotional support: you may need a bit of both at times along your journey.

CONCLUSION

This short chapter emphasizes the fact that research is commonly a collaborative process. There can be other people involved, not just you. It need not, and should not, be a lonely endeavour. Erase all ideas of self-sufficiency and think about how to proactively build a team around you. This will lead to better coping, more enjoyment and higher-quality research.

 Further reading and resources

Cooksey, R. W., & McDonald, G. M. (2011). *Surviving and thriving in postgraduate research.* Prahran, Vic: Tilde University Press.

This book provides some useful guidelines and tips around managing research relationships. Although this book focuses on postgraduate research and relationships with supervisors, many of the lessons can be applied more broadly to research teams. More specially, useful advice on clarifying expectations, maintaining relationships and handing problems are touched on throughout the book.

AVOIDING PITFALLS

HOW DO I AVOID PITFALLS COMMONLY MADE BY BEGINNER RESEARCHERS?

4

LEARNING OUTCOMES

In completing this chapter and related activities, you will be able to:

1. identify pitfalls commonly experienced by beginner researchers;
2. identify ways to prevent such pitfalls;
3. generate ways to address such pitfalls if they occur;
4. identify your own logical fallacies and when they appear.

WHAT ARE THE PITFALLS COMMONLY EXPERIENCED FOR BEGINNER RESEARCHERS IN COACHING AND MENTORING?

A pitfall is a hidden or unsuspected danger. There are several pitfalls that new researchers can fall into. Many coaching and mentoring beginning researchers may well have commenced as practitioners before coming to research, which also means that there are more common pitfalls for this type of beginning researcher. An assumption here is that as a new researcher you do not wish to become overly stressed about doing research. If this was to be turned into a hypothetical equation, then:

The stress of conducting research = the risk of data collection × time demands of methodology × fuzziness of research question.

If you want to have a stressful time, increase your risk of data collection, choose a very time-demanding methodology and leave your research question unclear or change it frequently. This chapter addresses these issues in terms of pitfalls and the interaction between risk, time demands and clarity of your project. It is useful to identify these pitfalls so they can be avoided or identified and remedied. In this chapter we outline seven pitfalls common for beginning researchers, in a coaching and mentoring context. The common pitfalls are that the project:

1.   is not sufficiently informed by the literature;
2.   is too big and lacking in focus;
3.   employs an unnecessarily complex design;
4.   is too dependent on a risky data source;
5.   involves poor data sampling;
6.   involves undeclared bias, hasty generalization and other logical fallacies;
7.   demonstrates a lack of critical thinking and writing.

PITFALL 1: THE PROJECT IS NOT SUFFICIENTLY INFORMED BY THE LITERATURE

The first pitfall is not informing the research from the **existing literature**. You may have identified a need for improving a coaching method, a different way of delivering mentoring processes or combined some ideas in a novel way. You now want to investigate this idea further. It is fine and often very beneficial that an idea is triggered from a need you have identified from practice. However, it is also important to ensure that you have examined the literature in a systematic way; there needs to be a corresponding need for your study in the existing literature.

Do the groundwork and use the library to research the foundation and relevant theories and evidence relating to your area of study (for more information here, see Chapter 9 on Reviewing literature). Remember, it is important to know where your research sits compared to what others in the field have already done. It may be that you are extending or further building on someone else's theory or research. Having an idea, while a good start, is simply not enough. Your idea may seem wonderful in the beginning, only for you to find that there is 10 years of evidence that directly refutes the claims you are making. Alternatively, there may be 10 years of evidence that already exists on your exact research question, meaning your study is just not needed. Alternatively still, you may find very little literature on your topic and this might partly justify the need for some research in this area. You will not know this unless you do an extensive search of the literature before beginning your project.

PITFALL 2: THE PROJECT IS TOO BIG AND LACKING IN FOCUS

The second common pitfall is designing a research project that is **too big and lacks focus.** Chapters 7 and 8 are dedicated to this issue directly. If your project is too big, you will have a huge amount of material to read and may unwittingly leave out important information, which can leave your readers or examiners thinking you do not really know the topic you are describing.

As a general rule, depth is generally better than breadth. Using the analogy of a photographic lens, there are wide-angled lenses and there are zoom lenses. The suggestion here is to use a zoom lens, but remember to keep it in focus – that is, scope the project so it is relevant and feasible (see Chapter 7 for scoping a project, and Chapter 12 for feasible timelines). Keep the project in focus, meaning that it is being described at sufficient depth but still at an understandable level.

In supervising many beginning researchers, we have witnessed student after student simply try to do too much at the beginning and some being unwilling to zoom into an area. Consider a new researcher, Charlotte, who ends up doing a study that examines the coaching of nursing staff to help them become more optimistic about patient prognosis. This is quite a nice project that is focused and allows Charlette to go deep (to zoom in). However, it did not start here. When the project started, Charlotte decided that she wanted to do a project working with management in medical organizations to enable patients to be optimistic. However, she soon realized that this was very broad and unfocused. What does 'working with management' mean? What practice will she examine? Who are the participants in her study (management or patients)? What will she do to enhance optimism? This prompted Charlotte to draw some circles on a page with key-words to 'mind-map' the key ideas she wanted to study. Thus, she wrote down words in the circles such as optimism, patients, coaching, medicine, nursing, management, organizations, training. She then decided to cross out a few circles (training, management, organizations) to try to focus her project. It moved from medical organizations to nursing staff, from patient optimism to nurse optimism (it is easier to get ethics approval for staff than patients, within the possible time frame – see Chapter 11 which covers risks in research ethics) and from the general idea of management training to a specific idea of coaching.

If you are currently prone to wanting to do too much, we suggest that you consider mind-mapping your ideas in this way and consider eliminating two-thirds of the circles. Which ones seem unimportant or peripheral? It is a cliché, but try to *learn to let go.* Reading can make this worse, as you keep discovering new and interesting ideas. Put these aside for later. Perhaps consider keeping an 'interesting ideas' folder or journal. Beware of any sentence you utter that beings with 'It would be interesting to also … ' Just because ideas are interesting does not mean they have to be formally in your project. Projects are harder to do than circles are to draw. Ideas have to truly deserve to be in your project. You do not let every nice person into your home and do not let every nice concept into your project design.

The process of focusing a topic takes practice, so be patient with yourself. It is challenging when you do not know too much about a topic. It will get easier as your knowledge base increases. Remember that the research process is an iterative one, which means that you may need to revisit your topic of choice more than once if you find it doesn't work out. Luckily, there are some strategies and methods to help you through this critically important part of the process (see Cooksey & McDonald, 2011: 603–4; also see Chapters 7 and 8).

PITFALL 3: THE PROJECT EMPLOYS AN UNNECESSARILY COMPLEX DESIGN

Just as in Pitfall 2, many beginning researchers try to include too many concepts and relationships between the concepts; they also make research designs unnecessarily complex. Sometimes beginning researchers think 'more is better', 'bigger is better' and perhaps 'if I make it look more complex, I look smarter and more like an authority in the area'. Unfortunately, the reverse of these statements reflects reality much more closely. The key message here is that research designs serve to answer your well-crafted research question. The design is the overall form of the project, particularly how and when data will be collected and, if relevant, when the intervention is provided. Ask yourself what key questions you are seeking to answer. Then ask yourself how you can do that – and just that? Chapters 8, 16, 17 and 23 explore research designs in more detail.

PITFALL 4: THE PROJECT IS TOO DEPENDENT ON A RISKY DATA SOURCE

The fourth common pitfall that is made by beginning researchers is relying on a **risky data source.** This is particularly relevant to applied research in a coaching and mentoring context. There are several types of risky data sources. These can include not gaining all the necessary approval processes in organizations to access the data source, or potentially having a relationship with only one member of the organization. If that person leaves the organization, you can kiss your access to your sample goodbye. Restructures and budget crises also happen in organizations. In business language, data is a critical success factor; there should not be a single point of dependence. The hypothetical equation at the beginning of this chapter includes risky data sources as a potential stressor for you. This is based on the experience of numerous projects we have supervised and conducted. When data flow is nil or slow, the stress on the researcher steadily rises as the project due dates get nearer. Data are gold, and have multiple ways and places to dig for them. These issues of risk and time are discussed in more detail in Chapter 12, Feasible timelines.

PITFALL 5: THE PROJECT INVOLVES POOR DATA SAMPLING

Poor sampling is pitfall number five. Sampling can relate to both qualitative and quantitative research. A common pitfall is that new researchers do not genuinely think about the reasoning behind their actual sample. Samples may be chosen purely for convenience purpose, and important concepts such as sampling frame, stratification, probabilistic sampling, purposive sampling and power-analysis are overlooked. If you do not know these terms, do not be concerned at this stage – they are technical terms from both the quantitative and qualitative realm. The key issue here is to understand that sampling – i.e., how to choose a sample of participants to answer your research question or test your hypothesis, is a decision-making task in its own right. Not only does the sample need to be an appropriate size (for example, to have sufficient statistical power to make generalizations), but it needs to have relevance to the question asked (for example, if you want a range of views and experiences, you may need to purposely sample people from different demographics).

PITFALL 6: THE PROJECT INVOLVES UNDECLARED BIAS, HASTY GENERALIZATIONS AND OTHER LOGICAL FALLACIES

A not uncommon experience for us as senior researchers in a university context is to be approached by practitioners (e.g., coaches with consulting businesses) who have developed practice models over several years. They often say that they wish to do a Master's or PhD-level research project to 'prove' or support their model because they know it works. The very obvious question that comes to our mind is this: if you already know it works, why do research on it in the first place?

While sometimes this is an issue of semantics, often it is a case of confirmation bias. Confirmation bias, which is sometimes called confirmatory bias or myside bias, involves the tendency to search for, recall and interpret information in a way that confirms one's pre-existing beliefs or hypotheses. People display this bias when they gather or remember information selectively or when they interpret it in a biased way. The effect of this bias is stronger for emotionally driven and personal values. For example, if you are involved in a mentoring programme for disadvantaged youth and you have strong values of equity, there may be pressure for a programme evaluation to demonstrate that the programme is effective (see Chapter 22 on Programme evaluation). Chapter 5 introduces ways of knowing (epistemology) and from some perspectives all research is necessarily biased. In this case, it is the declaration of your assumptions, preconceptions, context and values that are important.

Making rapid or hasty generalizations is a common pitfall. Much of the debate within the philosophy of science (see Chapter 5) and research methodology (see Chapter 6) is about the ability or inability to generalize beyond the immediate context of the research. In philosophy, and logic in particular, there are well-established rules for reasoning. It is useful for you as a beginning researcher to learn or refresh basic logic and some of the logical fallacies (mistakes) that people make in their reasoning. For a broader reading on heuristics, we recommend Tversky and Kahneman's (1974) work on heuristics and biases. This has been further popularized by the recent accessible book, *Thinking fast and slow* (Kahneman, 2011).

Examine the Challenges and problems box below, which includes a selection of the many logical fallacies, chosen because of their relevance to coaching and mentoring research. Before reading through them, it is useful also to refresh the basic principles of reasoning and logic.

Inferences are the steps in reasoning. They move from premises to logical consequences. If the reasoning is poor, the consequences are fallacious – that is, they are derived from logical fallacies. Here are two forms of reasoning that will be instrumental in helping you to understand what follows in this book.

Inductive reasoning (i.e., induction) is a form of inference that goes from a specific case to a general principle. It starts with the conclusion and ends up with a theory or hypothesis about what that conclusion means. Thus, inductive reasoning is more bottom-up, because it starts with the data and then makes inferences as to the meaning of the data. In research, inductive logic tends to be more associated with qualitative methodology (see Chapter 6), which tends to be more data-driven and exploratory.

Deductive reasoning (i.e., deduction), in contrast, is inference that derives logical conclusions by moving from general (often true) principles to the specific case. Thus, deductive reasons starts with a hypothesis and examines the plausibility or validity of that hypothesis to reach a conclusion. In scientific terms, we start with a theory and then predict (hypothesize) which observations should eventuate if the theory were correct. Thus, we start with theory and end up with a conclusion. In research, deductive logic tends to be more associated with positivism (see Chapter 5) and quantitative methodology (see Chapter 6).

CHALLENGES AND PROBLEMS

A challenge for coaching and mentoring researchers is that they may believe passionately in the benefits of coaching or mentoring. While passion is good, it can lead to logical fallacies that you might want to avoid when doing your coaching and mentoring research. Here are some possible fallacies.

1. **Hasty generalizations** are statements made without sufficient evidence to support them. They are a poor use of inductive reasoning. Not only may they be overgeneralized, inflated, exaggerated claims, they often occur quickly – hence the term 'hasty'. They are very prominent in society, as there are debates about what constitutes sufficient evidence. In the natural

sciences, particularly with experimental designs, high levels of evidence are required to make a claim seem acceptable. Academic and scientific writing is a genre that does not value over-generalization or hasty generalization. This is most relevant in the discussion and implications sections of your research reporting. A simple trick is to ask people to turn their claims into if–then statements and their generalizations become more obvious and open to scrutiny. This makes prejudice and stereotyping more transparent.

2. **Circular argument** (*petitio principi – assuming the initial*). A circular argument or circular reasoning occurs when the conclusion to the argument appears as one of the original premises. It is something that looks like an argument, but really is just a restatement of the original premise – that is, the argument goes in a circle. In quantitative research methods, some variables correlate very highly – perhaps they are the same thing with a different name. This is a context where circular arguments may appear. The word 'thesis' derives from place, meaning to place a proposition. Your research contains a thesis; you are placing a proposition and argument likely linking several propositions – sometimes in the form of an hypothesis. Be sure it is an argument rather than a restatement of the proposition. Avoid something that resembles the form, such as: *Coaching is good because coaching is good.*

3. **Straw man.** The straw man (or woman) fallacy is named after a lifeless scarecrow made from straw. The fallacy involves attacking a position that an opponent does not really hold. By using the fallacy, your position looks better compared to another untenable position, even though your opponent does not hold those claims. In coaching or mentoring research, comparisons to teaching and counselling may be openings for the straw man fallacy. For example, consider the claim that 'counselling is problem based and backwards facing, whereas coaching is solution focused and forwards looking'. Many from the counselling community may view this as a straw man characterization of counselling.

4. **Ecological fallacy.** This fallacy refers specifically to the interpretation of statistical data. Hence, for those using a quantitative methodology to investigate coaching and mentoring, this is quite relevant. The fallacy is when inferences about the nature of individuals are deduced from inference for the group to which those individuals belong. Much of quantitative research methods involves group-based data (e.g., the calculation of means). So, in a coaching pro-gramme compared to a control programme, the means of goal attainment may be higher for the coaching group after six weeks of coaching. An ecological fallacy would be to conclude that if you as an individual are in the coaching programme, your personal goal attainment will necessarily be higher. It assumes that your result as an individual is necessarily the same as the group. This is a very common fallacy that members of the general public often fall into, due to their misunderstanding of inferential statistics. Debates about differences between sexes and gender roles are relevant contexts to identify some ecological fallacies.

5. **Appeal to authority** (*argumentum ad verecundiam – argument from respect*). Overcoming this fallacy is to champion rationality and the enlightenment era. Because dad said it, god said it or the president said it does not make it so. This fallacy can occur in research when we cite only authorities rather than exploring evidence and argument from a range of

(Continued)

(Continued)

viewpoints. In coaching and mentoring research, there may be prominent scholars, with multiple books and publications, whom you cite. There may be an outstanding, well-noted coach practitioner. While their work may be worth including in your argument, appealing to their authority alone is a logical fallacy. This relates also to the critical thinking pitfall mentioned in this chapter. Some beginning researchers think: 'Who am I to question the work of Mr/Ms Famous Scholar?'

6. **Appeal to pity.** This fallacy occurs when we mistake feelings for facts. Issues of illness, death, poverty, abuse, violence, all can be deeply upsetting. However, if we are evaluating reasoning to ascertain whether it is true or false, the feeling about an event is not relevant as to whether the event is a fact or not. For example, consider the claim that 'this coaching programme is really effective because youth suicide is such a gut-wrenching thing'. The fallacy is evident in the word 'because'. While engaging oral presentations or movies often use 'pathos' (a communication technique of rhetoric, which engages people's emotions, particularly pity and sadness), this is different from factual claims using logic and reasoning. Consider a Shakespearean tragedy, the fact claim that Emilia is killed, is different from that claim that it is pitiful in the way in that she died. The value of logic and reasoning does not mean that emotions are not a useful and legitimate way of knowing (see knowing from in Chapter 5).

7. *Ad hominem* **(against the man).** The *ad hominem* fallacy is familiar to most who have done debating or studied introductory philosophy or critical thinking courses. Stated simply, it involves an attack on the person and not the argument. It is a fallacy because attacking the personal characteristics of a person presenting an argument is deemed as irrelevant to the quality of the argument per se. This is very common in political debates, where mud-slinging occurs between political leaders. Debates about gender may lead to this type of attack – for example, the assertion 'you would not understand as a man (or woman)' is *ad hominem* reasoning, as it attacks the speaker rather than the argument. While there may be information that is derived from the experience of not being a man or woman that is important to know, the reasoning by itself is fallacious (i.e., a fallacy), according to formal logic. It is notable in this example, however, that there are feminist critiques of formal logic. Think of debates where things turn from reasoning and following a line of argument, to hurling abuse at an opponent. We know that *ad hominem* has arrived. Social media provides many examples for you to observe this in action – just spend 20 minutes observing a politically sensitive topic unfold on Twitter.

8. **Bandwagon**. The bandwagon fallacy comes in several forms. It is commonly used in advertising: 'Many people do x, therefore you should also do x.' This is a version of the '*ad populum* – to the popular/populous fallacy', one of the examples of bandwagon. Jumping on the bandwagon comes from a wagon that carried a circus band. Jump on, join in or you will miss out. Consider the reasoning, 'coaching and positive psychology have become very popular; researchers should also appreciate its obvious quality'. This statement is not unfamiliar to many undergraduate essays and is an example of the bandwagon fallacy: everyone is doing it, therefore it must be good. The first part of the sentence is fine – everyone is doing it may be factual – the problem lies with the claim that follows.

PITFALL 7: THE PROJECT DEMONSTRATES A LACK OF CRITICAL THINKING

Closely related to Pitfall 6, the final pitfall is a lack of critical thinking and writing. If your reasoning skills are poor, it will be more difficult to use critical thinking. Hence, Pitfalls 6 and 7 travel together. Critical thinking and writing are essential for undertaking quality research in coaching and mentoring. In the emerging research literature of coaching, it is paramount as some researchers may have been too uncritical of coaching programmes and their effects. Note also that critical thinking is *not* synonymous with criticizing. For example, being uncritically favourable towards a coaching programme is evidence of absent critical thinking, but so is blindly dismissing a programme as 'rubbish' without a proper evaluation of the evidence. Critical thinking involves looking at both sides, strengths and limitations, and reaching a balanced conclusion. The most characteristic features of critical writing are:

1. a clear and confident refusal to accept the conclusions of other writers without evaluating the arguments and evidence that they provide;
2. a balanced presentation of reasons why the conclusions of other writers may be accepted or may need to be treated with caution;
3. a clear presentation of your own evidence and argument, leading to your conclusion; and
4. a recognition of the limitations in your own evidence, argument and conclusion.

There are many online resources for improving critical thinking, and universities and colleges provide many resources, human, paper and online, to assist students with this. Find them and use them. Also, other general resources are available (see Cohen, 2011). Critical thinking is also linked with good literature review skills, which are covered in Chapter 9, and not doing this is the first pitfall. Literature reviews should involve a critical element, not just what is there in the literature, but what is strong and weak with the interpretations, reasoning, evidence and methodology of the projects in the literature, with the implication that your project will contribute to making it better.

 **Activity**

How likely is it that you will meet one of these pitfalls in your research?

Using the methods of GROW and coaching, let's explore your current reality. Assuming that you know yourself reasonably well, try to be as honest as possible and identify how likely it is that you will fall into these pits. Consider the following questions.

(Continued)

(Continued)

- Do you tend to be over-inclusive in your writing and explanations?
- Are you someone who cannot always decide, so end up including something for everyone? Are you prone to jumping to conclusions?
- Do you commit deeply to one position and inadvertently avoid alternative views?

Then, have a go at rating each of the following pitfalls out of 100, where 100 represents that you are certain that you will make this mistake (or already have) and 0 represents no chance or that you have already avoided it:

1. Is not sufficiently informed by the literature.
2. Is too big and lacking in focus.
3. Employs an unnecessarily complex design.
4. Is too dependent on a risky data source.
5. Involves poor data sampling.
6. Involves undeclared bias, hasty generalization and other logical fallacies.
7. Demonstrates a lack of critical thinking and writing.

Now let's consider how to avoid these pitfalls. Focusing particularly on your three highest numbers from the previous part of the activity (e.g., you may have rated Pitfall 5 as 80), let's explore your options to overcome the pitfalls. What are two things you could do to avoid that pitfall? Who could you talk with? What could you read?

WHAT NEXT?

What next? from this chapter is up to you. After completing the Activity above, there are likely actions you will need to take, which we will leave to you. Also, after being exposed to the logical fallacies, there are also things you need to be careful about. Further reading and accessing resources to ensure that you are being sufficiently critical in your thinking and writing is important. What three things do you wish to commit to at this moment? Who can assist you?

CONCLUSION

Research reviewers and doctoral supervisors who have had much experience describe patterns and common pitfalls that researchers in general make, and more recently there are some trends in coaching research. This chapter identified seven common pitfalls that coaching and mentoring researchers may face, and how to address or avoid these problems.

 **Further reading and resources**

Cohen, M. (2011). *Critical thinking skills for dummies*. New York: Wiley.
Cooksey, R. W., & McDonald, G. M. (2011). *Surviving and thriving in postgraduate research*. Prahran, Vic: Tilde University Press.

For definitions of sampling

http://socialresearchmethods.net/kb/sampterm.php

Writing resources

www2.le.ac.uk/offices/ld/resources/writing/writing-resources/critical-writing

Critical thinking resources

www.brainpickings.org/2014/01/03/baloney-detection-kit-carl-sagan/

Logical fallacies

https://thebestschools.org/magazine/15-logical-fallacies-know/

THEORIES OF KNOWLEDGE

HOW DO I KNOW?

5

LEARNING OUTCOMES

In completing this chapter and related activities, you will be able to:

1. describe how different ways of knowing (epistemology) influence the production and consumption of coaching and mentoring research;

2. identify your own preferred ways of knowing;

3. understand the relationship between ways of knowing and approaches to methodology.

WHAT IS THE CURRENT REALITY OF RESEARCHERS' VIEWS ON KNOWLEDGE IN COACHING AND MENTORING RESEARCH?

For the practically oriented person, broader philosophical discussions about what constitutes knowledge, whose view is given status and ethics, may seem irrelevant, particularly given that you are so busy. However, coaching and mentoring research very much needs to have these discussions. Consider the following claims.

1. We need to make coaching more evidence-based.
2. There are many charlatans in the coaching industry who do not know what they are doing.
3. I want a mentor because they have actually done it, not just in theory.
4. I already know what I'm doing works, I'm just using research to validate it

All of these claims have an embedded view of what constitutes knowledge, how we know in general, and points out that some views are more valid than others. For example, Claim 1 values empirical evidence. Claim 2 infers that there is a particular 'in group' (i.e., non-charlatans) who know what they are doing, such as a professional body. Claim 3 values practical knowledge and experience – a view very common in practitioners, not surprisingly. Claim 4 represents something you often hear from practitioners, be they from business, health or education, when they come to do research at a university. Research for them is an instrument to be used to give the knowledge claim status, and they need it to join the powerful club with legitimate knowledge.

Currently, there are calls among some coaching and mentoring scholars for more research, as well as for more research of a particular type, based on a particular epistemology – namely, we need more randomized controlled trials to show that coaching and mentoring works, based on a positivist epistemology.

Beware, enter this chapter at your own risk. There may be big words that are cumbersome to work through. However, if you do not yet know what epistemology or positivism means, this chapter is for you. Any time you see an 'ism' attached to the end of a word, it is usually traceable to an intellectual tradition, which shares a set of assumptions. For example, positivism is a tradition within the philosophy of science about what constitutes a legitimate way to know. Any time you see an 'ology' – for example, method*ology*, psych*ology*, etc. – it just means 'reason', theory or account, deriving from the Greek word *logos*. Hence, what is the reason behind your method, what is the reasoning of the psyche, etc. Well equipped with your 'isms' and 'ologies', you will have more tools to approach research in general, but also to identify which are the most important to coaching and mentoring research. Like all aspects of this book, take a coaching approach to the learning and work your way through.

The following quote illustrates why you need to clarify your position on knowledge to be a better researcher:

> how we come to ask particular questions, how we assess the relevance and value of different research methodologies so that we can investigate those questions, how we evaluate the outputs of research, all express and vary according to our epistemological assumptions (p. 1, Johnson & Duberley, 2000).

Coaching and mentoring are practices and processes, things that we 'do', and hence we should use approaches to knowledge that are best suited to this. For example, what is the epistemology (way of knowing) most appropriate for practice? These are not simple questions to answer, nor are they unique to coaching and mentoring. Similar questions are asked of medical practice, nursing practice, counselling practice and any other form of practice (Ferry & Ross-Gordon, 1998).

Theories of knowledge studied in the discipline of epistemology (a subfield of philosophy) are difficult to do justice to in half of one short chapter. However, it is important to surface some of your assumptions about how knowledge is judged and why, before going too far into the research journey. Epistemology, alongside ontology and philosophy of science, are all subfields of philosophy. Philosophy of science examines and debates what qualifies as science in general, and within particular disciplines. This also leads to discussions about methodology in general and what is appropriate for what is being investigated. An ongoing debate is about whether the social sciences (psychology, sociology, economics, etc.) should use the same methodologies as the natural sciences (physics, chemistry, etc.) (Alexandrova, 2017). Coaching and mentoring research is located more within the social sciences, where interpretivist and constructivist approaches are more prominent, but so is positivism, particularly in psychology.

Arguments about what constitutes science, knowledge and how we know (i.e., epistemology) have very significant consequences. You are encouraged not to dismiss it as irrelevant in the name of being practical – remember what we wrote about fatuous pragmatism. How you assume you can know impacts on theories, models and claims you will use, which will impact on the questions you ask, and then the methods you use to answer them.

What is considered legitimate knowledge, including scientific knowledge, has powerful effects. It then relates to who is considered an expert and considered to have expertise. This is the important relationship between knowledge and power. If those who have knowledge are more powerful, it is not a surprise that there are arguments about what is considered knowledge and what is the best way to know. Consider the distinction between 'witch doctors' and contemporary Western medical specialists. The first group were just as powerful in their community during their time, as are medical specialists in the current day. So, in addition to influencing methodology, questions and ways to answer them, there is also an issue of power and privileging of types of knowledge. In some contexts, qualitative researchers feel disadvantaged that their work does not have the same epistemic status as quantitative researchers. Conversely, in some humanities and social science contexts, quantitative research may be viewed as inappropriate or shallow. Hence, research communities continue to argue about this. These debates are good if they are informed and considered. The question 'What is the right epistemology for coaching and mentoring research?' will yield a range of proponents and views. Join the conversation in general and, importantly for your project, at least know where your work sits in the debate. Just because you do a project this time with a particular epistemology and consequent methodology, does not mean that you cannot change and evolve beyond the current project. To start understanding 'ways of knowing', Shotter's (1993) typology helps us to begin to understand how different types of knowledge are privileged in different contexts.

- **Knowing that**: declarative knowledge, or declaring that something is true. For example, the claim 'Six sessions of coaching leads to better outcomes than four sessions': this type of knowledge is seen as more valuable in scientific research contexts.
- **Knowing how**: procedural knowledge (think of skills) or knowing how to do something. For example, 'When I mentor people, I know how to listen'. The type of knowledge referred to here is privileged in contexts that value practice. See Pragmatism within definitions, covered later in this chapter.
- **Knowing from**: Shotter (1993) referred to this as a third way of knowing, and it is knowing from experience in a particular situation: for example, knowing from a lived experience of giving birth. This type of knowledge is privileged in contexts where people wish to share or have an experience understood.

Definitions

Ontology is derived from 'ont', which means being, and *logos*, which means theory or account. Hence, ontology is theory or accountability of being/existing, of what is real. Some like to shorten the definition to 'what things exist'. A more accurate definition may be 'the study of what things exist, and what other things are similar or different and their classification'. Ontology is often coupled with epistemology, as we cannot know something if it does not exist. For example, does coaching exist as separate from counselling, or is it just a relabelling? This question is, in part, an ontological discussion.

Epistemology is derived from 'episteme', which means knowledge, and *logos*, which means theory or account. Hence, epistemology is the theory or accountability of knowledge. It is the study of how we can know and what constitutes legitimate knowledge, particularly scientific knowledge. Some like to shorten the definition to 'ways of knowing', but a more accurate definition may be 'the study of the relative legitimacy of ways of knowing'. Scientific ways of knowing are often seen as very legitimate and are therefore said to have high 'epistemic status: for example, what is the best way to know whether or not coaching works?

Positivism is a philosophical theory of knowledge (i.e., an epistemology) that states that all information that is derived from sensory experience (i.e., observed) forms the basis of knowledge, and is interpreted through reason and logic. These sensory experiences become empirical facts. It rejects theism, metaphysics, intuition and introspective knowledge. In much of the Western world positivist assumptions to knowledge are now taken for granted. Researchers using quantitative methodology often, but not always, have positivist assumptions about knowledge generation. In a coaching and mentoring context, terms like 'evidence-based coaching' assume a version of positivism in their aim to establish general principles based on observable evidence.

Relativism in the context of knowledge is that all positions are relative to the perspective from which they are viewed, and that all claims to truth have equal legitimacy. For a large number of philosophers and most scientists, it is something to be avoided – that is, how does your view avoid 'anything goes'? For example, if a mentor claims that they have the most effective mentoring approach ever, which includes the use of herbs and trampolines because in their knowledge system sedation and elevation are of the highest order, is this acceptable? Or do we need some accepted claims to existence (ontology) and accepted ways to know (epistemology) to proceed? There are similar debates regarding ethical and cultural relativism.

Realism in philosophical terms (not to be confused with art) is the belief that an object exists (i.e., ontology) independent of the observer, their concepts, perceptions, linguistic practices, etc. The well-known question 'If a tree falls in a forest and no one is around to hear it, does it make a sound?' directly points to the issue of realism. A major problem for those who do not hold a realist position is how they avoid relativism. There are degrees of realism – e.g., critical realism – although many people in the coaching and mentoring research world are likely to adopt a form of realism, while there may be significant debates about epistemology, how we know.

Constructivism as an epistemology (as opposed to art, education, etc.) is the view that scientists construct models of the world, a world that does not exist independently from the observer (i.e., they believe there is a real world). However, constructivists view our ways of knowing this world as mediated by our own constructions and we have no direct access to a world without our interpretations and constructions. It is a position which means that absolute objectivity is not possible.

Social constructionism is a theory of knowledge, derived from sociology and communication theory, that views much of knowledge as socially constructed – that is, what we accept as taken-for-granted reality, as interactions between social agents (i.e., people). For example, the majority of social constructionists would assert that language does not mirror reality, but constitutes reality. For this reason, social constructionism is viewed as a relativist position to knowledge. For example, if a professional coaching body asserts that they will only allow evidence-based practice in coaching, a social constructionist position may be that 'evidence-based approaches' are socially constructed agreements to enact in-group and out-group membership, rather than knowledge representing an external reality.

Pragmatism within philosophy derives from the Greek word *pragma*, which means deed, and refers to a theory of knowledge where a proposition is held to be true if it works satisfactorily. Pragmatism examines the real effects of claims to ascertain their meaning and truth. Pragmatism assumes a changing universe and emphasizes that knowledge is for acting, not only describing. Many practitioners, including coaches and mentors, make claims that imply a pragmatist position: 'I've used it several times and it works' (imply, therefore it is true). For example, a coach or mentor who is only interested in learning about things that can be changed (i.e., tractable) is one who is taking a pragmatist stance.

Contextualism, within the context of epistemology, is a view that a claim made about knowledge concept or truth, needs to be anchored to the relevant context. For example, debates about what coaching is and what it is not, are similar to debates about what well-being is and is not, and philosophically the same as the question of whether temperature hot is the same as hot chilli pepper hot. They are concepts in different contexts, but are they the same concept? Is executive coaching actually the same as life coaching? Contextualism would require these questions to be explored deeply and claims made about knowledge to be carefully anchored to the context. Many feminist approaches to knowledge champion situational knowledge and context, and will reject universal claims and laws.

WHAT IS YOUR CURRENT REALITY IN TERMS OF WAYS OF KNOWING IN COACHING AND MENTORING RESEARCH?

Often, beginning researchers, if they think and write about epistemological assumptions and consequent methodology, will use something they have most recently read, report it and move on. Beware of this approach. A coherent piece of work will consider linking epistemological assumptions, theoretical assumptions and methodological assumptions with use of methods.

For example, if you have a relativist, social constructionist or post-modern worldview and epistemology, it makes sense to use a theory consistent with that approach, and the associated methodological assumptions and methods (e.g., discourse analysis). So, within your context, of coaching or mentoring research in which coaching or mentoring is the phenomenon under investigation or the practice used relating to the phenomenon under investigation, what are your assumptions about reality and how to know it? Complete the Activity below to surface some of your assumptions.

 **Activity**

Write some responses to the following questions or discuss them with an interested person who knows a little about your work.

- Do you believe a reality (e.g., a mentoring session) exists independently from observers? Why? What supports your view?
- If yes to (A), do you believe that this reality (e.g., a mentoring session) can be directly observed and understood without bias? Why? What supports your view?
- If no to (A), do you believe that this reality (e.g., a mentoring session) is constructed by language? Why? What supports your view?
- Do you believe the issues regarding reality and knowing exist on more of a spectrum and not simply yes or no? Explain with reference to research on coaching or mentoring.

WHAT ARE YOUR OPTIONS IN TERMS OF WAYS OF KNOWING?

Having completed the Activity, you may have wrestled a little with the big questions about whether an independent reality exists and whether it can be known directly. Take some time to read and think about the definitions within this chapter. Many of the definitions represent key options as ways of knowing. Sometimes people believe they use different epistemologies depending on what they are trying to know. For example, they take a positivist epistemology towards their health, a pragmatist epistemology towards their family life and constructivist epistemology at work. Most people haven't thought about it. Focus on the coaching or mentoring research piece and examine what your options are for that.

What approaches to ways of knowing are most relevant to you? Examining the definitions, do you identify your work with positivism, constructivism, pragmatism, social constructionism, contextualism or something else? They are not always mutually exclusive. For example, quantitative methods derived from positivism may be used in the service of more constructivist-based work. For now, it is useful at least to know what attracts or repels you and why. Rather than foreclosing on an option too quickly, which would not be dissimilar to choosing a religion in one day, keep working on this. Consider the questions in the What next? section that follows.

WHAT NEXT?

Apart from additional reading, it is useful to discuss these concepts with someone, as they may be difficult in the first instance to understand and, for some, it may be difficult to see their relevance.

Find an interested friend, possibly someone on your course, and explore the following questions.

- What is the difference between ontology and epistemology?
- What is the dominant epistemology that is given preference in your environment (e.g., university, college, workplace)?
- What is the difference between positivism and constructivism?
- How much do you believe that language influences reality?
- Why is understanding epistemology important to becoming a good researcher in coaching and mentoring?

Also, you are encouraged to take the online quiz: What's your epistemology? (see Further reading and resources at the end of the chapter).

CONCLUSION

This chapter introduced the study of epistemology from the discipline of philosophy. The theory of knowledge, or how we know, is relevant to how we seek to create new knowledge (i.e., to know), in this case in coaching and mentoring research. You were encouraged to identify, as best as you can at this time, your own assumptions about knowledge. This importance of epistemology was emphasized as it influences how you will frame your overarching enquiry and the methodologies (quantitative or qualitative) and hence the methods you will choose. Remember to use your coaching skills to break this into actionable steps, work on it, seek support and repeat. These are not simple ideas to understand, particularly if you have never studied philosophy.

 **Further reading and resources**

Johnson, P., & Duberley, J. (2000). *Understanding management research*. London: SAGE.

(The book focuses largely on epistemology underpinning applied research.)

Online quiz. What's your epistemology?

www.qzzr.com/c/quiz/49304/17d1b70c-c863-4d2c-a5ed-4968c92773cf

PART II
PHASES OF THE RESEARCH PROCESS

CHOOSING A RESEARCH METHODOLOGY

6

HOW DO I CHOOSE A RESEARCH METHODOLOGY?

LEARNING OUTCOMES

In completing this chapter and related activities, you will be able to:

1. describe a research methodology;
2. identify factors that help you to choose a research methodology;
3. describe advantages and disadvantages of quantitative and qualitative methodology;
4. identify the best choice for your current situation.

WHAT IS THE CURRENT REALITY IN TERMS OF CHOOSING A RESEARCH METHODOLOGY?

Before we unpack how to choose a research methodology, let's quickly recap where we've been so far. Research generally begins with an epistemology (see Chapter 5) that governs the assumptions we make about the research process. Usually, but perhaps not always, we do not choose the epistemology. Instead, the epistemology chooses us. This might sound bizarre, but it reflects the reality of much research. For example, if we enrol on a course in the natural or medical sciences, then we are likely to develop a positivist epistemology because positivist assumptions underpin these research fields. In the humanities and social sciences, it could be one of many different epistemologies (see Chapter 5). Different epistemologies shape our research questions and also give rise to different methodologies that form the basis of different methods we use to carry out the research. In this respect, methodology differs from method. A *method* is essentially a tool, strategy or technique that we use to carry out our research, whereas a *methodology* is the justification or theory about why we are using such methods. For example, we might have a textbook on statistics which is likely to detail the theoretical principles behind different statistical analyses (statistical methodology), whereas within that textbook it is also likely to detail several different statistical methods that might be used to carry out the data analysis (correlation, factor analysis, etc.). Thus, methodology is a higher order concept than methods.

Table 6.1 Typical decision sequence in the research process

Process of key decisions by researcher	Wei Chang (example researcher 1)	Ananya Ahuja (example researcher 2)	Relevant chapters
Epistemology	Constructivist	Positivist	**Chapter 5**
Research question	*What is the experience of mentoring among middle managers?*	*Does mentoring increase perceived middle-manager suitability for promotion?*	**Chapter 8**
Methodology	Qualitative	Quantitative	**Chapter 6**
Inference and reasoning	Inductive	Deductive	**Chapters 4, 15**
Methods of data collection/ generation	Semi-structured Interviews, focus groups	Subjective data (e.g., self- or other report surveys), objective data (e.g., actual performance)	**Chapters 17, 18, 20**
Sampling	Small samples chosen for specific purposes	Large representative samples	**Chapters 17, 20, 23**
Analysis/ interpretation	E.g., narrative analysis	E.g., correlation, regression, factor analysis	**Chapters 18, 21**
Communication of results	Tables, figures, narrative samples	Tables, figures, graphs	**Chapters 14, 21**

Table 6.1 is designed to show how this all fits together by distinguishing two sample researchers with different starting epistemological assumptions. The downward arrow in the table reflects the fact that decisions made in the upper levels of the table have downstream effects and typically govern more micro- or lower-level decisions in the research process. Table 6.1 is oversimplified for pedagogical reasons, as research does not always play out in such a linear fashion. In particular, there is feedback between the decisions at each level that can lead to iterations in the decisions made at earlier stages, but the table does show the sequence of decisions that is typical from different researcher perspectives.

Take Wei Cheng, for example, who is shown on the middle-left of the table. Wei Cheng is a researcher from a UK-based university, and due to his connections he is able to draw data from a large global corporation to study mentoring. He is particularly interested in examining the experiences of middle-management employees who are undergoing mentoring as protégés. Wei Cheng is a constructivist who starts with the belief that scientists construct models of the world, a world that does not exist independently from the observer. Hence, absolute objectivity in the research process is not possible for Wei Cheng. For this reason, his research tends to be based on qualitative methodology, which by its nature is typically inductive in the inferences made about the world – that is, his research tends to be more concerned with the generation of new ideas in a fairly exploratory nature. Inductive reasoning lends itself to qualitative methods, such as interviews or focus groups, through which text-based data such as narrative samples are retrieved for later analysis. Because interviews and focus groups are quite resource intensive to actually do, among other reasons, they tend to be performed with relatively few participants who are selected for a specific purpose. Thus, Wei Cheng plans to recruit about 30–50 middle managers for interviews in this global corporation, with equal representations of men and women. Wei Cheng will analyse his data with typical methods designed for the text-based data collected in focus groups or interviews (e.g., narrative analysis), which he will then report in tables, figures or narrative samples in his research outputs.

Wei Cheng differs from Ananya Ahuja, who is shown on the middle-right of the table. Ananya also works at a large UK-based university and also has connections with the same global corporation. Ananya is interested in whether middle managers who receive mentoring are rated as more competent, which in turn helps them to be perceived as more suitable for promotion. Thus, Ananya is a positivist and therefore believes that all information about the world is directly observable. Observation then forms the basis of knowledge and is interpreted through reason and logic. Because Ananya is a positivist, her research tends to be based on quantitative methodology, which in turn tends to be more deductive in the inferences it makes about the world. Hence, Ananya has designed testable *a priori* research hypotheses (predictions) that she will test once her data are collected. In particular, after reviewing the research literature, Ananya hypothesizes that middle managers who receive mentoring will be rated as more competent by their supervisors, which will increase their perceived suitability for promotion. Ananya therefore plans to give validated questionnaires to the supervisors of a large representative sample of middle managers (about 200–500) to measure the *perceived competence* of the middle managers, as well as their *perceived suitability* for promotion. She also plans to identify how much mentoring each middle manager has received by asking them directly via a different survey. Because there are more men than women in this particular corporation, Ananya will aim to have her sample reflect this imbalance in the genders recruited in her sample so that it is representative. She will examine her hypothesis with correlation and regression-based techniques, the results of which she will report in various forms with tables, figures or graphs in the research outputs.

These two examples are designed to show how different epistemologies inform our research questions and hence affect our choice of methodology through which we address our research questions: qualitative or quantitative. You will notice in these two examples that Wei Cheng's research question is much more open-ended, which lends itself to inductive inferences, whereas Ananya Ahuja's research question is more closed-ended and lends itself to a particular set of possible conclusions. Such conclusions are typically predicted in advance via research hypotheses. While no *one* epistemology or methodology is 'correct', they do have important consequences for other decisions made downstream in the research process.

WHAT IS THE CURRENT REALITY FOR YOU IN TERMS OF CHOOSING A RESEARCH METHODOLOGY?

Sometimes it is not clear what our epistemology is or what particular methodology we should opt for. It may be helpful to take stock of your current situation and work backwards from your research questions. In doing so, try to answer the following questions.

- Do you currently have a research question/s? If so, what is it?
- Is your research question/s more open-ended or closed-ended? For example, the question 'What value do senior leaders see in mentoring programmes?' is an open- ended question that could generate a variety of different insights and perhaps might lend itself to qualitative methodology, based more on inductive logic.
- Are your research questions focused on *description*, *comparisons* or *relationships* between variables? Such questions tend to yield a narrower set of possible answers and also lend themselves to the development of hypotheses (predictions) and thus might be more suitable for quantitative methodology. Examples of each are as follows.
  - **Relationship-based** question: What is the association between mentor gender and protégé ratings of mentoring effectiveness?
  - **Comparison-based** question: Are senior mentors more effective than peer-mentors from the perspective of protégés?
  - **Descriptive** question: Since 1990, what growth has occurred in the use of executive coaching among senior leaders in corporate environments?

We delve more into the different types of research questions in Chapter 8.

WHAT ARE YOUR OPTIONS IN TERMS OF CHOOSING A RESEARCH METHODOLOGY?

To help us further unpack the general differences between quantitative and qualitative methodology, we explore some key characteristics of each below. We will touch on these points again in Parts III and IV of this book, which are each specifically focused on these two methodologies and the methods used within them. **Qualitative methodology** is concerned more about theory and principles to understand human experience or behaviour from the perspective of the participant. It generally assumes a dynamic and changing reality. In contrast, **quantitative methodology**, because it is typically rooted in positivism, is more concerned with uncovering observable facts about phenomena. It thus assumes an objective and measurable reality and is particularly interested in cause-and-effect relationships. Table 6.2 unpacks some of the key differentiating characteristics between quantitative and qualitative methodology a little further. If some of this language is unfamiliar to you, it might become more familiar to you as you progress through Parts III and IV of the book.

Table 6.2   Quantitative and qualitative methodology key characteristics

Key characteristics	
Quantitative methodology	**Qualitative methodology**
Data are collected through operationalized measurement.	Data typically collected via participant observation, interviews or focus groups.
Data are analysed through numerical comparisons and statistical inferences.	Data are analysed around themes that are organized from descriptions of participants.
Data are reported in tables, figures, graphs and associated statistical tests.	Data are reported in the language of the informant, which can also be organized into tables and figures.
Can be used in descriptive, correlational, experimental or quasi-experimental research designs.	Lacks any coherent typology of designs into which studies are pigeonholed.
Common data-collection methods used: Subjective measures might include rating scales in surveys, which can be self-report or other report (see Chapter 17). Objective measures might include performance data, absenteeism, biological swabs or another metric that does not draw on the options or perspectives of participants (see Chapter 17).	**Common data-collection/generation methods used:** Participant observation, open-ended questions, structured and unstructured interviews, focus groups. Generally qualitative data is text-based, though this does not always have to be the case. Other data-types could be photos, sound recordings, etc.

So which one is better? There is no answer to that question, as both quantitative and qualitative methodology have important strengths and weaknesses, and each is more suitable in different contexts. Carr (1994) identifies a number of strengths and weaknesses for both forms of research methodology, summarized and expanded in Table 6.3 below. Note that we recap these advantages and disadvantages of quantitative and qualitative methodology in Parts III and IV of this book.

Table 6.3   Strengths and weaknesses of quantitative and qualitative methodology

Quantitative methodology	
Strengths	**Weaknesses**
Considered more objective.	Can ignore experiences of the individual.
Involves numerical data that is orderly and numerically comparable.	Individual experiences are often not well captured with numerical data.
Deviant (outlying) cases are typically eliminated.	Sometimes outlying cases are of valid scientific interest.
More easily replicated, as they are often derived from standardized protocols.	As the data are reliant on numerical descriptions rather than detailed stories and narratives, they typically don't allow for deep exploration of human experiences.
The researcher has more control over extraneous or unrelated factors (confounds) that could impact the findings.	The research can be carried out in an artificial lab environment that lacks external validity (generalizability).
Large samples are designed to make the research more generalizable.	Large samples can be resource intensive and onerous on the researcher to collect.
It is the best way to test for causality.	Data are generally focused on a narrow question.
It can allow for higher levels of precision in the results.	If survey methods are used, pre-set answers may not necessarily reflect how participants actually feel and thus might miss important information.
Qualitative methodology	
Strengths	**Weaknesses**
Rich descriptive data allows researchers to go into much depth into human experiences. It might find issues or experiences commonly missed with positivist research.	Not always generalizable due to smaller, less representative samples.
Is inherently flexible.	Researcher has much less control over the research process.
Is generally more capable of capturing the actual thoughts and feelings of participants.	Conclusions need to be tentatively drawn.

Qualitative methodology	
Considered more holistic as the human experience is considered in greater detail.	Is less reliable, as results may differ depending on the day/the sample.
While qualitative methodology cannot be used to test for cause-and-effect relationships, qualitative descriptions can suggest possible relationships, causes, effects and dynamic processes that are later tested.	Reliability and validity (see Chapter 17) are generally major criticisms. Because the data are very subjective, findings are not replicable and different conclusions may be reached by different researchers.

This is not an exhaustive list, but the key point to consider is that for every strength, there is generally a corresponding weakness associated with the methodology (Carr, 1994). Hence, no one methodology is 'best', but each instead serves a different purpose and is linked with different research epistemologies, as well as research questions.

Note, it is common practice to combine qualitative and quantitative research methodologies, which could each yield different and complementary insights into a research question. This is known as mixed-methods research. Interested readers can explore this in more depth in Chapter 24.

WHAT NEXT?

Go back to Table 1.1 in Chapter 1 for a distinction between the different types of coaching and mentoring research: process, outcomes, implementation and non-intervention research. Also flip forward to Chapter 20 and read further about these different types of research. Then, consider the following two points.

- Which of the four types of research does your own project best align with?
- How might these different types of research support your choice of quantitative or qualitative methodology?

 Further reading and resources

We recommend you locate and read the following book which has much more detailed information on quantitative and qualitative methodology. In particular, Chapters 7–9 deal with qualitative methodology and Chapters 10–12 deal with quantitative methodology.

Punch, K. (2013). *Introduction to social research: quantitative and qualitative approaches* (3rd ed.). London: SAGE.

RESEARCH SCOPE

WHAT IS THE SCOPE OF MY RESEARCH PROJECT?

7

LEARNING OUTCOMES

In completing this chapter and related activities, you will be able to:

1. define the concept of research scope;
2. describe the difference between research area, topic, question and hypothesis;
3. understand how to frame or position your research.

WHAT IS THE CURRENT REALITY IN TERMS OF SCOPING A RESEARCH PROJECT?

The process of scoping a research project involves identifying testable research questions that are feasible to test within the time, resources and access to data that a researcher (or team of researchers) has available at their disposal. The scope of projects will vary depending on who is undertaking the research and the resources available to them. For example, a PhD project will possess a different scope from a collaborative research project that involves teams of researchers with millions of dollars in research funding. The former will generally be smaller in scope, due to more limited resources. Indeed, projects that delve into territory out of scope will put the project at risk of *never being completed* (see Chapter 4, Avoiding pitfalls). Hence, scoping is a fundamental step in the research process.

So that we can better equip you to scope your research project, we need to distinguish some important details in this area. Below, we distinguish 'area of research' from 'topic of research' from 'research questions' and then 'hypotheses'. Each is important for you to learn in terms of determining the scope of your project, as each comes with a level of specificity that allows you to pinpoint your thinking to develop sound research questions and hypotheses to evaluate.

AREA OF RESEARCH

The area of research refers to the context and broad category within which you may seek to find your actual topic. For example, 'coaching in organizations' or 'mentoring at universities' is an area within which a research project might proceed. They are not topics, which are more targeted and specific, as we shall demonstrate shortly.

We find that many students of ours, particularly when they begin their research careers, bring a research area to the table that they want to study, rather than a topic. This can be problematic because it ultimately makes it very difficult to determine what fits within the scope of the research and what sits outside. This is because research areas are very broad by their nature. Instead, what we tell them is that they need to identify a research topic, which is more focused. After they do that, they need to identify one or more meaningful research questions, which are more focused again. Figure 7.1 illustrates how moving from a research area, to a topic, to a research question, effectively funnels our thinking towards more specificity in the research process.

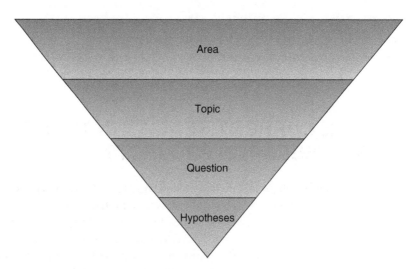

Figure 7.1   The funnel towards a research question or hypothesis

TOPIC OF RESEARCH

The topic of a research project is the specific issue it investigates within the broader area. Thus, within the research area of 'coaching in organizations' some workable topics might be: 'Solution-focused coaching in "high potential" staff at university'; or 'The rise of coaching interventions in organizations since the 1990s'; or 'Life coaching for employees with clinically diagnosed depression'. You will notice that these topics take up noticeably more words than 'coaching in organizations'. This is natural, because a research topic is more specific than a research area. If you see potential topics consisting of only a few words, they most likely are not research topics, but rather research areas. A topic is distinguished by its focus and precision. It will typically consist of a short statement from which a research question can easily be derived.

When selecting a research topic, it will be essential to choose an area that interests you. It is also important to keep it manageable. This means that it has to be feasible to complete within both your time frame and budget. If a topic is too broad, it will be problematic to research, because the parameters for the research project will not properly distinguish what sits inside and what sits outside your scope. Some common ways to funnel from a research area towards a research topic are:

- by geographical area: e.g., the growth of coaching for well-being in the United Kingdom;
- by culture: e.g., the efficacy of coaching in East Asian cultures;
- by time frame: e.g., mentoring approaches in commercial organizations during the global financial crisis;
- by discipline: e.g., the contribution of coaching principles to performance management processes;
- by population group: e.g., coaching for those nearing retirement;
- by theoretical orientation: e.g., solution-focused coaching.

While these examples are still far too general for research topics, using these strategies to focus your question will narrow your topic so that it becomes distinguishable from an area alone. Also, it will be important for you to justify the significance of your research within your narrower topic. For example, if you decide to narrow your research area by studying the growth of coaching for well-being in the UK, it will be important for you to identify why this is important knowledge that is worthy of scientific enquiry (remember **significance** from Chapter 2). Doing so will be instrumental for you in justifying your contribution to the literature. It will also be instrumental for you in being able to speak to the urgency of the project and therefore put together a very solid research proposal (see Chapter 10).

If you have any difficulties or questions with focusing your topic, it is often useful to discuss the topic with your research supervisor (if you have one), or with someone else who can help make your topic more focused. Generally, this person will require at least some expertise in the area.

RESEARCH QUESTIONS

Research questions can be either exploratory (open-ended) or confirmatory (derived from hypotheses, which we will describe shortly). A research question is a concise, targeted and testable question around which you can focus your research. Typically, it will take your research topic and rephrase it into a specific question so that it becomes testable. For example, you might ask 'What is the effect of solution-focused coaching for the well-being and academic performance of university students?', or 'To what extent have coaching courses grown in the Western hemisphere since 1990?' or 'Does life coaching alleviate depressive symptoms in clinical patients?'.

As we will emphasize throughout this book, research should be driven by research *questions* rather than research *methods*. This means that the methods you choose will serve the research questions that you ask and not vice versa. The opposite of this is when your research questions are designed around the research methods you would like to use, which is problematic. Research should be driven by your research questions because it will ensure that your research methods are the right fit for what you want to test empirically. It also ensures that your research questions are more likely to make a contribution to the literature. We often see students and beginning researchers who will design their research question around a method with which they are comfortable or one that they want to learn. This can be problematic because not all methods are the right fit for a research question. For example, sometimes qualitative methods will not yield the right information to evaluate a coaching or mentoring programme and at other times we need to know more than quantitative data can tell us. In applied contexts, such as coaching and mentoring, however, research questions may be constrained by what is possible due to data and resources.

HYPOTHESES

Research hypotheses are derived from the research question and are specific **testable predictions** made about what you expect to find in the study. Usually, a study or research proposal will begin with a brief literature review that covers relevant background material, such as theory and prior research. This will inform and justify the particular hypotheses that are to be tested. Hypotheses will represent the particular outcome you expect to find, and which you will confirm or disconfirm at the conclusion of your research study. Hypotheses are established at the beginning of the research process and they are then used to help inform the research design and methods you will use, which ultimately need to be carefully thought through in order to adequately test hypotheses. A study can have one hypothesis or potentially several hypotheses. Importantly, not all studies will state hypotheses, particularly if they are based on inductive logic (see Chapter 4).

 **Activity**

What is the current reality for you in terms of scoping your research project?

Now that you know more about research areas, topics, questions and hypotheses, let's look at your current situation. See if you can respond to the following questions.

• How focused is your current project?
• Is it a research area, a topic or a question?

If it is too broad, can you rephrase it into a focused and testable question?

Below we have three tips to help you develop research questions. In Chapter 8 you will find further detailed information that can help you to shape a good research question.

Tip 1: Formulate a few questions on what you would like to know about the topic in which you are interested. For example: What do you hope to find out? What is known and not known already? In what are you most interested?

Tip 2: Now narrow your question to the *most* important thing you want to find out (this will help to keep you focused when your project becomes more complicated later down the track).

Tip 3: What are the time and resources available to you? Does this limit what you can do? Answering this question will help you in terms of shaping your question around what is possible for you to achieve. As an example, a sole practitioner will generally have more limited time and resources than researchers who are a part of a larger research team, with ample funding, who generally have the luxury of asking more complex and 'bigger' questions that can take years to study.

 **Activity**

What are your options in terms of scoping your project?

We invite you to go through a process that is colloquially termed 'gaming out your study'. In other words, we invite you to ask yourself the following questions and to record your answers to them.

1. What are the possible findings you hope to learn from your research study?
2. What impact do you expect these findings to have? That is, how will they make a difference either to the research literature or to the real world?
3. Which ones will make a difference to how you think about the topic you are researching?
4. Will you use pre-set hypotheses or predictions that will guide your analysis in your study?

Reflecting upon your answers to the above questions, consider whether your thinking is currently at the level of a research area, a research topic, or do you have a more specific question in mind? Question 4 will be very important for you to consider, as it will ultimately shape whether your research will be inductive (exploratory) or deductive (confirmatory). As we briefly outlined in Chapter 4, inductive reasoning in the research process typically starts with the data, and then uses this as a starting point for evaluating trends or patterns one finds, which might later shape hypotheses or theory. Deductive reasoning, in contrast, usually starts with verifiable predictions (hypotheses) that are derived from theory and then uses empirical data to confirm or disconfirm these predictions. Choosing between inductive or deductive research traditions is among the most important options you will have and it will depend heavily on the type of study you wish to carry out. We discuss this further in Chapter 9, which is where we cover the basics of research design.

The above reflective questions will help you focus your project into more targeted research questions, with possible accompanying hypotheses. This is a crucial step in the research scoping process. A tight research scope will no doubt help to keep you on track throughout your project. However, you should also beware of a phenomenon known as 'scope creep'. Scope creep is common in project management and refers to a process whereby a project sees its original focus expand while it is still in progress. Scope creep is also common in research and, as the term suggests, can ultimately result in projects that are expanded to such a level that they are no longer feasible, leading to the researcher or research team failing to deliver. Even if the research is completed, scope creep can result in a final project that resembles nothing like what was originally proposed. Thus, we recommend that you do the following.

1.   Develop a clear research scope that you can later revisit if necessary.
2.   Revisit your research scope throughout your research project to ensure that it stays on track.
3.   Develop some feasible time lines, which will help to ensure that you stay on track and within scope (see Chapter 12 for research time lines and planning).

WHAT NEXT?

Have a go at scoping your own research project. Identify a) a research area, b) a research topic, c) one or more research questions, and d) clear and testable hypotheses that relate to your research question. This may take some time, but it is fundamental in both putting together a research proposal that is clear and focused, and actually carrying out your research project.

CONCLUSION

This chapter has differentiated between an *area* of research, a *topic* of research, a *research question* and a *hypothesis*. This distinction is fundamental to 1) writing a proposal for your research and 2) actually completing your project. A lot of confusion is created when people new to research bring a research area to the table, when they should have a clearly articulated topic, question and hypotheses. It is fundamental to have a clear scope for your research, which will help you to stay on track and will also help to ensure that you have a clear focus for your research. However, beware of scope creep which may expand your project into one that will become unmanageable.

 **Further reading and resources**

Read Chapter 5 of the following text, which provides a good discussion of research questions and hypotheses. It will also help to prepare you for what is to come in this book, including reviewing literature (Chapter 9) and testing for causality (Chapter 16).

Punch, K. F. (2013). *Introduction to social research: quantitative and qualitative approaches* (3rd ed.). London: SAGE.

RESEARCH QUESTIONS

8

HOW DO I SHAPE A GOOD RESEARCH QUESTION?

LEARNING OUTCOMES

In completing this chapter and related activities, you will be able to:

1. understand the importance of research question/s;
2. describe the features of well-defined research question/s;
3. formulate a well-defined research question/s.

WHAT IS THE CURRENT REALITY IN TERMS OF WRITING RESEARCH QUESTIONS?

Writing clear, concise and legible research questions is fundamental to the research enterprise. This is because research questions state the specific issue or problem that your project aims to address, and without research questions it is difficult to determine the boundaries for the research study. To be meaningful, research questions need to be clear, concise and relevant, and focused on a novel issue that is of substantive importance to either theory, practice, methods or something else. A research question will help you to focus your research by laying the path to a specific, arguable thesis.

So what, then, makes a 'good' research question? Many universities have excellent introductory materials about how to write meaningful research questions. While a synthesis of these materials is beyond the scope of this book, we do direct readers to ones that we find most helpful and ones that we will direct our higher degree research students to. For example, Queensland University of Technology (2016) has created a range of useful materials that may guide you to develop well-defined research questions. Specifically, they recommend that research questions contain several properties, which we have adapted here for the purposes of this book. We stress that many other resources are available and that readers should consult *a number of* resources to provide guidance on writing research questions.

IT WILL IDENTIFY THE PHENOMENA OF ENQUIRY

The phenomena of enquiry reflect what you will be studying. For example, imagine a project with the following research question:

- 'What is the effect of solution-focused coaching on employee mental health in Australia?'

In this project, the phenomena of enquiry are solution-focused coaching and employee mental health. This title also lays out the population of interest (which differs from the phenomena of enquiry), who are Australian employees. More specifically, it is the combination of all these things that is of most interest to the researcher and either one used in isolation would likely serve to make the project too broad. Identifying the phenomena of enquiry helps you to focus your research into a more targeted set of parameters that help set the boundaries for the study. For those working from a positivist epistemology (see Chapter 5), it is often useful to contain the following specifics within a research question:

1.   the **independent** variable (IV: the variable you will be manipulating or the variable under study);
2.   the **dependent** variable (DV: the outcome variable; see Chapter 15 for deeper discussion of IVs and DVs);
3.   the **study population** of interest.

Note that these specifics are particularly useful for confirmatory, rather than exploratory, research questions. See later in this chapter for a discussion of this distinction.

Activity

Try to identify which are the independent variable, dependent variable and the study population from the research question described above. Then, think of your own possible research question and see if you can identify these three specifics: the IV, DV and study population.

IT WILL ASSIST WITH THE CODING OF RELEVANT LITERATURE

The research question will help you to determine what is within scope and what is out of scope for your research project. For example, using the same research topic in the previous example, it is clear that an evaluation of *solution-focused coaching* on *employee* mental health in *Australia* is of interest, and therefore you do not need to look into other interventions (e.g., virtual mentoring), or other populations (e.g., children), or other outcomes (e.g., learning), or investigate nations other than Australia. Thus, the research question helps you to determine what is relevant and what is not relevant to your study.

IT WILL DRAW ATTENTION TO THE SIGNIFICANCE OF THE RESEARCH

Your study should increase knowledge in an important way on whatever topic you are studying (see Chapter 2). If possible, try to identify what will be different about the literature after the completion of your project. Using the previous example, it is clear that the study contributes evidence about the evaluation of a solution-focused coaching programme on employee mental health. To be satisfactory, such a project should yield new insights that were not available before the project, and this should be clear from the research question. After reading your research question, a reader should get an idea of what he or she could learn if you were to proceed to complete the full study, and that knowledge should excite them.

IT HAS THE CAPACITY TO SURPRISE THE RESEARCHER

The research question should hint at surprising new possibilities to the literature, which will increase the chance that your project will make a contribution. In this example, our research question hints that after the study, we will know more about whether solution-focused coaching improves (or doesn't) employee mental health in an Australian context.

IT SHOULD GENERALLY NOT BE ANSWERABLE WITH A SIMPLE 'YES' OR 'NO'

A well-written research question should generally not be answerable with a simple 'yes' or 'no', or easily obtained facts. Instead, it should require both research and analysis on the part of the researcher. In our case, perhaps the solution-focused coaching programme improved employee mental health, or perhaps it didn't. Perhaps solution-focused coaching works, but only under particular circumstances, such as the type of occupation, characteristics of the participants, the type of organization in which it was delivered, or something else. Your research question should allow for complex theses to be built that address the research problem.

COMMON CHALLENGES AND PROBLEMS

An important point to keep in mind when formulating a research question is that it should be specific rather than general. Bless, Higson-Smith and Kagee (2006: 29) write that, in some cases research questions are too vague and too general to be of much use to a researcher.

When a question is specific and focused, it is easier to answer than if it is general and unfocused. This is because such questions identify the boundaries for the research and make it easier for the researcher to identify what is relevant and irrelevant to the study. Moreover, if the research question is too general and vague, it will be difficult to distinguish it from a research area (see Chapter 7).

Working from our example, let's imagine we proposed the following research question: 'Does solution-focused coaching work well in organizations?' In this example, our research question is lacking focus, as well as complexity. From the question, it is clear that solution-focused coaching is of interest and it also has something to do with organizations. But the question tells us nothing about what our key dependent variable is (i.e., our outcome of interest was employee mental health). Instead, it seeks to address the vague problem of whether 'solution-focused coaching works well …'.

WHAT IS THE CURRENT REALITY FOR YOU IN TERMS OF WRITING RESEARCH QUESTIONS?

Now that you know some of the properties that clear and meaningful research questions commonly contain, have a go at drafting a research question for your own project that incorporates each of these properties. Table 8.1 identifies some useful sentence structures that might be helpful as they offer phrases that help establish complexity in the question.

Table 8.1 Useful sentence structures for writing research questions

What is the nature of …?	How do … differ?	What are the functions of …?
How do … perceive?	What factors affect …?	What strategies are used …?
How do … respond?	How do … affect?	What are the effects of …?
How are … defined?	Under what conditions do …?	What is the relationship between … ?
What are the mechanisms by which …?		

Sourced from: http://airs.library.qut.edu.au/1/3/

WHAT ARE MY OPTIONS IN TERMS OF FORMULATING A RESEARCH QUESTION?

Depending on your epistemology (Chapter 5), there are several different ways in which one can formulate a research question. We focus on two different types of research questions here because we find this distinction particularly useful. Specifically, Barker, Pistrang and Elliott (2015: Ch. 3) distinguish **exploratory** from **confirmatory** research questions. Let's have a look at a plausible example of each.

- **Exploratory question:** What do new protégés find helpful about virtual mentoring in the workplace?
- **Confirmatory question:** What makes virtual mentoring more effective in enhancing the work performance of early-career compared to middle-career employees?

The fundamental difference between these two examples is that the former is more open-ended, descriptive and, importantly, follows inductive logic. The latter lends itself to the development of specific testable hypotheses (see Chapter 6) and therefore follows deductive logic. For this reason, confirmatory questions are commonly (but not exclusively) addressed with quantitative methods (see Chapters 16–19). Barker et al. (2015) note that it is appropriate to develop exploratory research questions under the following circumstances.

1. When a research area is relatively new or little is known about it.
2. When the phenomenon of enquiry is a highly complex process, event or experience, requiring in-depth description and definition.
3. When a research area is contradictory, confusing or not moving forward. Sometimes this happens when the research area skips the open-ended descriptive work and goes straight to quantification.

WHAT NEXT?

We recommend you read Barker et al. (2015: Ch. 3), which will help to consolidate your skills in writing research questions. In Ch. 3, entitled 'Doing the ground work', you will learn further about how to formulate research questions, and learn in more depth the difference between exploratory and confirmatory research questions.

We also recommend you revisit Cooksey and McDonald (2011) who provide further useful information on formulating a research question.

CONCLUSION

Building on Chapter 7, this chapter explored how to formulate clear and meaningful research questions, which are fundamental to the research enterprise. Clear and meaningful questions are specific, focused, evidence-based and hint at surprising and complex answers. This chapter also distinguished exploratory from confirmatory research questions, and identified situations in which exploratory research questions might be more appropriate.

 **Further reading and resources**

The following resources provide further information on writing research questions.

Cooksey, R. W., & McDonald, G. M. (2011). *Surviving and thriving in postgraduate research.* Prahan, Vic: Tilde University Press.
Queensland University of Technology, 'The six properties in detail': http://airs.library.qut.edu.au/1/2/ (accessed on 2.11.2016).
Punch, K. F. (2013). *Introduction to social research: quantitative and qualitative approaches* (3rd ed.). London: SAGE.

REVIEWING LITERATURE

9

HOW DO I DO A GOOD LITERATURE REVIEW IN COACHING OR MENTORING?

LEARNING OUTCOMES

In completing this chapter and related activities, you will be able to:

1. describe common types of literature reviews;
2. generate useful search terms for your next literature review;
3. identify criteria to critically evaluate coaching and mentoring research studies and literature reviews;
4. construct an annotated bibliography for your research study.

The skills associated with literature reviewing are central to those of a researcher. This chapter will address the techniques of literature review for coaching and mentoring researchers, including narrative reviews and systematic reviews, and will touch on meta-analyses. The chapter will include practical exercises for the researcher to apply to their own literature searching, and will identify checklists to ensure that one is conducting rigorous reviews using solid search strategies and efficient information management. Literature reviews are ubiquitous and are typically performed to introduce any empirical research study. However, literature reviews are also commonly done in their own right, in which case the review itself will become the research study and provides the basis from which knowledge is created. In this chapter, we focus primarily on this latter type of literature review.

WHAT IS THE CURRENT REALITY IN TERMS OF LITERATURE REVIEW IN COACHING AND MENTORING? A REVIEW OF KEY CONCEPTS

Before we can evaluate your own current reality with respect to a literature review, we first need to unpack a few key concepts. Below, we describe the key components of the narrative review and systematic review.

WHAT IS A LITERATURE REVIEW?

A literature review is a critical analysis and synthesis of the literature on a particular topic. The review should describe and evaluate what is currently known and what is not known within a given research area. A literature review, by its nature, will tend to be broader than an individual empirical study. A literature review will not only synthesize and evaluate what is known and what is not known on a topic, but it will also *create new knowledge* in doing so. This is a key characteristic of a literature review that helps distinguish it from a generic summary of the literature. Whereas a summary of the literature will summarize what is currently known, a literature review will use the literature in such a way that it develops a new argument or 'way of thinking' that serves as new knowledge.

Literature reviews are not typically very easy to write, but they can be very influential. This is because literature reviews serve as a bridge between the vast and scattered assortment of articles on a topic, and readers who do not have the time or resources to locate and synthesize them themselves (Baumeister & Leary, 1997). Thus, literature reviews can be instrumental decision-making devices for policy makers, practitioners, clinicians, leaders or textbook writers who will generally go to literature reviews as their first point of call to identify best-practice or 'the current state' for a particular field (Borenstein, Hedges, Higgins, & Rothstein, 2009). Literature reviews can also be a helpful way for you to learn about a research topic or research area, and are a great way to learn new skills relevant to research. Writing a literature review will likely let you develop skills in three areas.

1. **Information seeking**: the ability to scan the literature efficiently, using manual or electronic methods, to identify a set of useful articles and sources for the review.
2. **Critical appraisal**: the ability to apply principles of analysis to identify unbiased and valid studies.
3. **Synthesis**: the ability to synthesize findings, which includes creating a picture of what is known and not known.

The synthesis step is key to a literature review, which is where an author integrates the available sources included in the review in a way that provides new insight on a topic. A literature review will not simply list studies relevant to a topic and describe each one in turn. The literature needs to be woven together and integrated (i.e., synthesized) to build informative arguments.

WHAT IS THE CURRENT REALITY FOR YOU IN TERMS OF WRITING A LITERATURE REVIEW?

It is important to note that literature reviews come in many shapes and forms, and this will be an important point for you to consider when reflecting on your own situation and goals for your review. Importantly, literature reviews can be *stand-alone research projects*, in which case the literature review will form a research project in and of itself. In a lot of these cases (but not always), such reviews will follow the structure of a typical research study (e.g., introduction, methods, results, discussion). Literature reviews can also *be part of larger research projects*, in which case the literature review generally forms part of the introduction before the methods and results are detailed, or the background material to be covered in a larger project, such as a doctoral or Master's thesis. The skills we present in this chapter will allow you to approach your literature review systematically and exhaustively, and will thus be helpful for whatever your objective is for the literature review. This is because the skills needed to do a literature review (i.e., developing meaningful search terms and protocols, criteria for inclusion, etc.) are complementary for different types of literature review. Nonetheless, before we detail the different types of literature review as stand-alone projects, which involve heavy amounts of synthesis, let's turn to some useful steps that may help you organize the literature. We detail in particular the annotated bibliography.

WHAT IS AN ANNOTATED BIBLIOGRAPHY?

A useful prelude to the synthesis step in a literature review is to complete an annotated bibliography. The purpose of an annotated bibliography is to provide a brief account of the available research on a topic. It does so by establishing a list of research sources that includes concise descriptions and evaluations of each source. Typically, an annotated bibliography contains a brief summary of content and a short analysis or evaluation of each primary study that will be included in the review. So how, then, does one write an annotated bibliography? Consider the following tips.

1. Consider your research question and then generate search terms for a literature search to find sources relevant to your literature review.
2. Decide which sources/studies will be included or excluded from your review (see later in the chapter for guidance on these two steps).
3. Summarize each item concisely, but still include themes and concepts, and do some critical assessment of the material. As a guide, your annotations should not extend beyond one paragraph. Remember, this is not an essay, but just a summary of the most relevant details for you to create an overview of the literature.
4. Use an overall introduction and conclusion to state the scope of your coverage and to formulate the question, problem or concept your material illuminates.

5. If you can, try to identify characteristics of the research, such as the design, participants, aims and research methods the authors used.
6. Background materials and references to previous work by the same author are generally not included; because you are addressing one text at a time, there is no need to cross-reference or use in-text citations to support your annotation.

Sample annotation

We have developed a sample annotation for you to use as a guide (see Table 9.1). You will see that the citation goes first and is followed by the annotation. The summary needs to be concise – about a paragraph long – and in our example we use a key to show each element. For presentation simplicity, we show the annotation in paragraph format here, but others might find it more helpful to put all this information into a spreadsheet where each citation appears on a different row and the key (see below) appears as the column headings. This way you organize your annotated bibliography in tabular form; bibliographies become very easy to organize and manage in this way. Note that while an annotated bibliography does not involve a synthesis of the literature, it will be very helpful to you in completing the synthesis step of the review. This is because an annotated bibliography will allow you to see connections between studies, such as the design used, or participants recruited, or other characteristics of your review that will help you to make connections and integrate the literature into a legible and cohesive picture.

Now that you know more about the annotated bibliography, which can be incredibly valuable to get a grasp on a literature, consider your own situation and why you might like to write a literature review. Try to answer the following questions.

- Are you intending to write a literature review as a research project in itself?
- Are you intending to write a literature review as a part of a larger project?
- Do you currently have some literature that you could organize into an annotated bibliography before you begin the synthesis part of your review?
- How systematic was the process you used to locate this literature (we cover systematic processes later)?

WHAT ARE YOUR OPTIONS IN TERMS OF WRITING A LITERATURE REVIEW?

We have already discussed two options for literature review: the stand-alone literature review and the literature review that forms part of a larger project. Let's now turn to some different types of literature review that could form options for stand-alone research projects, as well as some of the steps involved in conducting one of these reviews. Note that a

Table 9.1 Sample annotation for conducting an annotated bibliography

(1) Grant, A.M. (2014). Autonomy support, relationship satisfaction and goal focus in the coach–coachee relationship: which best predicts coaching success? *Coaching: An International Journal of Theory, Research and Practice*, 7(1), 18–38.

(2) This article examines four aspects of the coach–coachee relationship to investigate which is more related to specific measures of coaching success: (1) autonomy support; (2) the extent to which a coachee feels satisfied with the actual coach–coachee relationship; (3) the extent to which the coaching relationship was similar to an 'ideal' coach–coachee relationship; and (4) a goal-focused coach–coachee relationship.

(3) The aim was to inductively explore features of the coaching relationship that predict measures of coaching success (see point 2 for the four features). The authors use multiple measures to compare the relative efficacy of different aspects of the coach–coachee relationship.

(4) Participants were 49 coach–coachee dyads who conducted four coaching sessions over a 10- to 12-week period.

(5) Results indicated that satisfaction with a coach–coachee relationship does not predict successful coaching outcomes; instead, a goal-focused coach–coachee relationship was a unique and significantly more powerful predictor of coaching success.

(6) The article is useful to my research topic on exploring coaching methods to enhance teacher satisfaction, though it is not central to the topic.

(7) Participants were mature-age university students who were enrolled in a coaching psychology postgraduate degree and these findings may not be generalizable to other contexts.

(8) The authors emphasize the importance of goals in the coaching process and highlight important differences between psychotherapeutic and coaching working alliances.

(9) This article will not form the basis of my research; however, it will be useful supplementary information.

Key
(1) Citation
(2) Introduction
(3) Aims, design and research methods
(4) Participants and scope
(5) Findings
(6) Usefulness (to your research/to a particular topic)
(7) Limitations
(8) Conclusions
(9) Reflection (explain how this work illuminates your topic or how it will fit in with your research)

requirement of any literature review is that literature must be available on a topic for you to locate and then to synthesize. If you are doing research in a brand-new research area or topic which has no prior studies available, then the literature is unlikely to be established enough for you put a literature review together. Note also that while we focus heavily on the systematic review in this section, we do so because the systematic processes used in a systematic review are invaluable for conducting any type of review. This is because they will a) help you to find literature, b) identify its relevance to your purpose, c) critically appraise the literature, and d) organize your study in such a way that others can follow and replicate what you did. But first, we introduce the subject of narrative reviews.

NARRATIVE REVIEWS

Narrative reviews are commonly used in the social and behavioural sciences. The narrative review provides an in-depth discussion of the state of a science on a particular topic. A narrative review will not typically detail methodological approaches that were used to conduct the review, such as the literature search strategy or eligibility criteria about what gets included in the review. This is more the terrain for the systematic review.

 **Activity**

Why do a narrative review?

There are a variety of motivations or goals that you might have to write a narrative review. Baumeister and Leary (1997) identify five possible goals of the narrative review, listed in Table 9.2.

Table 9.2   Common purposes for writing a narrative literature review

Developing theory	The most ambitious goal of a narrative review where an author will try to propose a novel theory regarding a phenomenon of interest.
Theory evaluation	This review will not offer a new theoretical perspective, but will review the literature to test the validity of an existing theory.
Survey of knowledge	Narrative reviews can survey the state of knowledge on a topic of interest in order to provide an overview or integration of research in a given area.
Problem identification	The review will seek to highlight contradictions, weaknesses, controversies or problems in a research area.
Historical review	This review will typically provide an historical account of the development of a theory or research area. Such reviews will typically be organized chronologically, and will also typically provide a commentary regarding the impact and limitations of the contributions within a field.

This is not an exhaustive list, and there may be other reasons that authors opt to write a narrative review. Nonetheless, it is useful to consider some different reasons to write a narrative review and how they might contribute to the literature.

Read Feldman and Lankau (2005), which is a narrative review on executive coaching. As you read it, try to develop answers to the following question.

- Using the table above, what was the essential goal of this literature review? Justify why you came to that conclusion.

It is important to note that the narrative review is a common type of literature review that graduate students are required to write. While a narrative review is easier to write when an author holds expertise in an area, it can also be used to develop expertise in an area, too.

A criticism of narrative reviews is their general absence of systematic processes and protocols, which can lead to biases in the review itself. For this reason, narrative reviews, in contrast to systematic reviews, tend to be more difficult to replicate (Cipriani & Geddes, 2003), but that does not mean they are worthless. Narrative reviews can be an essential tool for researchers due to their inherent flexibility. A narrative review can be useful to draw together studies, using different methods, on different topics for the purposes of interconnection and integration, which will ultimately push a literature forwards. A systematic review, in contrast, will tend to be more focused and precise about what it addresses. We turn to this type of review in the following section.

SYSTEMATIC REVIEWS

Systematic reviews provide an appraisal and synthesis of primary research papers, within a literature, using a rigorous and transparent methodology in both the search strategy and the inclusion of studies. This is designed to minimize bias in the results. The clear and transparent documentation of the processes and the decisions made are intended to allow the readers to identify potential biases in the conclusions made and, if need be, to allow the review to be replicated (Geddes & Carney, 2002). The systematic approach includes clear documentation of what is included and excluded, as well as why. A systematic review will also generally include a critical appraisal of the studies included in the review, and there are a variety of different methods to do this, which we touch on briefly later. For more information on the systematic review as a review technique, we recommend Gough, Oliver, & Thomas (2017), which provides a useful and comprehensive overview of the steps to undertake a systematic review.

META-ANALYSIS

A meta-analysis is a particular type of systematic review that uses statistical methods to aggregate findings on a topic across a literature. The aggregation procedure allows a researcher to identify overall patterns of findings, or to calculate overall summary effects that quantify the results of the review. Due to their quantitative focus, meta-analyses can only include quantitative studies (see Chapters 16–19) that report the needed information, such as an index of the strength of findings in each study (i.e., an effect size). For more information on meta-analysis as a literature review technique, we recommend Borenstein et al. (2009) and Schmidt and Hunter (2015) as two comprehensive textbooks on the subject. For more practical information about how to actually do a meta-analysis, we recommend Field and Gillet (2010) or Lipsey and Wilson (2001).

As a literature review technique, meta-analyses have exploded in the sciences since the 1970s, and there are now some focusing specifically on workplace coaching (e.g., Jones et al., 2016; Theeboom, Beersma, & van Vianen, 2014), mentoring (e.g., Allen et al., 2004; Eby, Allen, Evans, Ng, & DuBois, 2008; Eby et al., 2013), and a variety of other related topics: including leadership (e.g., Burke et al., 2006; Slemp, Kern, Patrick, & Ryan, 2018) and well-being interventions (Slemp, Jach, Chia, Loton, & Kern, 2019), which might help to support a coaching or mentoring relationship.

WHAT ARE SOME OF THE STEPS INVOLVED IN UNDERTAKING A SYSTEMATIC REVIEW?

We have briefly reviewed some common types of literature review, including the narrative and the systematic review. Meta-analysis is a more specialized type of systematic review that you might also adopt if you feel comfortable with that approach. All are important options for you to consider when conducting your literature review. However, due to the highly procedural and systematic process used to put together a systematic review, we feel the skills and steps involved are particularly useful for beginning researchers to learn because they will help you with any type of literature review you plan to write. While an exhaustive review of every step involved is beyond the scope of this chapter (and is the topic of several books in themselves; see Gough et al., 2017 as a good starting text), we highlight the steps that we find most helpful for beginning researchers. In particular, we include commentary on developing a search strategy, eligibility criteria, critically appraising the literature and a checklist of steps for the literature review.

THE SEARCH STRATEGY

A systematic literature review will be exhaustive and capture all available information in a literature. Typically, this will include both published and unpublished research studies, but some reviews will focus just on published literature, which is less desirable. There are many places you can search for resources for your literature review. Below are a few suggestions.

- Electronic databases, such as:
    o   PsycINFO;
    o   Web of Science;

- o   Business Source Complete;
- o   PubMED;
- o   ProQuest Theses and Dissertations Global, which is a useful resource to capture unpublished materials, such as PhD theses.

- Aim to use several relevant databases in conducting your literature search. Another important approach to capture available information on a topic is to:
  - o   scan the reference lists of existing relevant literature reviews and articles;
  - o   scan conference proceedings for relevant information and studies;
  - o   search key journals in your area of expertise. For example, if you would like to examine coaching or mentoring with the field of organizational behaviour, then it will be important for you to examine key journals in this field (e.g., *Journal of Organizational Behavior, Academy of Management Journal* or *Journal of Applied Psychology*). If your focus is in sports coaching, then you will need to examine relevant journals in this area, and so on;
  - o   contact scholars who possess expertise in this area;
  - o   internet search on general scholarly sites, such as Google Scholar.

Researchers might choose to do all or a combination of the above in order to find relevant studies.

IDENTIFYING BOUNDARIES FOR INCLUSION OR EXCLUSION

You will need to establish limits for what is included or excluded from the review, which are referred to as eligibility criteria. Eligibility criteria will help you narrow a large number of search results (potentially numbering in the thousands) to a smaller number of relevant studies which you will include in your review. A useful way to do this is to use a conceptual framework that guides the boundaries for your review. A variety of options are available for this and a full review of them all is beyond the scope of this book. However, one common approach that is widely used, especially for reviews of intervention studies, is to a conceptual framework such as a PICOT framework (Gough et al., 2017; see the Activity below).

 **Activity**

PICOT stands for:

- **Population**: What type of participants will the review examine (e.g., adult employees, adolescent tennis players, etc.)?
- **Intervention**: What is the nature of the intervention in the studies? Is it mentoring? Coaching? A specific type of coaching or mentoring?

(Continued)

(Continued)

- **Comparison:** To whom is your intervention group compared (skip forward to Chapter 16 to learn more about comparison groups in research)?
- **Outcomes:** What is ultimately being measured in the studies – that is, what is the dependent variable in which you are interested? Is it appropriate that there are differences between them or can you accumulate studies that have consistency in the outcomes measured?
- **Time:** What particular time frame is being examined – is it immediately after the intervention or will you also examine longitudinal outcomes (those that the primary studies evaluate over time)?

PICOT is useful because it requires authors of systematic reviews to pinpoint the specifics of target studies, which can then be synthesized to yield an answer to your research question. PICOT can also be used to inform search terms and ultimately identify the boundaries for the review. PICOT is particularly helpful when reviewing quantitative intervention-based studies that focus on outcome research (refer back to Table 1.1 in Chapter 1), but it can also be adapted where necessary to accommodate other types of studies with different research epistemologies (see Chapter 5).

Thinking about your own research question, try to have a go at using the PICOT framework to pinpoint the specifics involved with your own planned review. Try to identify your own target *population, intervention, comparison, outcomes*, and *time-frames* that might shape your review.

WRITING UP YOUR SEARCH METHODOLOGY

A framework such as PICOT may be useful in helping to develop a search methodology and search terms. A search methodology should document your search so that someone else can easily determine what you did and reproduce the steps involved to get similar results. Include the following.

- The names of the sources you search and which provider you accessed them through – e.g., Medline (Ovid), Web of Science (Thomson Reuters). You should also include any grey literature sources you used.
- The date on which you carried out the searches.
- Any search limits you applied – e.g., language, date ranges of publication, types of publications accessed.
- Any individuals or organizations you contacted.
- Any sources you searched by hand.
- Consider putting together a search diagram that shows the number of hits you began with, as well as how many were excluded at each stage to end up with your final number of eligible sources. Consider using Preferred Reporting Items for Systematic Reviews and Meta-Analysis (PRISMA) guidelines in completing this step, which contain templates that are freely available: http://prisma-statement.org/prismastatement/flowdiagram.aspx

Using a PRISMA search diagram will help you to ensure that you are being exhaustive and systematic in your search. Many databases also allow you to save your search strategies inside a free personal account area. We recommend that you do this, but remember to save your passwords and user names, which will differ between each database. This step is important, because if you do not do this, writing the search method in your review will become very difficult and cumbersome as you forget your many different passwords and saved searches.

ASSESSMENT OF LITERATURE

An informative part of a systematic review is to conduct a quality assessment of the included studies. We will refer interested readers to the following resources, which may help in this regard:

- QATQS; National Collaborating Centre for Methods and Tools, 2008;
- Jadad checklist (Jadad et al., 1996);
- Downs & Black (1998) checklist.

Your choice of quality assessment tool will depend on your purposes for the review, so we recommend that you familiarize yourself with all of these, as each contains different criteria that might or might not be relevant to your purposes.

SYSTEMATIC REVIEW CHECKLISTS

We stress that this chapter is only meant to introduce readers to some of the systematic protocols used in systematic review, which will be helpful in locating studies, determining their relevance for your purpose, critical evaluation, and ultimately organizing and synthesizing studies included in a literature review. Interested readers might want more complete information to review the 'A measurement tool to assess systematic reviews' (AMSTAR) checklist, which is a quality rating system that be used a) to evaluate the rigour involved in a systematic review, b) to guide the process of conducting a systematic review, and c) as an aid to teach about systematic reviews. See https://amstar.ca/Amstar_Checklist.php. Thus, the tool is valuable to enhance the rigour involved with any type of literature review and to learn about what makes systematic reviews rigorous.

WHAT NEXT?

We recommend that you do some more reading on literature review, because there are ample resources available that are useful to writing and reporting in literature review. In addition to the sources we've introduced you to in this chapter, we recommend that you do some reading of the following websites and resources, which will help you through the process of writing a literature review.

- The Cochrane collaboration has some excellent resources. In particular, they have available examples of prior systematic review that might serve to guide you about what is contained: www.cochrane.org/about-us
- PRISMA have other resources that are helpful to establish a minimum set of items to report in your systematic review: http://prisma-statement.org/
- If your review is health-focused, before you start you may want to register it on PROSPERO, which is an international prospective register of systematic reviews. The database is aimed at providing a comprehensive list of reviews that are registered at inception, which helps to avoid problems with duplication, reduce reporting bias and ensure that reviews are more replicable by ensuring greater transparency in the process: www.crd.york.ac.uk/prospero/

 **Further reading and resources**

The following resources provide in-depth discussions that build on what we have covered here.

Gough, D., Oliver, S., & Thomas, J. (eds). (2017). *An introduction to systematic reviews.* London: SAGE.
Ridley, D. (2008) *The literature review: a step-by-step guide for students.* London: SAGE.

RESEARCH PROPOSALS

10

HOW DO I WRITE A RESEARCH PROPOSAL?

LEARNING OUTCOMES

In completing this chapter and related activities, you will be able to:

1. define a research proposal;
2. describe a typical format for a research proposal;
3. identify what stage you are at and where to improve;
4. make some informed judgements on the quality of a research proposal.

WHAT IS THE CURRENT REALITY IN TERMS OF WRITING A RESEARCH PROPOSAL?

In this section, we provide a broad overview of research proposals and the typical sections to include. We also describe the current challenges and pitfalls that are commonly faced by researchers. We stress that there is no one format for writing a research proposal and there will be slight variations depending on the research context.

WHAT IS A RESEARCH PROPOSAL?

A research proposal is a *concise* and logical outline of your proposed project. It is designed to clearly describe a research question, persuade a reader as to its significance and importance, and then to describe a method that will adequately address it. In doing so, a research proposal will also provide a brief summary of the relevant literature within which the research falls.

A research proposal will show its originality by clearly articulating how the project will add to, develop or challenge existing literature in the field. It will also convince the reader (e.g., funding body, future research supervisor) that *you* are the right person to undertake the project. Research proposals may vary in length, but a typical length is around 5–8 pages, or 2,000–4,000 words, though there may be instances where they need to be either shorter or longer than this. If it is substantially longer, it may be difficult to distinguish from a literature review. Remember that your goal with a research proposal is to describe a project, outline why it is needed and to convince the readers that you are the right person to undertake the project. The goal is not to bombard the reader with every piece of research on a topic.

TYPICAL FORMATS FOR RESEARCH PROPOSALS

While there is no one way to write a research proposal, it will generally contain the following components:

- title;
- abstract;
- background, including:
  - outlining research questions(s);
  - theoretical frameworks;
  - significance of the research;
  - aims and hypotheses;
- project summary, including:
  - planned methods;
  - ethical considerations;
  - research plan and time line;
  - budget;
- biography and/or CV;
- references/bibliography.

Below, we discuss these areas in more detail.

Title

When formulating a title for your research proposal, ensure that you include important 'key words' that relate your proposal. These key words will ideally be meaningful for potential supervisors, funding bodies and any other audience for whom you are writing your proposal. Ideally, the title will be written in plain language and will not contain jargon that the intended audience will not immediately understand. Good titles are short and grab the reader's attention without losing the message of the study. Try to avoid titles that are longer than 15 words.

Abstract

An abstract is typically no longer than 100 words and includes a concise statement of the intended research. Stick to the research question and its significance. Unlike an empirical research study, the abstract for a research proposal will generally not outline methods in much detail (and in many cases not at all). An abstract is not a requirement of every proposal and will depend on the context, the discipline and the audience. Given titles and abstracts go at the beginning of a proposal, it is often assumed that these are the first sections you need to write. However, we suggest this is a mistake. Instead, we recommend that you write the title and abstract *last*. This is because the other sections will allow you to distinguish which are the key ideas or messages that you need to capture in the title and abstract.

Background

The background section will be one of the longer sections of the proposal and will generally do several things. First, it will outline the **research question(s)** and consider how these are underpinned by relevant **theoretical frameworks** in the literature. The background will clearly outline the **significance** of the research and how it will contribute to either theory, practice, methods or something else (see Chapter 2). You will need to make a very clear case about why your project is needed. Note that it is *not enough* to simply state that a study of this nature has never been done before. Filling a gap in the literature is *only* important when that gap is an important one to fill, and you will need to convince your audience that this is the case.

The significance of the research is one of the most difficult parts you will have to write, yet this section is often one of the most important. This is because unless the reader is sold on its importance, your proposal is unlikely to achieve its aim – which might be to receive funding, gain entry to a research programme or something else. Typically, the background to your research will get more specific and focused as you go, such that towards the end of this section you might narrow down to research **aim** and **hypotheses**.

Project summary

You will use this section to outline the **methods** that you will use to answer your research question. Will you do an experiment? Will you run a survey? Will you do focus groups? Outline it here and justify why it is necessary for your research question. It is imperative that you choose your methods wisely and that your intended audience sees the methods as the most appropriate, justifiable and feasible available to you. If the methods do not align with the research question(s), then your proposal is unlikely to achieve its aim (e.g., to receive funding, gain entry to a research programme or something else). Importantly, ensure that your methods are chosen in service of your research question and not the other way around – that is, we often see students select methods first and then try to write their research question in a way that allows them to use those methods. This is a mistake and inevitably gets them into trouble in the long run, because it becomes much harder to sell the contribution unless you can persuade the audience that the research question(s) are worthy of being addressed. If you are conducting your project on the basis of using a favoured method, then it limits the capacity you will have to make a contribution to the literature.

You may also cover in this section any **ethical considerations** that are relevant to your project, as well as strategies you will use to minimize and manage them. This generally only occurs if the project is likely to cause concerns in your audience that are worthy of commentary. These might involve considerations such as informed consent, sensitive topics, participant vulnerability or something else (see Chapter 11 for a discussion of considerations in research ethics). The project summary will also typically include a description of your research **timeline** and proposed **budget**. The timeline will describe the stages of the project and the associated deadlines. If you are applying for funding, then it will be important to describe why those funds are necessary for the research and how you will spend any funding that is awarded.

Biography and/or CV

A biography and CV may or may not form a part of your proposal and it depends on a number of factors, such as whether you are applying for funding, the discipline, and so forth. However, a biography is typically a short (~100-word) summary of you and your notable career achievements to date. The CV is similar, but a CV will typically go into more depth into notable achievements and provide them in list form. Your goal in these documents is to convince your audience that you are not only a capable researcher, but that you are *the best person* to carry out this important piece of research. It is thus important to use both the biography and the CV to include any notable achievements that are relevant to the reason you are writing your proposal. For example, if you are writing your proposal to apply for funding, then it will be a good idea to outline any previous instances where you have been awarded funds that you have successfully used to deliver a project.

References

It is important to list all the references you cited in your proposal in a reference section, which will appear at the rear of your proposal. At this stage, it need not and should not be the full set of references that will be used in the complete research.

Activity

What is the current reality for you in terms of writing a research proposal?

Take some time to reflect and write on the following questions.

• Have I ever written a research proposal before? If not, have I even read a research proposal before?

- How confident am I feeling now about writing a proposal?
- What would make me more confident?
- Where could I access a proposal that might boost my confidence?
- Is there a more experienced mentor I can approach who may be able to offer useful advice and guidance with the process?

WHAT ARE MY OPTIONS IN TERMS OF WRITING A RESEARCH PROPOSAL?

A research proposal can be difficult to write and you will be required to make several important decisions along the way. If it is your first time in putting together a research proposal, you might benefit from having someone who is more experienced to help you with the process. There is much that needs to be considered in a research proposal, but it may not be immediately obvious about what should go in and what should stay out at first. It might be tempting to be over-inclusive in writing your background material, in which case authors can get carried away in showing that they are 'on top' of a literature by citing and commenting on every study they are aware of. This is generally a mistake and will only overwhelm the reader and potentially dilute the key message you are hoping to communicate. Instead, ensure that your proposal has a clear problem or question that you are addressing, and only information and literature directly relevant to that need be included. Aim for conciseness and get straight to the point.

So, if you feel you have a fairly solid and well-grounded idea, then have a go at writing your proposal. If it works for you, use the subheadings we outlined earlier. To help guide you through the process, we have also developed the checklist (shown below) to work through as you go. If this is not your situation yet, that's OK. We recommend that you again read through Chapters 6–9, which will help you scope your project and develop clear and convincing research questions. This may help you to develop strategies to refine your ideas before writing a full-blown proposal.

 **Activity**

Checklist prior to submitting

We offer the following checklist to keep in mind as you progress through your journey of putting together your research proposal. Tick all that apply and ensure that you have as many ticked as possible.

- Your title is less than 15 words and does not contain unnecessary jargon.
- Your research question(s) or problem is clearly stated and is convincing.

(Continued)

(Continued)

- You have made it clear that your project not only addresses a gap in the existing literature, but addresses a gap that is worthy of scientific study.
- Your aim and/or hypotheses are clearly stated and justified.
- The theoretical and conceptual underpinning of the project is clearly documented.
- Your proposal shows that you understand the research design and methods you have chosen, and you have demonstrated that these are appropriate to the research question(s).
- The scope of your project is feasible – that is, the size and complexity of your project can be completed in the time that you have available and within the budget you are requesting.
- Your writing is engaging and easy to read. Ensure that your writing is crisp and concise, and gets to the point quickly. A poorly written proposal is a quick and easy path to having your good ideas rejected.
- Have someone else read your proposal before it is submitted. We recommend that you have someone who is unfamiliar with the area of research, as well as someone who holds expertise in it.

Also consider the following questions, as you may need to comment on them to show that your project is feasible and practical within the specified timeline and budget.

- Do you need any additional resources, special equipment, software or material to make the study possible?
- How can you ensure that you get access to the necessary data or expertise?
- Are there potential barriers or pitfalls that may impede your ability to complete the project? How can these be overcome?
- Does your project involve human ethics, animal ethics or safety implications? How will you justify the risks involved?
- Will any travel or fieldwork be required? If so:
  - to where?
  - for how long?
  - at what intervals?

WHAT NEXT?

We recommend that you locate the following text (Cooksey & McDonald, 2011), which has an excellent resource for writing research proposals. Chapter 16, entitled 'How should I shape and defend my proposal', offers invaluable guidance on how to prepare and structure a research proposal, as well as discussing common problems encountered when writing proposals and how to make changes to them. While it is geared more towards postgraduate students, the principles will be similar for most contexts where you are required to write and defend a research proposal.

After you find and read this source, we recommend that you then have a go at completing Table 10.1 below. This will help you focus your thinking and put together the key pieces of information you may need for the research proposal. It will also help you to ensure that you can tick as many boxes as possible from the checklists outlined earlier.

Table 10.1   Key pieces of information typically used in a research proposal

Title:
Key members of research team (e.g., you, supervisor, etc.):
Key search terms in literature review:
Identified research gap:
Aims and objectives:
Significance to the literature:
The study is important because:
Theoretical and conceptual framework:
Research questions/hypotheses:
Design type:
Methods of data collection:
Key ethical issues:
Key milestone dates in timeline:

CONCLUSION

A research proposal is a concise and logical summary of your proposed project. A research proposal will outline a research question, persuade a reader as to its significance and importance, and then describe a method that will be used to adequately address it. There are several reasons you might need to write a proposal. Some common ones include attracting funding for your research project or gaining entry into postgraduate study. In this chapter, we discussed the common sections of a standard research proposal, and provided checklists and recommendations to help guide you through the process.

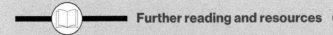 **Further reading and resources**

The following resources will provide further information about how to write a successful research proposal.

Cooksey, R. W. & McDonald, G. M. (2011). *Surviving and thriving in postgraduate research*. Prahran, Victoria: Tilde University Press.

Edelson, D. C. (2006). Balancing innovation and assessing design research proposals. In J. van den Akker, K. Gravenmeijer, S. McKenney & N. Nieveen (Eds.), *Educational design research* (pp. 100–106). Abingdon: Routledge. DOI: www.routledge.com/

The following resource focuses specifically on writing to obtain research funding:

Crawley, G. M., & O'Sullivan, E. (2015). *Grant writer's handbook: how to write a research proposal and succeed*. Singapore: World Scientific Publishing Company.

RESEARCH ETHICS

11

HOW DO I DEAL WITH ETHICS IN COACHING AND MENTORING RESEARCH?

LEARNING OUTCOMES

In completing this chapter and related activities, you will be able to:

1. describe generic ethical issues to be addressed in an ethics application;
2. describe common ethical issues in coaching and mentoring research;
3. list key ethical issues relevant to your current project.

WHAT IS THE CURRENT REALITY FOR RESEARCH ETHICS IN RELATION TO COACHING AND MENTORING?

In coaching and mentoring, like most of the behavioural sciences, research will involve human participants, and it is essential for research to be carried out with respect, purpose, integrity, justice and beneficence for those involved. These are just some of the values upon which research ethics are grounded, and are designed to ensure that ethical conduct 'is more than simply doing the right thing. It involves acting in the right spirit, out of an abiding respect and concern for one's fellow creatures' (NHMRC, 2007). Hence, most universities, hospitals and research governance bodies will have human research ethics committees (HRECs) whose responsibility it is to evaluate research proposals to ensure that they are ethically acceptable. If you plan to do a research project, you will need first to complete an ethics application and then to submit this to your appropriate HREC so that it can be evaluated and approved. In this chapter, we will show you how to practically structure and write an ethics application and how to identify common ethical issues in coaching research.

In coaching and mentoring, there are several key ethical principles to consider. Some of the primary ones are:

1.   informed consent;
2.   avoidance of harm;
3.   privacy.

We will discuss each of these in more detail below.

INFORMED CONSENT

Informed consent is an ethical and legal requirement for research involving human participants. It refers to the process by which a participant learns about and understands the purpose, benefits and potential risks of the research project, and then proceeds to make an informed decision to participate in the research. The concept of informed consent is embedded in the principles of the Nuremberg Code, the Declaration of Helsinki and the Belmont Report (Nijhawan et al., 2013). Therefore, informed consent is an essential requirement of every research project involving human beings as participants.

Obtaining informed consent involves informing the participant about his or her rights, the purpose of the study, procedures to be undertaken, potential benefits and risks associated with participation, expected duration of the study, the extent of confidentiality of personal identification and demographic data, so that the participation in the study is entirely voluntary. Typically, this will be done by providing paperwork (written in plain, easy-to-understand language) that each participant reads in order to minimize the possibility of coercion or undue influence, but there may be slight variations on this depending on the nature of the project. The participant must also be provided with adequate time to consider their participation.

In obtaining informed consent, it should be made clear that the process of consent is ongoing and participants have the right to 'withdraw' or to 'opt-out' of the study at any time, not just at the initial signing of paperwork (Nijhawan et al., 2013). The goal of the informed consent process is to provide sufficient information so that a participant can make an informed decision about whether or not they should enrol in a study.

AVOIDANCE OF HARM

All studies, including those in the field of coaching and mentoring, will generally involve some **risk**, which involves a potential for harm, discomfort or inconvenience to participants or others as a result of the project. It involves the likelihood that a harm (or discomfort or inconvenience) will occur, and will vary as a function of the severity of the potential harm caused. The assessment of risks involves:

- identifying any risks;
- determining their probability and severity;
- identifying whom the risks affect;
- assessing the extent to which they can be minimized;
- determining whether they are justified by the potential benefits of the research; and
- determining how they can be managed (NHMRC, 2007).

Research will be ethically acceptable only if its potential benefits justify the risks involved, and researchers have an ethical responsibility to both **minimize** and then **manage** risks created by their projects. The National Statement on Ethical Conduct in Human Research (2007) categorizes potential risks to research participants as follows.

a. Harms such as pain. This might include physical, psychological, social, economic and legal harms, as well as a possible devaluation of personal worth.
b. Discomforts (such as the measurement of blood pressure or anxiety induced by an interview). If discomfort becomes distress, then it is considered to be harm.
c. Inconveniences, which might include, for example, the time taken for participants to complete a survey battery or to complete a form.

The ethical review of your research takes into account the varying level of risk to which participants are exposed.

ASSESSING RISK TO AVOID HARM

Assessing risk involves taking into account the following.

a. The kinds of harm, discomfort or inconvenience that may occur through the research.
b. The likelihood of these occurring.
c. The severity of any harm that may occur.

These judgements should be based on the available evidence, and the process used to arrive at each judgement needs to be transparent and defensible. An important distinction is the category of negligible risk. Negligible risk involves research in which there is no foreseeable risk of harm or discomfort to participants, and any foreseeable risk is no more than inconvenience. Where the risk, even if unlikely, is more than inconvenience, the research is not considered to be negligible risk. Instead, it might constitute what is referred to as low risk. Low-risk research is that which the only foreseeable risk is one of discomfort, and research in which the risk for participants is more serious than discomfort is not considered to be low risk. It is important to remember that all research, whether risks are negligible, low or greater, must still be reviewed by a human research ethics committee.

In designing a research project, coaching and mentoring researchers have a responsibility to minimize the risks to participants. Minimizing risk involves an assessment of the research aims, their importance and the methods by which they can be achieved (NHMRC, 2015). So, when another researcher, ethics committee or review body judges your proposed research proposal, they will consider whether the level of risk is justified by the benefits. Research is ethically acceptable *only* when its potential benefits justify any risks involved in the research. Benefits of research may include, for example, gains in knowledge, insight and understanding that improve social welfare and individual well-being, and gains in skill or expertise for individual researchers, teams or institutions (NHMRC, 2007).

When risks have been identified, assessed and minimized, and the research has been approved, then the research team have a responsibility to adopt strategies to manage the risks created by the project. This requires that researchers include in their research design mechanisms to deal adequately with any harms that occur, and a monitoring process is in place and carried out.

Imagine, for example, a senior manager (named Mal Practice) in a large company and a couple of years ago he designed a mentoring programme to help onboard young graduates. The programme pairs young graduates who are fresh out of university with more senior staff so they can quickly learn how to navigate things like the computer software, people they need to know, payroll, and so forth. He's been using the programme each year since he developed it and believes it is helping relieve some of the stress of the new graduates, but he can't really know for sure. So, Mal now wants to empirically test this possibility. He decides that he will just run a study on his own mentoring programme, since he designed it himself and is already doing it himself. To do so, he invites a group of fresh graduates who go through the programme to also be involved in the study. He also decides to withhold the programme from another group of graduates so that he can use this group as a comparison group (or a control group; see Chapter 16 for some methodological reasons one might do this). If the group who receive the mentoring record more favourable stress ratings at the end of the programme than those who do not go through the programme, then Mal will take this as pretty good evidence that his programme is working.

Can you identify any possible ethical risks here? There are several, but we will comment briefly on some of the main ones. First, if the research were to go ahead, Mal would have a dual relationship with the people he proposes to study – that is, he works with them and he will also study them. A dual relationship makes participants more vulnerable because they can be pressured or coerced into participating when they do not really want to. Given Mal is more senior to the new graduates in this example, this relationship is also an unequal one, which means he holds more power than those who are participating in the programme. He will have to be careful to avoid a situation where participants feel pressured into participating, which, of course, limits their ability to make an informed decision to consent. A second ethical issue is that Mal has proposed to withhold a programme that will likely benefit a group of participants, so that he can use this group as a control. As we will outline in Chapters 15–16, while there may be sound methodological reasons for this decision, the upshot is that it makes the study less ethically acceptable. He will, of course, need a strategy to deal with this if it were to go ahead. A third ethical issue is that of privacy. Mal may learn things through the research that compromise the privacy and confidentiality of those with whom he has a working relationship. He will need a strategy in place to both minimize these ethical risks and to manage them if the project is to go ahead.

In this example, the participants are adults and may be vulnerable because Mal is a senior manager and holds more power. However, there are a range of factors that could lead to participant vulnerability. Below, we list some populations that are generally considered to be more vulnerable, and because of this, the ethical risks involved will be more extensive. It is important to consider participant vulnerability when undertaking a research project.

PARTICIPANT VULNERABILITY

Does your research specifically target any of the following groups of people?

a. Women who are pregnant.
b. Children and young people.
c. People in dependent or unequal relationships.
d. People highly dependent on medical care who can't give consent.
e. People with cognitive impairment, an intellectual disability or a mental illness.
f. People who may have been involved in illegal activities.
g. Aboriginal or Torres Strait Island peoples.
h. People in other countries.

If you answered 'yes' to any of the above, it is unlikely that your ethics application will be considered 'low risk' and thus the application procedure that you complete for your local HREC is likely to be more extensive.

SENSITIVE TOPICS

It is also important to consider if your coaching and mentoring research project will cover any sensitive topics. Sensitive topics are generally those that might arouse discomfort or distress in the research participants. While these may be less common in the field of coaching and mentoring, researchers may still find themselves in a situation where the topics covered in the research stray into the terrain of sensitive topics. The following is a non-exhaustive list of possible topics that would be considered sensitive. If your research covers any of these, you will likely need a strategy to manage the risk involved. It is also unlikely that your research project can be considered low risk, and thus you may need to submit a more extensive application within a higher risk category.

a.   Parenting practices.
b.   Sensitive personal issues.
c.   Sensitive cultural issues.
d.   Grief, death or serious traumatic loss.
e.   Depression mood states or anxiety.
f.   Gambling.
g.   Eating disorders.
h.   Illicit drug taking or substance abuse.
i.   Psychological disorders.
j.   Suicide.
k.   Gender identity and/or sexuality.
l.   Race and/or ethnic identity.
m.   Fertility and/or termination of pregnancy.

PRIVACY

Privacy is an important ethical issue in coaching and mentoring research. Risks to privacy can occur in any context, such as in sport, parenting, teaching and the workplace, and commonly arise when one party, such as an employer, a teacher or a parent, or someone else has a vested interest in the coaching or mentoring programme, and thus they express interest in learning what has been covered within the coaching or mentoring relationship. In these situations they might request information that could be uncovered by the research, even though it could compromise the confidentiality and privacy of those who are involved. However, there are other situations where risks to privacy become an issue as well, and researchers need to consider how they can manage these risks, too.

To ensure that the project has considered privacy and confidentiality, researchers are required to provide specific information about how an individual's personal and health information is collected, used, stored and disclosed to the individual or others concerned. It is important to let your participants know that they have a right of access to the information you collected about them. As a researcher, you must strive to ensure that the privacy, confidentiality and cultural sensitivities of the participants and/or groups are respected.

The term 'deidentified' is used frequently, and refers usually to sets of data from which names or other identifying features of participants have been removed. It is important to provide and maintain secure systems to ensure that confidentiality and the privacy of participants is upheld. As well, these systems will need to be appropriate to allow for the adequate storage and release of data that you collected. It is important that the process of deidentification can be irreversible if the identifiers have been removed permanently. This means that if participants request their data, you will no longer be able to provide it to them, which is also an ethical risk. In this case, it should be made known to participants prior to the study that the data will go through a deidentification process, after which they will not be able to access or request their data.

WHAT IS THE CURRENT REALITY FOR YOU IN TERMS OF RESEARCH ETHICS?

Have you ever been a research participant in a study?
   Please write your experience here of being a research participant.

- What happened?
- What did you like?
- What did you dislike?
- Can you identify any possible risks that the researchers took into consideration before inviting you into the study? Can you identify any other risks yourself?

As you uncover your own experience, you may identify issues you need to consider for your own research project. Below, we discuss some key questions to ask yourself if you are hoping to determine the level of risk involved in your project.

WHAT ARE MY OPTIONS IN TERMS OF RESEARCH ETHICS IN COACHING AND MENTORING?

One important option for you is whether to go ahead with your project. This obviously depends a lot on the level of ethical risk involved with your project, and in many cases the risks involved with research can be overcome if they are minimized and then managed appropriately.

   First, however, you need to determine how much risk is involved. Barker, Pistrang and Elliott (2002) have created an ethics self-study exercise to help you do this. We recommend that you read this because it provides some useful guidance. In brief, their exercise requires that you do your best to answer the following three questions.

1. What are the potential risks associated with the proposed research?
2. Are they serious?
3. What is the likelihood that they will happen?

Then, you might consider how the risks can be minimized and how they are to be managed if the project is to go ahead.

Another useful activity that might help you to identify the risks involved in your project is to consider a reflective writing activity that requires you to place yourself in the role of a potential participant in your own project, and then respond to the following questions in deciding whether to participate in your study.

1.   What issues and concerns might you have about the project before agreeing to participate?
2.   What information and reassurances would you want a researcher to provide?
3.   Based on this reflection, how will you modify your design – e.g., recruitment, consent, information sessions, etc.?
4.   List the key ethical issues relevant to your proposed project.

Based on your answers, do you need to:

1.   Revise your project plan to adjust the level of risk?
2.   Continue as is, managing or mitigating the risk at hand?

WHAT NEXT?

There is much information related to research ethics that is important for you to know, but which was also beyond the scope of this introductory text. Thus, we strongly recommend that before you opt to do your own research, you first read through some more comprehensive ethics guidelines and/or policy documents that will be instrumental in helping you to uncover potential ethical risks and strategies to minimize or manage them. We list three important ones below and have selected them because they serve as useful guidance in different regions of the world. We stress that you should find the policy document that is specific to your location.

NATIONAL INSTITUTE OF HEALTH (NIH) ETHICAL GUIDELINES REGULATIONS

The National Institute of Health (NIH) in the United States of America has developed Human Subjects Policies and Guidance which provides information on the standards of ethical conduct for federal employees. For further information, see: https://humansubjects.nih.gov/ethical-guidelines-regulations.

THE NHMRC NATIONAL STATEMENT

The National Health and Medical Research Council (NHMRC) National Statement on Ethical Conduct in Human Research (2007) is the primary ethical guidance document for Australia. Its purpose is to protect the welfare and the rights of participants in research and to facilitate research that is, or will be of benefit to the researcher's community or to humankind. See: www.nhmrc.gov.au/guidelines-publications/e72

THE BRITISH PSYCHOLOGICAL SOCIETY CODE OF HUMAN RESEARCH ETHICS

First published in 1990, the BPS code of human research ethics is a widely used document that many institutions and funding bodies have used to build or inform their research ethics policies and practices. See: www1.bps.org.uk/system/files/Public%20files/inf180_web.pdf

 **Further reading and resources**

In addition to the resources given in the preceding section, the following resource will provide further information and considerations when examining the ethics of your project and covers ethics from a general perspective.

Farrimond, H. (2012). *Doing ethical research*. Basingstoke: Palgrave Macmillan.

FEASIBLE TIMELINES

HOW DO I PLAN AND MANAGE MY RESEARCH TIME?

12

LEARNING OUTCOMES

In completing this chapter and related activities, you will be able to:

1. describe how coaching skills can be applied to research project management;
2. identify key project milestones;
3. create a visual project plan based on realistic time estimates;
4. identify key contingencies that can impact timely completion of projects.

WHAT IS THE CURRENT REALITY IN TERMS OF MANAGING TIMELINES IN RESEARCH?

As a student or practitioner of coaching and mentoring, you already have a range of key skills that can be used to manage your project. Consider the following and think of others that are also relevant.

SELF-REGULATION

Self-regulation of time, emotions, writing and attention are all relevant to research. How would you coach a person who won't stop reading and start writing? How would you coach a person who keeps adding to their research design with no regard to time limits? These are all issues of self-regulation.

STRUCTURING YOUR OWN SESSIONS WITH KEY ADVISERS

The GROW model – Goal, Reality, Options, Wrap-up (or whatever various labels people prefer) – is very relevant to working with your supervisor or adviser regarding your project. Treat discussions with your adviser as a coaching session. You may have more explicit coaching skills than they do. Take responsibility for structuring the session so that you leave with key and relevant actions.

FOCUSING ON THE NEXT ACTION

Research can be overwhelming to new researchers. So many uncertainties, new things to learn and, after all is done, the data may not behave as hoped. It is common, and perhaps necessary, that researchers get lost in the forest, cannot see the forest for the trees. Consultation discussions/supervision are useful to help lift the gaze and then give you the next relevant action. This is the same as the coaching process. Each time you work on your research, be very clear on the action to be achieved. Often there is not the luxury of having half a day to work on your project. Your work may be taken in 30-minute blocks, so what can you achieve? Writing can be very much like this and can be similar to exercise behaviour.

DELIBERATELY CREATING CYCLES OF FEEDBACK AND REVISION

One thing that predicts good research outcomes is how well students seek and act upon feedback. This is the same as goal review cycles. Deliberately seek and act upon feedback from informed sources. The more review cycles you can build into your project, the better the outcome will be, particularly in the written work.

BUILDING CONFIDENCE

Self-efficacy (the perceived sense of personal control to perform an action), referred to popularly as similar to confidence, is well known to many coaches and mentors. Confidence is of major importance to learning and doing research. Chapter 2 addresses this issue directly as it relates to approaching statistical analysis.

STRENGTHS-BASED APPROACH

While not all coaching and mentoring emphasizes being strengths-based, it is very useful to think this way towards your research project. How can you bring your personal strengths to your project? By this, we do not just mean technical skills – we mean your whole personal strengths. For example, you may be a good connector of people. If so, be the person who organizes research review sessions with peers and benefit that way.

GOAL SETTING, PLANNING AND REVIEW

Goal setting and review is common to many aspects of coaching. Bring these skills directly to your research project. While there are many technical aspects to research, it is, after all, a project. A project ends. A project has subsections, critical tasks and can be broken into tasks. The progress is reviewed. By taking this generic goal-striving approach to your research, it becomes perhaps more like something you know (i.e., coaching) and less like something you may not know (i.e., technical aspects of research).

TIME ASPECT OF SMART GOALS

SMART goals – Specific, Manageable, Attractive, Realistic and Time-framed (or whichever slight variation coaches use based on Locke and Latham's goal research) – clearly includes time. This is a key issue for this chapter. Many research students start with big questions and argue about preferred methodologies, etc. The hard reality, however, is that they have limited resources, particularly time.

FROM SMART TO RESEARCH PROJECT MILESTONES

Research projects have very common milestones, irrespective of specific methodologies or research questions. For PhD projects, which may vary from three to five years in completion time, it is useful to break down projects into smaller parts – for example, publications, studies, etc. Many of the readers of this volume may be pre-PhD research dissertation and hence likely to have time frames of 12 months or less.

Chunking the project into smaller milestones creates a sense of control and hopefully confidence.

WHAT IS YOUR CURRENT REALITY IN TERMS OF YOUR PROJECT TIMELINE?

Let's consider your project timeline. Examine the following list and consider whether they are relevant milestones for your project. At this stage, just write notes next to each as to its relevance, or you may have already completed some of these milestones. This is not to plan how to complete the milestone, just to assess whether it is relevant for your situation.

1. Locate an adviser.
2. Develop an agreed topic area.
3. Conduct a preliminary literature review.
4. Create an annotated bibliography.
5. Write a summary of literature review.
6. Write a full research proposal.
7. Complete additional reading/training on your particular methodology.
8. Write and submit a research ethics proposal.
9. Gain approval from the respective ethics board.
10. Gain approval for data collection for relevant partner/industry organizations.
11. Phase 1 of data collection.
12. Phase 2 of data collection.
13. Data analysis.
14. Phase 1 of writing – e.g., Chapters 1–3 or article 1.
15. Phase 2 of writing – e.g., Chapters 4–7 or article 2.
16. Complete an oral presentation of your research.

WHAT ARE MY OPTIONS IN TERMS OF CREATING FEASIBLE TIMELINES?

The options open to you are (a) how you plan and prioritize your time and (b) how you create a project so as many things as possible are under your control – i.e., you are not totally dependent on outside factors such as a single data collection opportunity, or sole dependence on one expert for methodology advice.

In terms of planning and prioritizing your time, you can use the key project milestones to create a visual project plan mapped onto time. Think of it as a 'time budget' where there is a plan, and then the plan is adjusted like forecasting in financial budgets. These plans are useful for you as a researcher and are also expected by those assessing your research plan, be they academic advisers or funding bodies. For those with project management backgrounds, Gantt charts will be very familiar and many versions are available on the internet. For most shorter dissertation projects, however, the full complexity of such software may not be necessary.

In most cases, creating and revising spreadsheets will be enough. Some people are very visually oriented and will like to create other mind maps, diagrams, etc. to assist their planning.

The six key principles in creating your 'research time budget' recommended are, however, that it:

1. includes detailed and specific time frames;
2. is based around the key milestones;
3. has milestones that are achieved in parallel, rather than just one before the other;
4. is based on feedback from people who have done it before;
5. is represented visually to give an overview of the whole project;
6. is revised regularly as the 'time budget' changes.

Now it's your turn. Use the following steps to create your own project plan.

1. Using the revised project milestones from above, insert them into the first column of a spreadsheet, making them the titles for each row of the new spreadsheet.
2. Decide on your overall time frame and whether you want to break that down into months or weeks. For projects less than six months, using weeks is recommended.
3. Block out the cells where it is intended to work on each project task. The end of the coloured cells represents milestone completion.
4. Remember that this is a living document and it is likely that some revision will be needed, and often the 'colour blocks' migrate to the right.

A very simplified example may look like this (Table 12.1), but you are encouraged to add more detail to your own.

Table 12.1 Example Gantt chart for establishing a research project timeline

Time	February	March	April	May	June	July	August	September	October	November
Literature Review	████	████	████							
Ethics Proposal Acceptance			████	████	████					
Writing Introduction and Method				████	████	████				
Data Collection						████	████	████		
Data Analysis								████	████	████

In terms of creating a project to maximise your amount of control, ask yourself, 'What are the key rate limiting factors in this project?' – that is, if something is going to slow this project up significantly, what might it be? For many projects, there are two common answers to this question.

1. Ethics review board acceptance.
2. Data collection.

A key principle for a feasible project with the time frame and resource constraints that you have, is to make as much of the project under your control as possible.

To mitigate the risk of over-running, ask yourself the following questions.

1. How reliant am I on external individuals or organizations for my data?
2. Could I use existing data rather than collecting new data?
3. How risky is my project in the eyes of the ethics review board?
4. How many things in this project are new to me – for example, am I learning a new theory, a new method and trying to reach a difficult or minority sample?
5. Do I really need to do an intervention study, or is that just my preference because of my background as a practitioner?

While research proposals are often written in a linear fashion and appear definite in their convictions, it can be useful to have contingency plans. In quantitative contexts, this may be construed as poor science akin to changing one's hypothesis to fit the data. This is not what is being proposed here. Rather, the question is, what meaningful question can be asked in the time frame and resources available? If the world changes, which it often does, what alternative question can be asked for a meaningful answer? As most coaching and mentoring research is applied in nature, it is useful to explore contingencies of what can and often does go wrong in terms of data collection and how to work around it in a timely fashion. This is addressed more directly in Chapter 13 to follow.

WHAT NEXT?

You are invited to do one or all of the following actions.

1. Seek feedback on your timeline ('time budget') from someone who has completed a similar project in a similar context.
2. Further, discuss with your adviser or similar risk mitigation strategies regarding rate limiting factors, particularly data collection and ethics approval.
3. Explore online resources for timeline templates (see Further reading and resources below).

CONCLUSION

While many new researchers may be experienced in skills of programme management or creating Gantt charts, it is not uncommon for these skills to be overlooked when a researcher becomes immersed in literature reviewing or data analysis. By using coaching methods, as a coaching or mentoring researcher, you are likely to be skilled in setting detailed plans and review cycles in conjunction with their research team members. Setting, reviewing and revising research plans is an ongoing process and needs to be done in conjunction with the scope and research question as discussed in previous chapters.

 Further reading and resources

https://en.wikipedia.org/wiki/Gantt_chart
www.vertex42.com/ExcelTemplates/timeline.html

DATA COLLECTION AND ANALYSIS

13

WHAT ARE THE LIKELY ISSUES I WILL FACE DURING DATA COLLECTION AND ANALYSIS?

LEARNING OUTCOMES

In completing this chapter and related activities, you will be able to:

1. understand ways to position your research so it is seen as relevant to key stakeholders, particularly participants;
2. describe common issues and challenges that coaching and mentoring researchers may face during data collection/generation;
3. describe common issues and challenges that coaching and mentoring researchers may face during data analysis/interpretation;
4. brainstorm 'Plan B' options for your current research design and data collection.

WHAT IS THE CURRENT REALITY FOR DATA COLLECTION AND ANALYSIS IN COACHING AND MENTORING RESEARCH?

As a starting point, it is useful to remember that most people do not care about your research project as much as you do – that is, the participant and their organization may not have the purpose in mind that you do. Attitudes towards research are often not positive, particularly in action-based environments, relevant to coaching and mentoring (e.g., health services, business). People feel busy and many see research as too abstract for their real-world concerns. These attitudes may be even worse if your project is seen as 'just another student project'.

CURRENT CHALLENGES AND PROBLEMS

In practical and sometimes fast-moving environments where coaching or mentoring may be relevant, doing research may not be viewed as valuable by organizations or participants. At times, the role of a researcher collecting data may resemble more of a salesperson having to persuade others, and using optimism and perseverance to deal with rejections. However, with good research planning and design, good industry relationships, 'cold calling' to collect data is well avoided. Your data source may be one of the most important factors as to whether your project is completed on time (as discussed in Chapter 12 on Feasible timelines).

Several ways to position your research so that it is relevant in the minds of participants and possible organizational partners, include the following.

1. Find stakeholders as part of your research (see Chapter 3 on Research teams). If no one else has a 'stake', you have a problem.
2. Develop relationships with key stakeholders (e.g., it may be that a 30-minute coffee chat is enough to garner their support).
3. When appropriate or possible, involve people in the research process – e.g., scoping, design, communication, etc.).
4. Be disciplined and avoid creating long surveys or long interviews.
5. For beginning projects, try to join an existing research programme or organizational partnership. You may not have time to build it all on your own, so join something existing (e.g., a researcher who you wish to work with already has a research relationship with the major city hospital).
6. Have a clear view yourself on why your project is important to something bigger than yourself and show your excitement.
7. Learn to communicate about your research in ways that other people need to hear – i.e., use their language schema. For example, business environments may need to hear a story that mentions return on investment.
8. Be clear on what makes you, your organization and your research appear credible – e.g., you are working with a well-reputed unit.
9. Use key statistics to state why your project is important – e.g., one in five people have a mental illness and ...
10. Use stories and key analogies to make your key idea understandable. Have an elegantly brief, five-word statement that captures the essence of the idea – for example, 'Coaching coaches to protect goals'.

See Chapter 14 for further ways to communicate in an ongoing way with stakeholders in your research.

While this chapter refers to data collection, as will be described in Chapter 20, many qualitative researchers use the term 'data generation', as collection is seen as not acknowledging the role of the researcher. Similarly, the term 'analysis' is not preferred by some qualitative researchers whose use of the term 'interpret' is one common example of an alternative. Rimando et al. (2015: 2026) assert that 'data collection, usually occurring simultaneously with data analysis in qualitative research, is defined as the systematic gathering of data for a particular purpose from various sources, including interviews, focus groups, observation, existing records, and electronic devices'. For quantitative research, as discussed in Chapter 17, this will often involve survey designs using self-report scales. As discussed in Chapter 1 and illustrated in the Appendix, it is useful to locate whether your research is an intervention study or not, and, if it is an intervention study, is it focusing on outcome, process or issues of implementation/fidelity? This will impact on how data is collected and analysed, and hence the likely issues faced during data collection and analysis/interpretation.

The challenges faced may be related to the researcher, the participant, the data collection environment or the method used (Rimando et al., 2015). Beyond the results from Rimando et al.'s (2015) study, it is useful to use this four-part framework to consider data collection issues in general (see the Activity below).

Table 13.1 illustrates common issues faced during data collection/generation for researchers using both quantitative and qualitative methodology. Of course, a mixed-method approach may involve both. Do not let these challenges overwhelm you – they represent a list of the many things the first author has experienced in conducting and supervising research for 20 years. By reading and considering the issues in the other chapters, these challenges can be managed or prevented. Data is, however, gold and most researchers go through a challenging period during the data collection/generation phase of their project. It is through the experiences described in Table 13.1 that people come to understand how difficult 'applied', also known as 'difficult, applied research' such as coaching and mentoring research can be.

Table 13.1 Common data collection/generation challenges for coaching and mentoring research

Quantitative methodology (see Part III)	Qualitative methodology (see Part IV)
1. For intervention research, quantitative researchers may underestimate the time and risk involved in setting up quasi-experimental designs to collect data.	a. Participants are unwilling or unable to commit the longer time required for interviews or focus groups.
2. Sampling is done poorly, yielding data that is biased, skewed, non-representative, etc. depending on the inference required.	b. Sampling is done poorly, not yielding the breadth or richness of narrative consistent with the assumptions of the methods.

(Continued)

Table 13.1 (Continued)

Quantitative methodology (see Part III)	Qualitative methodology (see Part IV)
3. In the search for reliability and validity, scales used may not be as relevant to local situation and language of participants.	c. Visual or audio-recording devices malfunction or there are poor-quality recordings.
4. In the search for reliability and scope, the time to complete scales becomes too long for participants.	d. Researcher is not able to keep the participants on topic or conclude interviews leading to major unnecessary narrative transcription.
5. For organizational research, the organization restructures or key partner staff leave and the commitment to the project may be reduced.	e. For organizational research, the organization restructures or key partner staff leave, and the commitment to the project may be reduced.
6. The response rate from participants is nil, which is too slow or simply not enough to achieve reasonable statistical power.	f. Prospective participants do not understand qualitative research and believe it may not be valuable as it is not quantitative or 'controlled research'.
7. For research involving multiple data collection points (repeated measures), participants gradually drop out leaving less data (attrition).	g. The team or organization is so small that serious concerns about confidentiality stop or concern participants.
8. Participants want to choose to be involved in coaching or mentoring programmes, but because research is optional, they opt out.	h. Participants want to choose to be involved in coaching or mentoring programmes, but because research is optional, they opt out.

Table 13.2 illustrates the common analysis or interpretation challenges for coaching and mentoring research. If the research has been well planned, many of these challenges can be prevented. The work of data entry and interpretation is time-consuming and, despite huge improvements in technology, persistence and motivation remain an important ingredient.

Table 13.2 Common data analysis/interpretation challenges for coaching and mentoring research

Quantitative methodology (see Part III)	Qualitative methodology (see Part IV)
1. Due to smaller sample sizes or attrition, the types of analysis used may need to be modified.	a. The researcher underestimates the sheer time and labour required for data interpretation.

Quantitative methodology (see Part III)	Qualitative methodology (see Part IV)
2. Once calculated locally, the reliability (internal consistency) of the scales is not as high as in previous studies, 'lost in objectivity'.	b. The researcher struggles with the relativism of interpretations, 'lost in subjectivity'.
3. The researcher chooses statistical analyses which are too complex and difficult to learn in the time they have.	c. The researcher has not developed a system of managing, interpreting and reinterpreting the data.
4. The researcher becomes very concerned that the hypotheses are not confirmed – e.g., no gains in intervention – and feels as though there is nothing to write about.	d. The source of the information being interpreted becomes unclear due to knowing the participant, what others have said, etc.

 **Activity**

What is your current reality in terms of collecting and using these data?

Write a few sentences in response to each of the following questions. Be honest and candid in your answers. This may prove critical in the success of your project. People get enamoured with theory, their pet idea, their personal cause or the technical aspects of their particular methods. However, not adequately addressing these eight questions may lead to big problems downstream.

1. Where will you get data from?
2. Do these data relate directly to the questions you are asking?
3. How realistically can you get these data in the time frame you have?
4. How realistically can you analyse/interpret these data in the time you have?
5. Which issues about you as a researcher may help or hinder data collection/generation?
6. What are issues for the participants that may help or hinder data collection/generation?
7. How may the environment/location that you are using/intending to use help or hinder data collection/generation? For example, online versus face-to-face, too noisy, privacy, etc.
8. How may the methods used for data collection/generation influence the quality, consistency and amount of data generated/collected? For example, is your scale too long? Try to make scales brief and relevant, with acceptable language and easy to understand.

What are your options in terms of a back-up plan for data collection?

For projects less than one year in a time frame, it is highly recommended to try to attach projects to existing larger projects, avoiding the lone-researcher when possible. If possible, you may also seek to use existing data sets – that is, data that has already been collected. Different departments and disciplines have different views on this and hence you need to investigate it locally if you are doing a student level project. Open your possibilities for a moment and write down three possible sources of data. Before reading on, do it now.

WHAT NEXT?

Now that you have considered a 'back-up plan' for data collection, it is useful to work out what comes next in terms of overcoming data collection/generation risks and problems. If you have already 'locked in' a data collection/generation site/source, then you should focus further attention on Rimando et al.'s (2015) four areas impacting data collection – e.g., researcher, participant, data-collection environment and method. Explore in more detail how each one of these (i.e., including you as the first one) may help or hinder data collection. If you are still pre-commitment to a major data source, keep exploring the respective data source options, and their relative risks and benefits.

CONCLUSION

Many new coaching and mentoring researchers enter research from the practitioner world where they have been coaches, and the primary focus is on assisting the coachee/mentee to achieve relevant goals, clarify values or improve performance. Coachees/mentees are accessed because they are available and issues of 'stratified sampling' have never been a concern. Common issues of response rates, participant retention, missing data and organizational restructure have been outlined within this chapter. Managing risk by having 'Plan B' designs and samples was emphasized.

 Further reading and resources

Rimando, M., Brace, A. M., Namageyo-Funa, A., Parr, T. L., Sealy, D., Davis, T. L., Martinez, L. M. & Christiana, R. W. (2015). Data collection challenges and recommendations for early career researchers. *The Qualitative Report, 20*(12), 2025–2036. Retrieved from: https://nsuworks.nova.edu/tqr/vol20/iss12/8

DISSEMINATION OF RESEARCH

14

HOW SHOULD I EFFECTIVELY COMMUNICATE MY RESEARCH FINDINGS AND INFORMATION?

LEARNING OUTCOMES

In completing this chapter and related activities, you will be able to:

1. describe the importance and range of options for disseminating your research findings and information;
2. describe common issues for written communication of research;
3. develop a personal plan for your individual research writing, including use of feedback;
4. describe steps in publishing your work.

WHAT IS THE CURRENT REALITY IN TERMS OF DISSEMINATING RESEARCH INFORMATION?

The English proverb 'Don't hide your lamp under a bushel', in contemporary language means 'Don't hide your light under a bowl'. While this was derived from a parable of Jesus, and light is interpreted as the message of Jesus, it remains relevant today, including your research project. Although you may or may not believe that your message is as important as that of Jesus, or be of this worldview, the parable is paramount for researchers. You have something worthwhile to say.

Thesis means argument, contention, proposition – derived from the Greek meaning 'to place … a proposition'. To remould the parable, you could say, 'Don't hide your proposition within course requirements only'. Your project is your claim to the world. It is not that useful to have a claim and not to inform anyone. At the time of writing, there are multiple knowledge claims, many non-factual, circling in the world via social media, traditional media or otherwise. Fact checks have been added to media to guard against erroneous claims. And yes, some coach and mentoring practitioners are also making these claims. Reasonable claims need to be shared and good research means that your claims are reasonable. Your project, however seemingly small, is important. If you do not think your project is important, you have not read Chapter 2 and perhaps you should reconsider your project, so you believe it is worthwhile sharing it with the world.

Do not just create a plan for doing your research, but also create a plan for disseminating your research. Also note, not just your research findings (i.e., data, conclusions), but rather any aspects of the research process that relevant stakeholders may be interested in.

When working with industry partners, this also is a professional and ethical issue. Partners have the right to be informed and sometimes educated about the research process. Applied research has moved increasingly to a collaborative model and it is not acceptable to come, take data and leave.

At a more instrumental level, research often requires additional funding through grants or philanthropy. The communication of research information is essential in this regard and Chapter 2 on Impactful research is directly relevant to why research may be funded, but the communication of this in multiple ways is paramount.

In terms of contemporary scholarly research, there are a range of dissemination options open to you, including and beyond those needed for course requirements if the project is being completed as a student. The first two methods of journal-style publication and oral presentations are common and traditional approaches in academic settings. They remain useful and important; however, there are many other approaches for different purposes and audiences.

Table 14.1   Possible methods to disseminate your coaching and mentoring research

- Refereed journal publication (see below for coaching and mentoring journals)
- Oral presentation – e.g., academic conference
- Industry publications – e.g., newsletter, magazine
- Workshop presentation – e.g., industry conference
- Podcast – e.g., invited industry – podcast
- Blog – e.g., personal blogging
- Video-storytelling – e.g., YouTube
- Webinar – e.g., professional body
- Email lists – e.g., psychology or human resources listserv
- Social media – e.g., LinkedIn, Facebook
- Website – e.g., personal website or institutional website

With the rise of technology and social media, there are more ways to communicate and disseminate research, even since 2010. However, most researchers have limited time and resources to have comprehensive dissemination strategies for large projects often run by senior university researchers (see Further reading and resources, below). While your project may not be as large, the principles are the same, however. Ultimately, in terms of prioritizing, working on your fundamental written and oral communication skills would remain a priority, particularly if you are seeking a university qualification.

Stated directly, can you write an academic piece? Can you effectively deliver an oral presentation to scholars of coaching and mentoring? This is different from a business-style presentation; it has a different purpose and there is likely to be more scrutiny of every knowledge claim being made. Coaches and mentors are practitioners by definition; some may also do research. Practitioners are often interested in what they can do next and this is where the misconception may occur when in scholarly contexts – i.e., if you are required to present your research project to academic professors. Academic contexts, while interested in applications and implications of research, start with the question: 'What will this research add to the academic literature?' The question of application and implication is secondary. Whether you agree with this or not, it is the genre expected in that context. Present the work in a way they can understand it, rather than in a way you understand it and want it to be. The key message here is to be very clear about the audience you are communicating with each time you communicate.

Written communication skills remain a key success factor for most researchers, and particularly research dissertations. While a full coverage of academic writing skills is well beyond the scope of this chapter and this book, there are some key issues to consider in the context of coaching and mentoring research.

WHAT IS YOUR CURRENT REALITY IN TERMS OF DISSEMINATING RESEARCH INFORMATION IN A WRITTEN FORMAT?

Given its importance, this chapter now focuses on written communication, and particularly academic writing. Here are five key questions to help locate where you are with academic writing.

1. Is English your first language?
2. How regularly do you write?
3. How familiar are you with the expectations of the academic writing style and genres (as compared to other genres such as business writing style or the genre of a novel)?
4. How skilled are you with referencing and citations?
5. If you are a student researcher at a university, there will likely be help with academic writing available. Do you know what is available? Have you contacted the relevant unit/searched online?

Now let's discuss each of these questions and answers in turn.

1. **English as your first language**. If English is not your first language, written English can be an extra challenge. In our experience, new researchers, particularly students, usually have a particular area they need to keep working on as a skill, in addition to the topic of research. If English is not your first language, it may well be writing in particular. For others, it may be statistics, for others it may be theory and conceptualization. As per the key message of this book, use your coaching skills to approach what is needed. Also discuss with someone who has done it successfully.

2. **How regularly do you write?** Writing is something that does improve with practice, particularly if you receive and act on feedback. It is similar to exercise; it takes some motivation, gets easier with habit, can take a while to warm up and is very important. Often you may be asked, 'How much have you written?' A different question is, 'How regularly do you write?' Often people will say they do not have much time and yearn for periods without interruption, just as they say regarding exercise. Consider writing five times a week, even if it is only one paragraph each time. The development of good writing habits is a key skill for early researchers.

3. **The academic writing style and genre**. The academic writing style is different from other styles – for example, the business writing style. The academic writing style values being precise, concise and, in scientific disciplines, a perception of objectivity and impartiality. It is explicit in style and often highly detailed to reduce ambiguity. Within this context there are genres, which involve narrative technique, tone, content and length – for example, the journal article genre; they have an accepted structure, a tone of authority, expected content and length, which is often between 3,000 and 5,000 words.

4. **Academic referencing**. Academic referencing is a professional expectation, recognizing the source of the original scholarly work. At a practical level, references are like 'rules of the game'. If, as a research student, you do not comply with these expectations (be it APA style, Harvard or other), a reviewer may simply deem it as low quality and be distracted by this rather than your important argument. There are many resources online about how to do this. A strong recommendation is to *learn it, do it, move on* – there are many other more important things to be doing than recorrecting poorly done referencing.

5. **Local resources for academic writing**. Most resources and colleges have additional assistance available with academic writing, and often journal article writing for postgraduate students. Unfortunately, students often view these as only for remedial situations rather than as a generalized skill that everyone can develop. The resource may vary from some useful tip sheets that you can download through to a series of one-to-one consultations where you receive feedback on your written work. Champions feast on feedback.

WHAT ARE YOUR OPTIONS TO PUBLISH YOUR RESEARCH?

Now let's consider whether you can indeed publish a written piece of work from your current research. For some coursework research students, this may seem a long way from your thinking; for doctoral-level research students, it may be mandatory.

So what are your options regarding publishing a journal article? Let's consider the steps in publishing in a refereed journal.

1. CHOOSE TWO OR THREE JOURNALS TO TARGET

Rank them in the order you intend to pursue them. This anticipates that the first journal may not accept the publication. This is common. Similar to a sports team that may not win every game, you may not win the first game. Choosing journals is a very important step and its importance is often overlooked. University libraries often have people who will systematically assist you with your journal choice. There are a range of things to consider in choosing a journal, including the impact factor of a journal (a number which indicates its likely citations in the discipline, turn-around time (i.e., how long it takes to publish) and where similar articles have been published before.

Examine the article types within these journals. Check that the journal accepts the type of article you are intending to publish. For example, let's look at what one coaching journal says with regard to types of articles.

Coaching: An International Journal of Theory, Research and Practice accepts the following types of article:

- paper;
- brief report, technique or interview;
- case study.

The journal welcomes original contributions with relevance to coaching from all parts of the world. It seeks to publish work that develops, tests and advances theory, research and practice in the domain of coaching. The following are examples of contributions that are suitable for publication:

- empirical studies, quantitative, qualitative or mixed methods;
- short case study reports (for more detail, please see this example: www.tandfonline.com/doi/full/10.1080/17521882.2012.684695);
- review articles providing either a meta-analysis or a comprehensive literature review which makes an original contribution to a subject;
- reports on innovative practice, such as technique reports;
- book reviews;
- special issues or sections are occasionally published on a particular thematic or regional focus, normally edited by guest editors. Suggestions for such issues are welcome.

www.tandfonline.com/action/authorSubmission?journalCode=rcoa20&page=instructions#about

Based on the above description, could you send something from your completed piece of research to this journal? If so, what type and example does it correspond with? For example, is it a paper and a mixed methods empirical study?

Below are some coaching and mentoring research journals to start the process of choosing a journal. Also consider that because of your topic or methodology, it could be published somewhere else. For example, if your project involves coaching youth, it may be better published in a journal focusing on adolescence. Likewise, if your project involves an innovative new methodology, a journal focusing on innovative methods may be appropriate.

- *Coaching: An International Journal of Theory, Research and Practice*
- *Coaching Psychology International*
- *International Coaching Psychology Review*
- *International Journal of Evidence Based Coaching and Mentoring*
- *International Journal of Mentoring and Coaching*
- *International Journal of Mentoring and Coaching in Education*
- *International Journal of Coaching in Organizations*
- *The Coaching Psychologist*

2. FIND TWO ARTICLES THAT ARE SIMILAR IN FORM TO THE ONE YOU WISH TO PUBLISH

If your article is a paper and mixed-methods empirical study, find two similar ones from that journal. Use them as a template for structure, style and tone. Remember that a journal is like a club, with a subscription. Readers often expect to see things in the same format and style. The more your paper as a new member looks like a club member, the more likely it will be accepted into the club.

3. WRITE A FIRST DRAFT ARTICLE TO THE STRICT REQUIREMENTS OF THE JOURNAL

Notice that writing starts at step 4, not step 1. So many research students say they are writing an article and they draft it without even knowing for which journal it is intended. This is like speaking to an audience without knowing what type of audience it is. Start with the journal choice and then write the article.

4. SEEK FEEDBACK AND EDITING BEFORE SUBMISSION

Seek as much feedback from external reviewers and co-authors when relevant.

5. SUBMIT AS SOON AS POSSIBLE AND START AN ELECTRONIC CONVERSATION WITH THE EDITOR

Beware of perfectionism. It is easy to hold on to papers for too long trying to make them perfect. Submit them, seek feedback and keep the conversation going with the editor. Do not submit the same article to two different journals at one time. This is considered very unprofessional and can lead to a professional reprimand.

6. TRACK THE STATUS OF YOUR SUBMISSION ONLINE WHEN POSSIBLE AND/OR FOLLOW UP AFTER TWO MONTHS

Have patience and work on other things while you wait. Full-time researchers often have multiple manuscripts under review at any one time.

7. RESPOND TO EDITOR AND REVIEWER COMMENTS

Most reviews will come in the form of: a) desktop rejection; b) rejection; c) revise and resubmit; d) acceptance with major or minor edits. Reviewers can be very critical and it is the editor's job to smooth the reviews and provide tangible ways forward. A desktop rejection means that the paper is examined by the editor for its quality and relevance to the journal and deemed not appropriate. While this is not desired, it is at least quick, enabling you to move straight on to your second chosen journal in step 1. Revise the manuscript based on the comments and provide a number of comment-by-comment responses to the editor regarding the revisions made.

If you are asked to revise and resubmit the article, it means that the journal is interested in publishing the work per se, but there is much work to be done. It is like an orange light rather than a red light. This is a stage where one needs to be resilient and optimistic and not take comments too personally. This may be easier said than done for new researchers. Repeat from step 4 above. Persist and then persist again.

WHAT NEXT?

Now that you have explored the importance of the dissemination of research, including academic writing in journal format, it is important to go back to the basics of your situation. Take some time to answer the following two questions. Write a short paragraph response to each.

- What is my plan for writing?
- Who will give me feedback and how will I best use it?

Also, see Spence et al. (2016) in the Further reading and resources section as an example of how student researchers can publish their work together.

CONCLUSION

Finding a worthwhile research topic, articulating a clear research question, designing the research, collecting and analysing data are all essential steps in the research process. If the research process and outcomes are, however, insufficiently disseminated or poorly communicated, the work is often futile. This chapter aimed to enable you to understand and improve in the common dissemination areas of oral presentations, journal articles, social media and research blogs. This chapter provided examples of the steps in research writing and submission for publication, and the need for receiving multiple sources of feedback on written work. This will apply to journal publications and traditional thesis formats.

 Further reading and resources

Silvia, P. J. (2007). *How to write a lot: a practical guide to productive academic writing.* Washington, DC: American Psychological Association.

Spence, G. B., Armour, M. R., Driessen, D., Lea, R. P. & North, J. (2016). Contributing to coaching knowledge whilst learning how to research: a review and discussion of four student-coaching studies. *Coaching: an international journal of theory, research and practice, 9*(2), 169–184.

Woods, P. (1999) *Successful writing for qualitative researchers.* New York: Routledge.

www.wikihow.com/Publish-a-Research-Paper

Example of writing coaches

www.publicationcoach.com/writing_coaching/

Resource of multiple academic and industry coaching and mentoring publications

www.peer.ca/Best_Pubs.html

Example of larger scale research dissemination planning

www.uq.edu.au/evaluationstedi/Dissemination/Planning_a_Dissemination_Strategy.pdf

PART III
QUANTITATIVE METHODS FOR COACHING AND MENTORING RESEARCH

CHOOSING QUANTITATIVE METHODS

15

WHEN SHOULD I USE QUANTITATIVE METHODS?

LEARNING OUTCOMES

In completing this chapter and related exercises, you will be able to:

1. understand the concepts of internal and external validity;
2. describe the limitations of uncontrolled studies;
3. describe the advantages and limitations of quantitative methods for coaching and mentoring researchers;
4. identify key issues in the decision of whether you should or should not use quantitative methods for your current or future project(s).

WHAT IS THE CURRENT REALITY FOR CHOOSING AMONG TYPES OF QUANTITATIVE RESEARCH DESIGNS?

In this chapter, we will focus primarily on intervention studies, but we stress that non-intervention research is also a large area within which quantitative methods are used. Refer back to Table 1.1 in Chapter 1 for a reminder of the different types of studies available in this field. We will address non-intervention quantitative research in Chapters 17 and 18.

To assess the current reality of quantitative research, there are several different study designs you could use to evaluate whether your coaching/mentoring programme or intervention has had an 'effect' on participants. It is important to understand some of these designs and the fact that some of them provide more information than others. Furthermore, each design contains a different degree of **internal validity**. Perhaps the simplest and one of the most common designs to use, albeit a limited one, is the single sample pre-test and post-test (uncontrolled) design, depicted graphically in Figure 15.1 below.

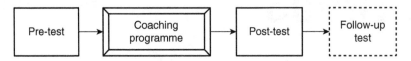

Figure 15.1   Process diagram of a single-sample (uncontrolled) study.

Put simply, this design involves: 1) administering measures to participants to obtain a baseline assessment on an outcome of interest; 2) running your coaching or mentoring programme with those same participants for a pre-designated period; and 3) readministering your measures to evaluate whether your outcome of interest has changed over the duration of the programme. More sophisticated versions of this design will include: 4) a follow-up test (depicted in Figure 15.1 in the dashed box), which will take place at some point after the programme, usually several months, to see if the observed changes were sustained over time. Follow-up might occur just once or multiple times. This step appears in dashes as it is frequently omitted from the research process, primarily because it is onerous on the researcher as well as resource-intensive to follow up people over long periods of time.

Before we address the very important limitations of this approach, let's review its advantages. First, this approach is *comparatively* simple to implement. Compared to more sophisticated designs, it is less onerous on the researcher as it involves following up and managing only one group of participants, which is generally easier than following up and managing two (or potentially several) groups at once. A second advantage is that it is generally easier to get such a design passed through an ethics committee review. This is because it does not involve withholding what is likely to be a beneficial programme from a group of participants who would otherwise benefit from it. Third, it can be a very useful way to evaluate how participants respond to your coaching or mentoring programme before you run a more complete controlled study. For example, participants might identify that there was too much (or insufficient) coaching in the programme, or that they did not understand the content of the coaching, or that they found the process irrelevant to their context. The researcher could then use this information to improve the programme before running a larger, controlled study.

Now for the limitations of the programme. The design is *low* in internal validity. The key piece of information you will obtain from this type of study design is whether the participants changed on some outcome of interest after going through your programme. It will *not* tell you whether that change was *caused by* the programme. This is because it is impossible to rule out other unrelated influences (confounds) on the observed changes. It could be, for example, that your participants changed naturally over the duration of your programme and that this would have occurred irrespective of whether they participated in your programme. Equally, it is possible that an unrelated event occurred concurrently with your programme and that this event might be explaining the changes you're observing. It is perhaps ironic that many researchers opt for this design as a quick and easy way to assess whether their intervention had an effect, yet it is this very design that does not allow one to answer that question. Given the low internal validity, this design generally leaves open too many unanswered questions, including causality (i.e., the extent to which we can claim that *our intervention* led to an increase or decrease in our outcome of interest), and thus it is often more helpful when it is used to evaluate the coaching process, information that can be used to enhance the programme before a controlled study is completed.

To address the important question of causality, we generally need to use more sophisticated designs, such as an experiment. While it is likely an overstatement and oversimplification to suggest that an experiment is *the* approach of choice to evaluate causality, it is safe to say that the logic and practicalities of establishing causality in an experimental design are somewhat more straightforward (Robson & McCartan, 2016). This is because an experiment will traditionally use a control group against which the experimental group can be compared. Still, causality is a high standard that depends on several factors, some of which we address in the next chapter, but a typical experiment is depicted graphically in Figure 15.2 below.

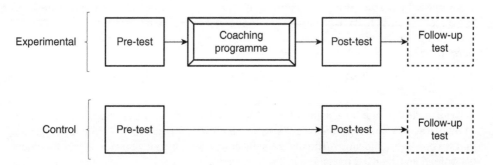

Figure 15.2 Process diagram of an experimental (controlled) study.

Here, two groups of participants are recruited into the study. One group is assigned into the 'experimental' condition and the other into the 'control' condition. It is the experimental group who will receive your coaching programme. The control group is for comparison purposes and will not receive your programme, yet will still be evaluated with the same measures of interest that the experimental group receives, at each time-point, as shown above. If it is indeed your coaching programme that is *causing* the change you're observing in the participants, then this change should be reflected in the experimental group (who receive your programme), but not in the control group (who do not receive your programme).

The follow-up portions of Figure 15.2 are shown in dashed lines because, again, these steps are often omitted from the research process. This occurs mostly for the control group, but sometimes for both groups.

With this design, we're getting closer to isolating the cause of the change to the coaching programme, but we're still not quite there yet. Before we can make claims about causality, there are at least two other very important issues to consider: random allocation and sample size. There are also several different types of control groups and each type has a different purpose. These issues, as well as other important considerations, will be described in more detail in Chapter 17, which focuses exclusively on experimental study designs.

In addition to intervention research that was described here, there are also different forms of non-intervention research, which may be useful for the researcher to establish which variables might be useful to bring into a coaching or mentoring programme. For example, if we determine that there is a relationship between the amount of coaching people receive and how effective they think the coaching process was (i.e., coaching is related to increased ratings of coaching effectiveness), then this can serve as important information when it comes to designing your coaching programme.

■■■■■■■■■■■■■■■ **Definitions** ■■■■■■■■■■■■■■■

Independent variable (IV): In research terms, an IV is a variable that you manipulate in your experiment in order to have an impact on a dependent variable (i.e., the outcome of interest). In coaching and mentoring studies, the coaching or mentoring programme itself is often considered the IV.

Dependent variable (DV): The dependent variable is what is being measured in the study (i.e., the outcome of interest).

Internal validity: Internal validity refers to how well a study was executed, and in particular whether it avoids unrelated variables (these are referred to as 'confounds') to cause the findings that we observe in the study. The more tightly controlled the study and the lesser the chance of confounding, then the higher it is in internal validity.

External validity: External validity refers to a study's generalizability. How well can the findings of a study be generalized to other groups of people in other situations, beyond the study participants themselves? Studies that are generalizable are high in external validity.

Note: There is often a trade-off in terms of internal and external validity. Some studies will be performed in a lab environment where unrelated variables can be very tightly controlled or eliminated (i.e., they are high in internal validity). But lab situations are unlikely to reflect the real world in which we live and thus may not be generalizable to the real world (i.e., they are low in external validity). Because coaching and mentoring studies are often performed in real-world settings, including work, schools, sports, and so on, it gives them higher external validity. Equally, however, it makes it more difficult to control for unrelated influences of the findings (confounds), because such influences are often out of the control of the researcher.

What's more important? Campbell and Stanley (2015) argued that internal validity is of primary importance within a study. Their reasoning was that if we cannot be confident in the findings within the study itself, generalization is then irrelevant. This is not to say, however, that every study should be performed in a lab environment so that they can attain internal validity. Inference is a primary goal of the scientific enterprise, and if we cannot generalize our findings to relevant populations, then questions may arise as to how relevant or valuable the research is.

WHAT IS THE CURRENT REALITY FOR YOU IN TERMS OF CHOOSING QUANTITATIVE METHODS?

Let's consider your current reality in choosing among quantitative methods, if indeed you wish to undertake a quantitative study. Refer back to Table 1.1 in Chapter 1 to reacquaint yourself with some different types of research studies in this area, and try to isolate which one your study fits into. Also, read and answer the questions below, which will be useful for you to identify your own motivation for undertaking quantitative research.

1. Do you have access to a potential sample to recruit into your study? If yes ...

    i   Is this a sample of convenience?
    ii Is it reflective of the population of interest (i.e., is it generalizable)?

2. Are you hoping to put your sample through a coaching or mentoring programme? If so ...

    iii Do you have access to a potential control group?

We will review more on the different types of control groups in experimental research in the next chapter.

WHAT ARE MY OPTIONS IN TERMS OF QUANTITATIVE APPROACHES IN COACHING AND MENTORING RESEARCH?

We have reviewed some of the types of quantitative research designs you might opt for in pursuing your study. You will first need to decide whether you want to take on a quantitative research study and, if so, you will then need to decide whether your study is intervention-based. If your study evaluates an intervention (or programme), you will need to select an intervention design that will yield the information you need. For example, if you're interested in causality, then perhaps an experiment will be your best choice. If you're more interested in piloting your programme to refine it before conducting a larger evaluation study, then perhaps a single-sample study will do just fine.

More generally, however, it should be noted that there are several advantages and limitations of quantitative research that you should be aware of. Many of the advantages and limitations are specific to the particular type of quantitative design one uses, and we discuss these in more detail within each of the chapters that follow, which each focus on a different approach. But first, to help you evaluate your options, here are a handful of very general strengths and weaknesses of using a quantitative research design. These are recapped from Chapter 6, but are shown again in Table 15.1.

Table 15.1   Strengths and weaknesses of quantitative methodology.

Strengths	Weaknesses
Considered more objective.	Can ignore experiences of the individual.
Involves numerical data that is orderly and numerically comparable.	Individual experiences are often not well captured with numerical data.
Deviant (outlying) cases are typically eliminated.	Sometimes outlying cases are of valid scientific interest.
More easily replicated, as they are often derived from standardized protocols.	As the data are reliant on numerical descriptions rather than detailed stories and narratives, they typically don't allow for deep exploration of human experiences.
The researcher has more control over extraneous or unrelated factors (confounds) that could impact the findings.	The research is often, but not always, carried out in an artificial lab environment that lacks external validity (generalizability).

In addition to this general list of advantages and limitations, there are some general points that we consider below which may help you decide whether to opt for a quantitative approach in your study. We address these points below in question-and-answer format. The questions reflect those that we often receive from our students or other people who are new to doing research and are deciding whether to use a quantitative approach. We stress that this is not an exhaustive list and suggest Creswell & Creswell (2017) for further reading on this topic.

FOR WHAT TYPE OF RESEARCH QUESTION(S) WILL A QUANTITATIVE APPROACH BE SUITABLE OR UNSUITABLE?

Again, we refer you back to Table 1.1 in Chapter 1 to locate the major types of research one might opt for, all of which can use quantitative methods. Your choice among the options in this table will go a long way towards isolating the quantitative approach you use. Generally, however, while there are other possible uses of quantitative research methods in scholarly research terms, quantitative approaches are most often used with one or more of the following purposes in mind:

- to test for relationships between variables (see survey methods, Chapter 17);
- to test for differences between groups (see experimental methods, Chapter 16);
- to test for changes within groups (see experimental methods, Chapter 16).

Further, the use of quantitative approaches will generally, but not always, involve:

- the selection of variables that can be measured in a reliable and valid way (see Chapter 17);
- the collection of numerical data that can be analysed using statistical procedures (see Chapter 19);
- the incorporation of protections against bias;
- controlling for alternative or unrelated explanations of findings;
- the presence of **deductive** research questions. Deductive reasoning generally uses verifiable predictions (known as hypotheses) that are derived from theory and then uses empirical data to confirm or disconfirm these predictions. In contrast, **inductive** research works the other way around and tends to be more open-ended – that is, inductive reasoning is more exploratory and generally starts with the data to explore patterns or regularities, which can be used later to form hypotheses or develop theories (Babbie, 2015). Hence, it follows that deductive quantitative research will include the presence of testable hypotheses.

Ultimately, the selection of a research design depends on the nature of the research problem being addressed, as each one serves a very different purpose. For example, if you're interested in the strength of a relationship between two variables, then a simple survey design (Chapter 18) is likely to be your best choice. If you're interested in the extent to which a coaching/mentoring programme 'worked', insofar as it causes an effect in participants, then a full experimental approach with a control group and random allocation will be required (Chapter 17). If you're interested in whether your programme 'worked', insofar as it causes an effect in participants, but are also interested in participant feedback about how to improve the coaching programme itself, then a mixed approach involving a full experimental design with some qualitative data collection will likely be necessary.

In contrast to quantitative approaches, qualitative approaches are generally more inductive and thus used to explore the meaning that individuals or groups attribute to a specific issue. The data itself is usually in the form of language or stories, which is evaluated for themes that allow the researcher to interpret the meaning of what is being said. For such a process, quantitative approaches are generally not suitable. However, qualitative methods are often combined with quantitative methods to form a mixed-methods study (see Chapter 24), as both approaches will often yield complementary information.

WHAT IS EASIER – QUANTITATIVE OR QUALITATIVE?

We live in a practical world where resources are limited, and so the time and resource commitment needed to adopt a research approach is of substantial importance to most researchers. That said, there is no simple answer to this question, and perhaps no valid answer at all, as it will depend heavily on the context for the research project, the participants, the researcher and, perhaps most important, the research question. However, we don't think it will be too controversial for us to say that both qualitative and quantitative approaches will confront the researcher with their own unique challenges. For example, in quantitative studies, statistical power (see Chapter 19) will be an issue, which generally requires the recruitment of large samples so one can more reliably address a research question. Recruiting, retaining and following up large numbers of people in a study requires a substantial investment of time, effort and resources by the researcher or research team. Because power is not an issue in qualitative studies, they generally need fewer participants, which is a plus. However, if long interviews or focus groups are conducted with as few as a dozen participants, it will require ample resources to transcribe and then analyse these datasets. In sum, both approaches will be challenging. At the same time, both are likely to yield interesting findings if they are done well.

WHAT NEXT?

We invite you to assess your motivation for undertaking quantitative research and then to determine whether your potential study is more deductive or inductive in nature. Here are some questions that may help you.

1.   What type of data are you hoping to collect? Will it be numerical or will it be more focused on language? Will it incorporate both?
2.   Do you have testable, verifiable hypotheses to test? If not, is it feasible for you to develop some? And what type of data will be required to test your hypotheses?

CONCLUSION

Quantitative studies can come in a variety of different shapes and forms, each of which has a different degree of internal validity. You must ensure that you choose the right design for your purposes. A large number of researchers opt for the single-sample study, which has a low degree of internal validity and will not yield information that addresses causality. To address causality, experiments are likely to be needed. Quantitative research has advantages, but it also has limitations and you need to consider these before undertaking a quantitative study.

Further reading and resources

Babbie, E. R. (2015). *The practice of social research.* Nelson Education.

Campbell, D. T. & Stanley, J. C. (2015). *Experimental and quasi-experimental designs for research.* Ravenio Books.

Punch, K. (2013). *Introduction to social research: quantitative and qualitative approaches* (3rd ed.). London: SAGE (see Chapters 10–12).

EXPERIMENTAL DESIGNS

16

WHAT ARE THE DIFFERENT TYPES OF EXPERIMENTAL DESIGN?

LEARNING OUTCOMES

In completing this chapter and related activities, you will be able to:

1. describe the advantages and disadvantages of using experimental and quasi-experimental designs in coaching and mentoring research contexts;

2. describe key types of experimental and quasi-experimental designs;

3. describe key concepts in experimental designs, including establishing causality, effect sizes, power analyses, protocol fidelity and implementation challenges.

WHAT IS THE CURRENT REALITY IN TERMS OF USING EXPERIMENTAL OR QUASI-EXPERIMENTAL DESIGNS IN COACHING AND MENTORING RESEARCH CONTEXTS?

We touched on single sample pre-test and post-test designs in Chapter 16. You would know by now that with this type of study design, it is not possible to evaluate causality. To do that, we need to employ experimental methods that allow for the evaluation of causal relationships. We also showed visually an experiment in the previous chapter, depicted again here in Figure 16.1.

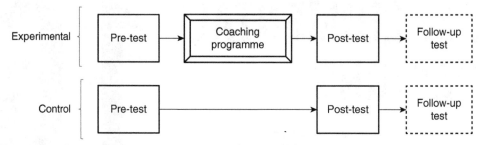

Figure 16.1 Process diagram of an experimental (controlled) study

We know that the design above is an experiment, but at this stage we do not know what type of experiment it is. The type of experimental design will have consequences for whether or not we can make claims of causality, and of key consideration is whether or not participants were *randomly* allocated into the different conditions of the experiment. Random allocation is essential because it is designed to ensure that all the different characteristics of participants (e.g., age, gender, experience, personality, etc.) will be approximately evenly distributed across the different experimental conditions. When this happens, it means theoretically that the only substantive difference between the two study conditions is the fact that one of them received your coaching/mentoring programme, whereas the other group did not receive your programme. Such a design is known as a **randomized controlled trial (RCT)**, and is depicted graphically in Figure 16.2 below.

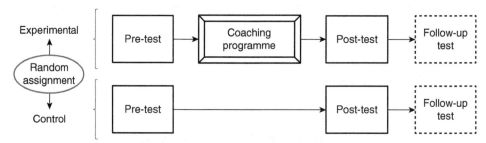

Figure 16.2 Process diagram of a randomized controlled trial study

If participants were not randomly assigned into experimental conditions, then the study is no longer an RCT. Instead, it will go by the name of a **quasi-experiment**, depicted graphically in Figure 16.3 below.

Although a quasi-experiment is generally preferable to a single-sample pre-test and post-test design (see Chapter 15) as it provides more information, it still does not allow for strong claims of causality. This is because in the absence of random allocation, important characteristics among the participants are unlikely to be evenly distributed across the conditions in the study. As an example, and for illustrative purposes, imagine you're designing a coaching

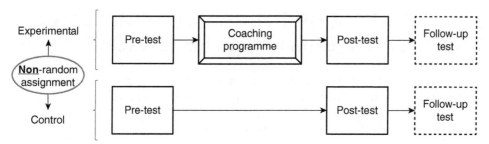

Figure 16.3   Process diagram of quasi-experimental study

study and plan to collect your experimental sample (who will receive your coaching pro-gramme) from your local law firm, which has about 50 staff, all of whom have agreed to participate. Let's further imagine that you aim to collect a control group, but this group will be drawn from the local fast-food restaurant, which also has about 50 staff – all of whom have also agreed to participate.

In this case, there are likely to be very important differences in the participant charac-teristics between these two organizations' staff, differences that may impact the results of your study. For one, the staff at the fast-food restaurant are likely to be younger than those at the law firm, as working at a fast-food restaurant is something people tend to do earlier in their careers. Second, the average level of education across the two organizations is likely to be very different, as working in a legal career requires several years of university educa-tion. Third, the employment status is likely to be quite different, with most people working in fast-food restaurants employed on a part-time basis, whereas those working at a law firm are more likely to be employed on a full-time basis. Each of these important differences is likely to have an effect on the results of the study. In practice, however, the differences between quasi-experimental groups are likely to be subtler than those identified in this example, but are often no less problematic. In cases where systematic differences between the experimental groups exist, they could act as 'hidden causes' of the findings and it is one of the key limitations with a quasi-experimental design.

Another key limitation with this approach is that there could be an unrelated event that confounds the programme, making findings difficult to interpret. Working again with the previous example, imagine you expect that your coaching programme will improve the job performance of your law firm participants. You then run your study, but during the coaching programme, the law firm decided to update its IT systems and also to increase the administration support it makes available to their staff. Neither of these changes were a part of your programme and neither took place at the local fast-food res-taurant. After the study, you indeed find improved performance in your law firm group, as you expected. Was it the coaching that caused that improvement? Perhaps, but we can't know for sure. It is certainly possible that the coaching had some impact, but it is also possible that these extraneous organizational changes are the real cause of the improvements.

WHAT IS THE CURRENT REALITY FOR YOU IN TERMS OF EXPERIMENTAL RESEARCH?

In considering your own situation, take a moment to consider the following questions which may help you to identify whether or not an experimental study is feasible.

1. Do you have access to a large sample and how will you monitor them over time?
2. Can you use a control group?

    i   Will you be able to randomly allocate participants into the different groups in your study?

3. How will you ensure that your participants adhere to your programme or treatment? Can you use a specific protocol? See the section on protocol fidelity below.

━━━━━ Definitions ━━━━━

Sampling. Sampling is a process of selecting a representative group (a sample) from a population under study. The population is the total group of individuals from which the sample might be selected. For example, let's say hypothetically that we're interested in CEOs in Australia. Let's further hypothetically assume that there are 10,000 CEOs in Australia. This group represents the population of CEOs in Australia. We could then select a sample from this group (say, $n = 200$) and we could use this sample of 200 to generalize to other CEOs in Australia. The larger the sample, the more generalizable it is. This process is known as sampling.

Sampling error. Sampling error refers to the random unrepresentativeness of a sample from the corresponding population. Using the same hypothetical example of CEOs in Australia, let's assume that on a life satisfaction scale that is rated from 1 to 10, where 1 is very low life satisfaction, and 10 is very high life satisfaction, that the average across this population of 10,000 CEOs was 7.4/10. Let's assume that our sample of $n = 200$ CEOs is a random subset that are drawn from this population of 10,000, and that we also learn that within this subset the average life satisfaction is 6.8/10. The difference between these two values is entirely due to the unrepresentativeness of our sample from the corresponding population (sampling error). The smaller the sample, the greater the influence of sampling error on the findings.

Random allocation. Random allocation is a process that involves the random assignment (by chance alone) of participants into the different experimental groups in the study. This is done to reduce bias in the distribution of participant characteristics, which is known to impact the findings in non-randomized studies. A randomized controlled trial (RCT) is a specific type of experimental study that involves the random allocation of participants into different experimental groups.

Quasi-experiment. A quasi-experimental study is a type of experiment that lacks the random assignment of participants into experimental groups. Let's say, for example, that you're designing a coaching study and plan to collect your experimental sample (who receive your coaching programme) from organization X. Let's further assume that you aim to collect a control group, but this group will be drawn from organization Y. In this case, it is the organization that determines whether each participant receives the programme, and thus the allocation is not random. This would be considered a quasi-experiment.

Non-intervention control. Some experiments will include a control condition where participants are not exposed to any type of intervention. This is known as a non-intervention control. A type of non-intervention control is a wait-list control, which is where control participants receive the intervention after the study has been completed. A wait-list control is typically used for ethical reasons, as it then means the study can proceed as normal without having to completely exclude a group from something that could benefit them.

Active control. Another type of control group is an active control, which is where the group receives another type of activity that is different from what the experimental group receives. For example, let's assume you're interested in testing a new type of coaching practice and would like to see if this new practice works better than practice as normal. In this case, your control group would receive the practice as normal intervention (an active control), whereas the experimental group would receive your new type of coaching programme.

WHAT ARE MY OPTIONS IN TERMS OF EXPERIMENTAL RESEARCH?

We have already identified one important choice that you will need to make if you are opting for an experimental research study – that is, you will need to decide whether you will randomly allocate participants to groups, or whether you will use some other non-random mechanism to determine who is and is not allocated to the experimental group. This is one of the most important options for you to decide on when conducting an experiment. However, another important choice is what type of control group you will use.

Let's imagine that you have developed a brand-new coaching methodology that you feel could be used specifically to improve employee well-being, and you would like to test whether the programme is indeed effective in improving employee well-being. Let's again imagine that you're keen to do this in the most rigorous way possible, and so you decide that you will run a full RCT with a group of participants you've collected across a large organization. You will randomly assign half of the participants into a coaching group, and other half into a control group. So far, it's looking very good.

However, an important decision for you to make is the type of control group you will use. As a general rule of thumb, if we are wanting to test a new variant of an existing practice, then we ought to then compare our new variant of that practice to the existing best practice to see if we find an improvement over what is already available. This means that we will use an **active control** group. They are **active** because participants in this condition will also receive 'something' during the intervention phase of the study, rather than nothing. But that 'something' will be different from what is given to your experimental group. A control group who receive nothing are referred to as passive and are less desirable. An example of an RCT with an active control group is depicted in Figure 16.4 below.

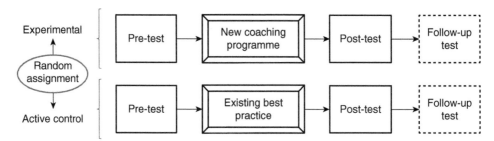

Figure 16.4   Process diagram of a randomized controlled trial study with an active control group

If you find that your new coaching programme does indeed outperform what is already available and considered best practice, you now have pretty strong evidence. Note that an active control group can be used within a RCT or quasi-experimental design. In practice, unfortunately, active controls are less frequently used – likely because they require yet more resources to implement properly. On the other hand, it is also worth mentioning that some experimenters will go one step further and recruit both active control and non-intervention control participants into the study, an example of which is depicted in Figure 16.5.

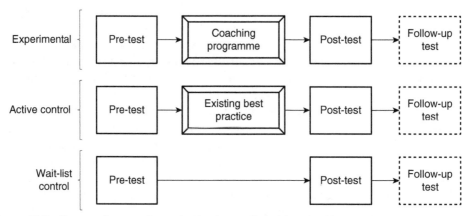

Figure 16.5   Process diagram of a randomized controlled trial study with an active control group

In the above diagram, you'll notice that experimental participants will be compared to participants who receive the existing best practice coaching methods, as well as a group who receive no intervention at all. Assuming random allocation was involved, this type of design will yield information about whether the new practice out-performed the existing practice, and whether each practice is better than nothing at all.

Further, you might have noticed that in this particular example, the group who are assigned to the no-intervention condition will form a part of what's known as a **waitlist control** group. What this means is that these participants will receive the coaching programme after the study has been completed (i.e., they are put on a waiting list) and thus they are not excluded from something that could benefit them. This is a useful way to ensure that your programme is more ethical.

OTHER IMPORTANT CONSIDERATIONS IN EXPERIMENTAL RESEARCH DESIGNS

Below, we identify a number of other important considerations for you, which will help you to identify among your many options the right type of study for your situation.

ESTABLISHING CAUSALITY

We will touch on two key requirements before one can make a solid claim of causality. We have already described the process of **randomization** (or random allocation), which is a key feature of an RCT design and a key requirement to produce 'equivalent' groups in your study. It is also worth noting, however, that randomization by itself does not guarantee the ability to make inferences of causality. In fact, randomization does not work properly unless the random samples are large, which they rarely are (Schmidt & Oh, 2016). Randomly allocated samples need to be large enough to produce 1) equivalent groups in your study and 2) groups that are representative of the population of interest (Tversky & Kahneman, 1971). Small samples are not representative of the population of interest because they are more greatly affected by **sampling error**. Sampling error refers to the degree to which a sample is randomly unrepresentative of its corresponding population. To reduce the influence of sampling error, large samples are required. The larger the sample, the closer your results will be representative of the corresponding population. If causality is really something that you are interested in, you will need to evaluate your current situation and determine whether randomization is possible (or feasible), and whether you have the resources to recruit a sufficiently sized sample into each of the groups within the study. Some useful resources for further reading are: Lenth, 2001; Fraenkel, Wallen, & Hyun, 1993.

Other important considerations for experimental studies are as follows.

POWER

The **power** of a study is the chance of finding a statistically significant effect if indeed an effect size of a given magnitude exists in the population of interest. Power is specified as a percentage (e.g., .80 would mean there is an 80 per cent chance of detecting the effect, assuming it exists). Power is determined by several factors, one of which is sample size. Larger samples yield more power. Another determinant is the size of the effect that exists in the population of interest. Larger effects are generally easier to detect, giving a study more power.

The lower the power of your study, the higher your chances of *failing* to detect a real effect (known as a **Type II error**; Schmidt & Hunter, 2015). Low power is also associated with an increased chance of a false positive, or concluding an effect exists when one does not (known as a **Type I error**). For more information on power, see Brickman & Rog, 2008; Faul, Erdfelder, Lang, & Buchner, 2007. A **power analysis** is used to inform the researcher about the sample size required to detect an effect size of a given magnitude with some specified degree of confidence. It is very important to perform power analysis before conducting an experiment as it tells the researcher how many participants will need to be recruited into the study.

EFFECT SIZES

When conducting an experiment, we are usually interested in some way of quantifying the degree to which our treatment/programme 'worked', often by comparing a treatment/experimental group against a control group. An **effect size** can be used to quantify the magnitude of this difference, but it can also be used to quantify the magnitude of change that occurred within groups. Further, an effect size can be used to quantify the strength of a relationship between two variables. An effect size should be accompanied by information about its precision or the degree of error associated with it. This is often referred to as a **confidence interval (CI)**. A CI will include a range of values that encompass the effect size and specify a probability (typically 95 per cent) that the effect size falls within the specified range. The wider the CI, the less confident we are in the effect size we've obtained. Smaller samples will be reflected by a wide CI, as more error is involved. The higher the power of your study, the closer your sample effect size will approximate to its corresponding population value.

PROTOCOL FIDELITY

Protocol fidelity refers to the degree to which the intervention will adhere to a protocol that was originally developed for that intervention. As ways to foster protocol fidelity, reporting checklists have been developed that are available publicly, including CONSORT and TREND, which researchers should adhere to when reporting RCTs or non-randomized studies. Unfortunately, however, in practice these checklists continue to be underutilized (Persch & Page, 2013).

WHAT NEXT?

We invite you to evaluate the following research studies (Grant, 2003; Green, Oades, & Grant, 2006) from the reference list and try to determine:

- what type of study each is (e.g., single-sample, randomized controlled trial, quasi-experiment, etc.);
- what type of control group was used (if any)?

CONCLUSION

Experiments are a useful form of research in the social sciences because they allow the researcher to come closer to establishing causality. However, to ensure that causal inferences are possible, you must ensure that participants are randomly allocated into the experimental groups, and that the samples are large to ensure equal distribution of participant characteristics that could influence the results of a study and to minimize the impact of sampling error on the findings. If random allocation is not possible, then the study will normally be a quasi-experiment, which contains less internal validity to the traditional RCT design.

 Further reading and resources

Bloom, H. S. (2006). The core analytics of randomized experiments for social research. *The handbook of social research* (pp. 115–134). London: SAGE.

Cook, T. D., & Wong, V. C. (2008). Better quasi-experimental practice. *The handbook of social research* (pp. 134–165). London: SAGE.

SURVEY DESIGNS

17

WHAT ARE THE DIFFERENT TYPES OF CROSS-SECTIONAL SURVEY DESIGN?

LEARNING OUTCOMES

In completing this chapter and related activities, you will be able to:

1. describe the advantages and disadvantages of using cross-sectional research in coaching and mentoring;
2. describe key types of survey-based research designs;
3. compare and contrast subjective and objective measurement approaches;
4. identify examples of useful coaching and mentoring research that use survey designs.

WHAT IS THE CURRENT REALITY FOR USING A CROSS- SECTIONAL RESEARCH DESIGN IN COACHING AND MENTORING CONTEXTS?

In a **cross-sectional study design**, researchers do not intervene in any way (e.g., by providing a coaching/mentoring programme), but simply observe and describe the participant behaviours, attitudes, health or lifestyle choices, within their natural setting. As the name suggests, a cross-sectional design is used to sample a 'cross-section' of the population of interest. Cross-sectional studies in coaching and mentoring research are often completed with surveys.

Cross-sectional surveys are a relatively quick, easy and inexpensive way to assess the strength of a relationship between variables of interest. For example, if you are interested in the number of hours of mentoring people received in company X in 2017, and you expect that those who received more mentoring will, generally, perform better on the job, you might administer a survey that will identify the number of hours of mentoring each employee received in company X in 2017, as well as their job performance in that year to see if the two variables are related. A **positive relationship** (referred to as a **correlation**, and most often denoted by r) means that the two variables moved in the same direction – that is, people who received more mentoring were generally the higher performers is a positive relationship (or correlation). If, in contrast, people who received more mentoring were generally the lower performers, this would be evidence of a **negative relationship** (or correlation). Correlations can vary anywhere from –1.00 to +1.00. The closer the value is to the minimum (–1.00) or maximum (+1.00) values, the stronger the relationship. A correlation of 0 indicates that the two variables are unrelated.

This is correlation in its simplest form, and there are much more sophisticated versions of this approach that will allow you to answer more nuanced research questions. Correlational approaches are often used with cross-sectional study designs. There are some advantages and limitations of using a cross-sectional design, and we detail some of them here. For the purpose of this discussion, let's assume that the cross-sectional research is administered with surveys (which is not always the case). Let's first discuss the advantages.

ADVANTAGES

- Cross-sectional surveys are generally quick, easy and cheap to do. They are less onerous on the researcher as they do not involve following up participants over long periods of time. There will be no 'loss to follow-up' because participants are only measured once.
- Cross-sectional surveys are generally easy to get through an ethics committee review, and indeed, are sometimes the only ethical way to conduct the research project. Occasionally, there may be situations where it is not considered ethical to run a programme and a potential alternative is to administer a survey.
- A cross-sectional design is well suited to estimating the prevalence of a certain behaviour or characteristic within a population. For example, imagine you're interested in knowing how often, on average, people in company Y conduct coaching conversations with their peers. You could build these questions into a cross-sectional survey to estimate this information.
- Cross-sectional surveys are typically performed earlier in the research process. This generally occurs because it is important to first establish that a relationship between variables exists, before you ascertain whether one causes the other. This cause-and-effect part of a relationship can then be unpacked further in later studies that use experimental methods.
- Cross-sectional studies tend to have larger samples than experimental designs. Larger samples are generally less affected by sampling error.

LIMITATIONS

- It is not possible to infer causality with a cross-sectional design. Just because two variables are related, it does not mean that one causes the other.
- Cross-sectional surveys are often affected by what is known as **common method variance,** especially when the same approach is used to measure each variable of interest. Common method variance is a well-known source of **measurement error** and is defined as 'variance that is attributable to the measurement method rather than to the constructs that the measures represent' (Podsakoff, MacKenzie, Lee, & Podsakoff, 2003: 879). Common method variance usually causes relationships (or correlations) to be larger than what their real value is (i.e., they are artificially inflated or biased upwards). Note, there are ways to reduce common method variance in cross-sectional data, which we discuss later in the chapter.
- Cross-sectional surveys are affected by **non-response bias** if participants who consent to complete the survey are different from those who do not consent. For example, imagine you have sensitive questions about participant income on your survey and people who have high salaries generally do not consent to completing your survey for this reason. In this case, you would have a sample that reflects a response bias towards lower income participants.
- Surveys are affected by **measurement error**. There are no perfectly accurate measures, and so we have to accept that when we administer a survey of a given variable, we are measuring both our construct of interest *plus error*, which is not of interest. There are no exceptions to this rule; all survey instruments are affected by measurement error. This is a concern that also affects experimental studies, too.

Definitions

Cross-sectional. In a cross-sectional study, a researcher will recruit a sample that is representative of a given population at a specific point in time – that is, in a cross-sectional study, data are all gathered at once and there is no time-lag between the collection of different pieces of data. A cross-sectional study will typically use a correlational design and evaluate the strength of relationships between variables using different forms of regression-based statistical techniques. A cross-sectional study can also be used to evaluate the prevalence of a variable of interest (e.g., an attitude towards the organization and awareness of a particular policy, etc.) A cross-sectional study cannot be used to infer causality.

Longitudinal. In a longitudinal study, a researcher will make repeated observations over time – which can range from very short periods of time (e.g., a week) to very long periods of time (e.g., decades). A longitudinal design can be used in correlational research and also different forms of experimental research. If causality is of interest, a longitudinal study will be preferred to a cross-sectional study because in longitudinal research, the temporal ordering of the variables can be established more clearly.

(Continued)

(Continued)

Measurement error. Measurement error refers to the difference in measurement of a variable and its corresponding true value. If this difference is large, then the measure will be less accurate than if this difference is small. Measurement error is always present in psychological instruments – there are no exceptions to this rule as there are no perfectly accurate measures. Measurement error can be both random (e.g., a respondent misreading a survey question) or systematic (e.g., flawed or biased measurement instruments).

Reliability. Reliability refers to the degree to which measurement instruments will produce similar results over repeated observations. If similar results are obtained over repeated observations, then a measurement instrument is said to be 'reliable' or high in reliability. If markedly different results are obtained over repeated observations, then the instrument is said to be 'unreliable' or low in reliability.

Validity. A measure is valid to the extent that it accurately measures what it purports to measure and not something else. For example, if we develop a measure of 'mentor satisfaction' to evaluate how satisfied protégés are with their assigned mentors and our instrument actually measures, say, job satisfaction (but not mentor satisfaction), then our measure is not a valid measure of mentor satisfaction.

Self-report. In a self-report measurement instrument, respondents will generally be asked a variety of questions with reference to themselves. For example, they might be asked to report how depressed they are, or how satisfied they are, or how engaged they are, or a host of other possible variables in which a researcher may be interested.

Other report. In an other-report measurement instrument, a respondent will be asked to report or respond to a variety of questions to evaluate someone else. For example, a typical scenario in which an other report is used, supervisors report on how effective (or ineffective) their subordinates' performance is on the job.

Objective data. Objective measures will generally capture data that can be directly and physically observed by the researcher. This might be, for example, outcomes from biological indicators (e.g., cortisol swabs) or actual performance data (e.g., number of sales in the previous week) or something else. Objective data is often considered more valid because it is less easily influenced by respondent biases. Researchers may opt to use objective data when they want to eliminate personal forms of bias that might creep into more subjective forms of measurement (e.g., measures that involve respondents answering a series of questions).

WHAT IS YOUR CURRENT REALITY IN TERMS OF SURVEY-BASED RESEARCH DESIGNS?

Let's consider your current situation and examine why you may want to undertake a survey-based research design. Refer back to Table 1.1 in Chapter 1 and decide for yourself which type of research your project will fit into. While survey-based research could be used across all of those types of research identified in the table, it is commonly used in non-intervention research. You will also need to determine what you're interested in and thus which variables you will measure in your study. Are you interested in well-being? Are you interested in learning? Performance? The process of coaching-mentoring itself? Your research interests will be key in determining what you actually measure in your study. There are also different types of survey-based studies, which means there are several options available to you in going about your survey-based research.

WHAT ARE YOUR OPTIONS IN TERMS OF SURVEY-BASED RESEARCH?

Once you know that you want to undertake a survey-based study, a variety of options are available to you. Below, we review some of these options and also examine some advantages and potential disadvantages of each, so that you can decide which option is the right one for you.

KEY TYPES OF SURVEY DESIGNS

We have already discussed in some detail the cross-sectional survey, as well as some advantages and limitations of this approach. As stated earlier, a major disadvantage of cross-sectional designs is that it is difficult to establish cause and effect. These designs are also highly affected by common method variance if the same procedure is used to measure each variable of interest.

One option available to you to strengthen a survey study is to administer it **longitudinally**, in which case each participant in the study will participate at two or more different time points. In other words, there is a **time-lag** between measurements. For example, imagine we suspected that work engagement causes better performance. Thus, if people are engaged in their work, we expect that their performance will be high. We could design a study to measure this and take a measure of work engagement at time 1, and then their job performance at time 2 (say, six months later). If we find a relationship using this time-lagged approach, we've now helped to establish that work engagement can predict better performance up to six months later, although we still cannot infer true cause and effect yet (see Chapter 16). Establishing a time-lag not only helps establish which variables are predictors and which are outcomes, but it also helps to lessen the impact of common method variance in our data. Common-method variance is generally a larger issue when the study is administered cross-sectionally (Podsakoff et al., 2003).

Another option available to you to lessen the effect of common method variance, and thus strengthen a survey study, is to have different sets of participants complete a measure. For example, using the previous example, let's imagine that we suspected participants were not the most accurate judges of their own performance. So, instead of using a **self-report** performance measure (where each participant rates their own job performance), we instead use an **other-report** measure and have their supervisors rate their job performance on their behalf. Given that we now have two different sets of participants to whom we administer our different measures of our different constructs, we have created an alternative method and thus error due to *common* method variance is lessened.

Yet another option available to you is to collect **multi-level** data, in which case parameters in the study will vary at more than one level. For example, imagine you're interested in doing a survey about the relationship between coaching and performance within organization Z. A multi-level study might measure 300 employees within this organization, but also measure 60 work-teams, within which these 300 employees are grouped. In this example, we now have two levels of data: individuals ($n = 300$) and teams ($n = 60$). In a multi-level study, data are typically **nested** – that is, the unit of analysis is typically individuals (at the lowest level), who are then 'nested' within a unit (which is aggregated) at a higher level (e.g., work-teams, business units, entire organizations, etc.). The same approach is often used in educational research, in which individual students (at the lowest level) are nested within classrooms (at a higher level), which are in turn nested within schools (at the highest level), and so on.

Multi-level data allows one to better take account of the fact that data are often clustered or possess a hierarchical structure. Thus, data observations are typically not independent. For example, two individuals working in the same work-team are more likely to be similar (in terms of age, skills, knowledge, personality and experience) than two individuals picked randomly from the population at large. Multi-level approaches better take account of this. These approaches can also be combined with longitudinal approaches, in which individuals who are then aggregated at a higher level are followed up and measured at various points over time.

There are several benefits to multi-level approaches. First, as noted above, they take into account that observations are typically not independent. An assumption of independence in non-independent data generally leads to greater error when making inferences from the data. Second, sometimes we're more interested in the group, rather than the individual. In coaching/mentoring research this is particularly true. For example, often, we are interested in the relationship (coach–coachee; mentor–protégé) just as much as we are interested in individuals within those relationships. Multi-level research will allow us to monitor group-effects, which might not necessarily match what we see for individuals within those groups. Third, common method variance is less of an issue in multi-level research. There are other advantages, too – which we will not delve into here. Interested readers might consider visiting the University of Bristol's Centre for Multilevel Modelling (www.bristol.ac.uk/cmm/), which has useful readings, videos and tutorials.

Another option available to you in this type of research is whether part of your study will partially evaluate a more objective type of measurement. **Objective measures** will generally capture data that can be directly and physically observed by the researcher. This might be, for example, outcomes from biological indicators (e.g., cortisol swabs to evaluate stress) or actual performance data (e.g., number of sales in the previous week) or something else.

Objective metrics are generally seen as more valid and reliable than survey-based research. Survey research, particularly that which uses self-reports, often gets criticized heavily in the behavioural sciences. While it is important to acknowledge the many limitations involved with self-reports (Podsakoff & Organ, 1986), it is a fallacy to think that other more 'objective' types of measures will provide you with data that is free of error. Ultimately, all data will contain measurement error. There are no exceptions to this rule (Schmidt, 2010).

It is also important to consider that some types of data are both expensive to collect as well as resource-intensive to administer. For instance, biological data (such as collecting cortisol) are becoming increasingly common as an index of stress. While certainly different from survey data, because such data are expensive and resource-consuming, the upshot is that researchers often recruit fewer people into their study, which then increases sampling error in their data. Ultimately, when considering how you will measure key variables in your study, you will need to consider a number of factors.

- What are the different ways to measure your constructs of interest?
- What is feasible for you to do?

  - What are the costs?
  - What are the resources involved?

- What has typically been done in the field to date?
- Will your study offer a unique contribution using new measurement approaches?
- Will you have to sacrifice some of your sample (therefore increasing sampling error) to accommodate a measurement approach that is resource-consuming? Is it worthwhile?

In sum, survey studies can be cross-sectional, longitudinal, multilevel, multisource, as well as contain mixed approaches to measurement.

WHAT NEXT?

You are invited to go to PsycINFO or Web of Science at your local university library and, using a combination of key words (e.g., coaching, mentoring, survey, cross-sectional, longitudinal, multilevel, etc.), try to:

1. locate some examples of coaching and/or mentoring studies that use different types of survey-based research;
2. evaluate the study and the measures the researchers used and determine how similar or different their method will be from the project you are proposing for yourself;
3. if you can't find examples yourself, examine the following research studies (Allen et al., 2006; Linley, Nielsen, Gillet, & Biswas-Diener, 2010) from the reference list, to identify whether each one is a) cross-sectional or longitudinal; b) individual or multilevel; and c) to identify the types of measures used.

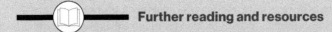

Further reading and resources

The following resources provide in-depth assessments of some of the challenges in conducting survey-based research.

Podsakoff, P. M., MacKenzie, S. B., Lee, J. Y., & Podsakoff, N. P. (2003). Common method biases in behavioral research: a critical review of the literature and recommended remedies. *Journal of Applied Psychology, 88*(5), 879.

Podsakoff, P. M., & Organ, D. W. (1986). Self-reports in organizational research: problems and prospects. *Journal of Management, 12*(4), 531–544.

Schmidt, F. (2010). Detecting and correcting the lies that data tell. *Perspectives on Psychological Science, 5*(3), 233–242.

COMMON QUANTITATIVE METHODS AND ANALYSES

18

WHAT ARE THE COMMON QUANTITATIVE METHODS AND ANALYSES FOR COACHING AND MENTORING RESEARCH?

LEARNING OUTCOMES

In completing this chapter and related activities, you will be able to:

1. describe the difference between quantitative methods and analyses;
2. understand the concepts of reliability and validity;
3. describe examples of common quantitative methods in coaching and mentoring research;
4. list advantages and disadvantages of some relevant quantitative methods and analyses for your current situation.

WHAT'S THE CURRENT REALITY WITH QUANTITATIVE METHODS AND QUANTITATIVE ANALYSES?

An important point to consider when conducting quantitative-based research is that your method decisions will be separate from your analysis decisions. Choosing the right methods (or designs) is among the most important, yet challenging decisions you will face during the research process. If you are opting for a quantitative study, there are many options available. A useful and accessible resource to get you started is Vogt, Gardner, and Haeffele (2012) who review a variety of different study methods and key decision points through the process. But do keep in mind that this resource is generalist and not focused on coaching–mentoring research.

We are assuming that because you are reading this section of the book, you are interested in using quantitative approaches, and two of the most common approaches to quantitative research in this field are survey designs and intervention/experimental designs. While neither of these designs requires the collection of quantitative data per se, quantitative data is very often used with these approaches. In this chapter, we outline a number of key decision points that you will need to consider in determining the approach that you use.

WHAT'S THE CURRENT REALITY FOR YOU IN TERMS OF QUANTITATIVE METHODS AND ANALYSES?

Before we answer the above question, another key decision point for you is that you will need to assess your current experience and comfort in using quantitative-based methods and analyses. We urge readers not to shelve the thought of taking on quantitative research because they think it is 'beyond their expertise' or that they are 'not a numbers person' – reasons we hear frequently. Instead, see it as a learning opportunity and as a new skill for you to master. Nonetheless, it will be helpful for you to evaluate the following.

- What is your current level of knowledge of quantitative research methods? If you answered 'none' to this question, then that's good – this chapter is for you.
- Do you even need to use quantitative research methods and analyses?
- How will you go about collecting and analysing quantitative data? Do you have access to someone who can help you through it in the beginning? Will you need someone?
- Does your computer have one of SPSS, MPlus, R or another platform you can use to actually evaluate your key findings?

WHAT ARE MY OPTIONS AND KEY DECISION POINTS WHEN DOING QUANTITATIVE RESEARCH?

By far the most common approach to conducting quantitative-based research in coaching–mentoring research is via the use of self-report scales. This is because they are relatively inexpensive, not onerous and easier than other types of measurement approaches. The downside is that they contain all the issues of self-report data (see Chapter 17), including self-report bias and common method variance if no alternative forms of data are gathered. Self-report scales will typically ask participants about their inner subjective states such as feelings, attitudes, motivations, thoughts and beliefs using an established set of questions (items) that have been evaluated for their **reliability** and **validity**.

Reliable scales measure constructs in a consistent and dependable way. If we use the same scale to measure the construct over time (assuming no intervention has been delivered), to the extent that we receive similar results on separate measurement occasions, the scale is reliable. Valid scales accurately measure the underlying construct of interest and not some other construct. To the extent that the scale measures what we think it does, it is construct valid. For example, if we have a scale of job satisfaction that does not really measure job satisfaction, but instead measures something similar but different (e.g., satisfaction with life), then the scale is lacking construct validity. When selecting scales, it is important to ensure that they accurately measure what we think they do and not something different. There are a variety of different ways to do this, and we refer interested readers to Clark & Watson, 1995; Drost, 2011; Mackenzie, Podsakoff, & Podsakoff, 2011 for a more in-depth discussion of procedures to establish construct validity.

There are several different analysis procedures that you can use to evaluate your data in coaching–mentoring research. These will generally flow naturally from the research design you opt for (e.g., survey design, experimental design, etc). A selection of approaches that will help you are described below. For space reasons, we *briefly* discuss those techniques most relevant to coaching–mentoring research and we remind readers that there are many other analysis options available.

TESTING FOR RELATIONSHIPS BETWEEN VARIABLES: CORRELATION AND REGRESSION

Perhaps the two most common procedures for analysing survey-based data are various forms of correlation and regression. Correlation analyses are used to examine the extent to which two measured variables co-vary and can be used to quantify the strength of the relationship. Such techniques are commonly used in non-intervention research, but are also used in process and outcome research (remember Table 1.1 in Chapter 1). For example, we might be interested in the relationship between mentoring received and protégé ratings of mentoring effectiveness.

We might expect that employees who received more mentoring (vs. those who receive little or no mentoring at all) will perceive the mentoring relationship to be more productive and beneficial. In this case, we measure protégé perceptions mentoring effectiveness (of which a variety of measurement approaches might be available) and also obtain information that quantifies the amount of mentoring employees received (e.g., number of sessions, number of hours, etc.), so we can calculate a correlation between the two variables.

Correlations are interpreted with a coefficient r, which is the effect–size metric used to quantify the strength of the relationship. A positive relationship – an observed coefficient – between 0 and 1.00 – indicates a trend that as one variable goes up, so does the other. In our example, a positive relationship would mean more mentoring is associated with higher protégé ratings of mentoring effectiveness. A negative relationship – an observed coefficient r between 0 and –1.00 – indicates a trend that as one variable goes up, the other one goes down. In our example, this would mean that more mentoring is associated with *lower* protégé ratings of mentoring effectiveness. The closer the observed coefficient is towards either 1.00 or –1.00, the stronger the relationship: positive or negative. When r is 0.0, there is no observed relationship between the variables. In our example, this would mean that mentoring received is unrelated to protégé perceptions of mentoring effectiveness.

Conventions for interpreting the strength of correlations vary depending on the subject domain (Bosco et al., 2015) but perhaps the most widely used correlation effect–size conventions were specified by Cohen (1988):

- ≥ .10 indicates a weak relationship;
- ≥ .30 indicates a moderate relationship;
- ≥ .50 indicates a strong relationship.

In organizational research, these metrics vary depending on the constructs (Bosco et al., 2015), so you must choose the right conventions for the practical and theoretical context of the area of research (Wilkinson, 1999). Correlations are often depicted visually with a scatterplot. Figure 18.1 shows a scatterplot at a correlation strength of (r = .60) between two variables for a fictitious sample of n = 228 employees going through a mentoring programme. By Cohen's (1988) conventions, this would be a 'strong' relationship. On the x-axis is plotted the number of mentoring meetings that protégés had with their mentor in the last three months. On the y-axis is plotted the protégés' average rating of mentoring effectiveness. You can see from the plot that the highest number of mentoring meetings over the three-month period was 7, whereas the lowest number was just 1. You can also see that greater numbers of mentoring meetings experienced over the three-month period was associated with higher average ratings of mentoring effectiveness overall. Thus, r is positive in this example.

Note that correlations can be meaningful, where the correlation reflects a genuine relationship between two variables. However, they can also be **spurious**, in which case the correlation does not reflect the actual strength of the relationship between two variables, but instead is caused by an unrelated third variable. An example of this is the positive correlation that is commonly observed between *drinking red wine* and *life expectancy*. Unfortunately, in this case, this is unlikely to be a real relationship (Schmidt, 2017). Instead, socioeconomic

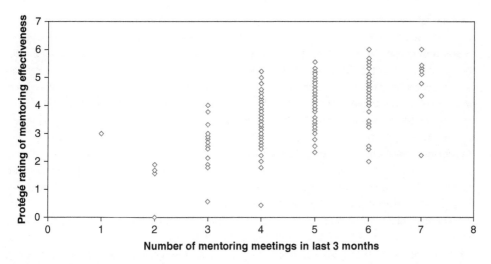

Figure 18.1   Scatterplot (Pearson correlation, r = .60) showing the relationship between the frequency of mentoring meetings over three months and protégé ratings of mentoring effectiveness

status (SES) is likely to be the real causal factor, because people who are higher in SES are more likely to drink red wine in place of other alcoholic drinks, and they are also likely to live longer. This is also an example why correlation does not imply evidence for causation.

Regression is similar to correlation, but differs insofar as it expresses the relationship in the form of an equation. This allows one to specify a 'line of best fit' through the data-points to facilitate prediction. Using the same example, we could use this equation and correspond-ing line of best fit to predict each protégé's rating of mentoring effectiveness (y) based on the amount of mentoring (x) they received (Figure 18.2). The line of best fit is derived from a formula that minimizes the error between the observed points in the scatter plot and that predicted by line (referred to as a residual).

The above are correlation and regression in their simplest form, but they are typically used in more sophisticated ways to answer more nuanced research questions. Below is a selection of common data analysis procedures that have their roots in correlation and regression, which are frequently used in coaching–mentoring research. A full review of all statistical procedures is beyond the scope of this book, and we encourage interested readers to explore our further readings after each technique to develop a much deeper understanding of each procedure. Common techniques include the following.

- **Multiple regression**: uses several predictors at once to predict the value of an outcome (y) (see Tabachnik & Fidell, 2007).
- **Path-analysis**: an extension of multiple regression that tests hypothesized paths between a set of predictors ($x1, x2$, etc.) and an outcome (y) (see Kline, 2015).
- **Moderation:** a regression analysis that evaluates whether a relationship depends on a third vari-able (i.e., a moderator). For example, we might expect that mentoring frequency will be related to

protégé ratings of mentoring effectiveness, but this relationship will be stronger for employees who are just beginning their careers (i.e., career-level becomes the moderator) (see Hayes, 2013).

- **Mediation:** is used to identify mechanisms or processes that underlie an observed relationship between two variables. For example, we might expect that mentoring frequency will be related to higher ratings of mentoring effectiveness, but the process through which mentoring 'works' is by increasing employee *competence* – that is, after receiving mentoring over a period of time, employees become better at their jobs and thus start to believe that their mentoring is paying off (see Hayes, 2013).

- **Moderated-mediation (or conditional path analysis):** sometimes mediation is conditional upon another variable – a moderator – which can be examined in moderated mediation (see Hayes, 2013 for an overview, and Lawn, Slemp, & Vella-Brodrick, 2018; Pollack, Vanepps, & Hayes, 2012 for examples of studies using this approach).

- **Factor analysis**: a statistical procedure for reducing a large set of items (i.e., survey questions) into a small number of factors that represent relationships among the clusters of items. For example, we might develop a bunch of items that we think measure *Work Satisfaction*. We collect some data for our new scale and after applying factor analysis we might see that some items correlate strongly to reflect *Satisfaction with the Organization*, others might reflect *Satisfaction with Pay/Remuneration*, and others might reflect *Satisfaction with Co-workers* – which are all different features of work. Factor analysis is often used in the development of scales to measure constructs (see Tabachnik & Fidell, 2007).

- **Structural equation modelling**: a powerful multivariate statistical technique which uses a combination of factor analysis and path analysis to test causal models. Through this technique, one generally proposes a hypothesized model and then examines how well this model 'fits' the data collected (see Kline, 2015).

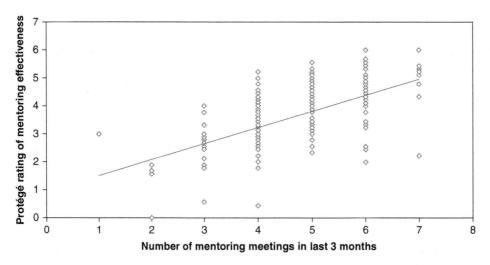

Figure 18.2   Scatterplot (Pearson correlation, *r* = .60) showing the relationship and line of best fit between the frequency of mentoring meetings over three months and protégé ratings of mentoring effectiveness

DESIGN CONSIDERATIONS FOR SURVEY-BASED RESEARCH

Now that you know more about survey-based research and analysis options, here are some design considerations for survey-based research. As you now know, survey designs are efficient, inexpensive ways to conduct research and are the single most widely used method in the social and behavioural sciences (Vogt et al., 2012). Important questions to ask yourself if opting for this design are as follows (see Vogt et al., 2012 for a fuller discussion).

1.   Are the questions something that could be asked to subjects directly (self-reports) or people close to them (other reports)?
2.   Can you evaluate the constructs of interest with brief answers (e.g., Likert-scale ratings) to structured and predetermined questions? Typically, these questions will address inner subjective states, such as attitudes, beliefs, feelings that are relevant to coaching–mentoring.
3.   Do you know how you will use the data? For instance, do you have established hypotheses that you will evaluate with your survey data?
4.   Can you expect an adequate response rate? The lower your response rate, the less generalizable your data will be. When sending out your survey, keep track of the number of distributions and aim for at least a 50 per cent completion rate (Vogt et al., 2012).

If you answer 'yes' to the above questions, then some important considerations for you are as follows.

1.   What constructs will you measure? Are there established measures available for those constructs and what is their reliability and validity?
2.   How will you measure them (e.g., self-report surveys, other reports?). Will you incorporate other information into your analyses, such as test scores or objective performance metrics?
3.   Will you include a time-lag between measurements? If so, how long will it be? Why?
4.   Will your study be focused on individuals, dyads or groups?
5.   How will you minimize common-method variance?

TESTING FOR DIFFERENCES: WITHIN GROUPS AND BETWEEN GROUPS

Just as correlation and regression are often used for survey-based research, other analysis techniques tend to be used for intervention-based research. Differences tests are used to test for differences in means: between-groups tests for differences *between* means if more than one group is used; within-group tests for changes in the same group over time. Such options are very useful when conducting outcome-based research (remember Table 1.1 in Chapter 1). We will explore each of these in more detail below.

   Within-group analyses are typically used when examining the extent to which a group of participants have changed over time (from time 1 to time 2, time 3, and so forth) on a variable of interest, typically after receiving some type of coaching–mentoring intervention. Analyses are often performed with t-tests or within-groups analysis of variance (ANOVA), depending on the nature of the data. A discussion of these analyses is beyond the scope of this book, but we refer readers to the following excellent sources for further information on univariate (Gravetter & Wallnau, 2016) or multivariate statistics (Tabachnik & Fidell, 2007). Typically, changes on some predetermined measured variable (e.g., performance, well-being, engagement) are expected after participants have received some type of coaching–mentoring intervention. If a change is observed from pre-intervention to post-intervention, then this change is often attributed to the intervention. While this sounds promising for the intervention, remember there are design limitations with this study that limit our capacity to infer cause and effect – see Chapter 15 about internal validity issues and inferences of causality with single-sample studies.

Due to the internal validity issues with single-sample studies, within-group differences often become more meaningful when explored between groups – that is, we evaluate whether two or more groups have *differed in their degree of change* over time. If we are to use an RCT design (Chapter 16), we might expect that our intervention group will improve more on our variables of interest than our control group, and we can quantify whether the improvement is meaningful. Here, our effect size is a metric that quantifies the degree to which the observed changes *differed between* the two groups. The greater the difference in the degree of change, the larger our effect size will be.

There are a variety of different metrics used to quantify effect sizes of group differences, but perhaps the most common in the behavioural sciences is a metric that quantifies the standard difference between the means, such as Cohen's *d* (Cohen, 1988). Unlike correlations, Cohen's *d* can exceed 1 and is interpreted as follows according to Cohen's (1988) conventions:

- ≥ .20 indicates a small effect;
- ≥ .50 indicates a moderate effect;
- ≥ .80 indicates a large effect;
- ≥ 1.30 indicates a very large effect.

However, similar to correlations, the benchmarks will need to be considered with respect to each field of interest (e.g., Bosco et al., 2015). Effect sizes should *always* be reported with a measure of the error associated with it, such as a confidence interval (CI). In small sample studies, sampling error will be larger, which will be reflected in wider CIs and thus indicates less confidence with our estimated effect size. In large sample studies, CIs will be smaller, indicating more confidence with our effect size.

Using differences tests, one can also test for differences in means between groups. For example, we might be interested in whether any of our variables of interest differed between our intervention group and our control group at baseline (before we deliver the coaching–mentoring intervention). This process is useful to help establish whether our random allocation was effective. If random allocation was effective, we would expect all variation to be randomly distributed between the groups, and thus in theory, groups should be equivalent on all variables of interest prior to the intervention.

This is a very brief snapshot of testing for differences; a more detailed discussion is beyond the scope of this book. However, we refer interested readers to Field (2009) and Field, Miles & Field (2012) for an accessible discussion of possible ways to analyse data after intervention-based studies, using widely known statistics packages for the behavioural sciences.

DESIGN CONSIDERATIONS FOR INTERVENTION-BASED RESEARCH

Now that you know more about testing for differences between groups, here are some design considerations for those who might choose to adopt this type of study. As you now know, intervention-based research comes in many shapes and forms, which vary in their degree of internal validity. Important questions to ask yourself if opting for intervention-based designs are as follows.

1. What type of measures will you use?
2. How many groups will be in your study? What is feasible?
3. How many participants can you recruit into your different groups? What is feasible?
4. If using several groups, can you randomly allocate participants to your intervention group and others to a control group? If so:

    i   What will your control participants do? Nothing at all? Another type of intervention?
    ii   What can you realistically pass through a human research ethics committee and how will you confront issues that arise? Often, withholding an intervention that might otherwise benefit people is difficult to pass through an ethics committee review without a proactive strategy to address it, so it is useful to have a strategy up your sleeve to deal with this, such as using a waitlist control (Chapter 16).

5. Will you follow up participants over time? For how long?
6. What is the state of the literature? Is it necessary to do an intervention or is other work needed first, such as survey-based research that can be used to identify variables to use in your intervention?

ADVANTAGES AND DISADVANTAGES OF RELEVANT QUANTITATIVE METHODS AND ANALYSES

While all the statistical tests mentioned are widely used, it must be noted that they are not without their disadvantages, especially those that are based on null-hypothesis significance testing (see Activity, below). It is important to realize that even the most sophisticated statistical analysis procedures will not make amends for poorly designed studies that are lacking in internal or external validity. One must ensure that their study is designed effectively with possible confounds well ruled out before getting to the data-analysis stage. One must also ensure that the right design is chosen for conclusions about cause and effect.

An advantage of all the statistical analysis approaches covered in this chapter is that they provide the researcher with a way to make sense of their data. Tests can be used to evaluate whether data are meaningful, if used in an exploratory manner. The tests can also be used in a confirmatory manner, in which case the researcher will use them to confirm or disconfirm *a priori* predictions (hypotheses) that are derived from sound theory. A disadvantage is that when quantitative methods are misapplied, it can lead to erroneous conclusions. For example, quantitative approaches can facilitate binary (all or none) thinking, meaning that researchers can fall into the trap of making conclusions based solely on the presence or absence of statistical significance (see the following Activity). Instead, researchers are encouraged to think about their findings in matters of degree, which is facilitated by point estimates of effect sizes and confidence intervals (Schmidt, 1996).

NULL HYPOTHESIS SIGNIFICANCE TESTING: PROBLEMS AND PITFALLS

Null hypothesis significance testing (NHST) is a common method of statistical inference where an observation is tested against a hypothesis that there is no effect or relationship (the null hypothesis). NHST is used to determine whether the observed results are different from chance findings – that is, they are 'significant'. Significance cut-off levels are generally predetermined at fixed values, referred to as the alpha-level, and are indicated by a p-value: $p < .05$, .01, or .001 indicates a 5 per cent, 1 per cent and .1 per cent chance of a false positive result, respectively. A false positive is when we conclude that there really is an effect or a relationship, when in fact there is not – that is, we have committed a Type I error (Chapter 16). In a nutshell, if our findings are accompanied by a p-value that is less than our set alpha, then we are to conclude that our findings are statistically significant. See Gravetter and Wallnau (2016) for a basic overview of statistical significance testing as applied to the behavioural sciences.

NHSTs are frequently used in the behavioural sciences – some would argue too frequently. Problems occur when researchers rely too heavily on significance tests to interpret findings. In fact, interpreting statistical significance in isolation is a flawed approach and should be avoided. Researchers are now being encouraged to move beyond NHST to other more recommended practices, such as estimation based on effect sizes, confidence internals and meta-analyses (Cumming, 2014). Statistical significance is determined by a number of factors (e.g., alpha level, sample size), most of which have little to do with the magnitude of the effect size. Indeed, some people believe that significance testing offers no positive contribution to scientific enterprise and should be avoided in favour of these other methods (e.g., Cohen, 1994; Cumming, 2014; Schmidt, 1996, 2010; Schmidt & Hunter, 2015).

To avoid these problems, it is becoming more common practice to report effect sizes with CIs. In fact, some journals now require that researchers report effect sizes with CIs (Schmidt & Oh, 2016). P-values, if they are even reported at all, should always be a backdrop to these more important and meaningful pieces of information, and should never be the central focus.

Now that you know a bit more about the different approaches available in quantitative research, the following are some important options you will need to decide on.

1. Will you ever need to conduct a quantitative study? If yes ...
2. Refer back to Table 1.1 of Chapter 1 and identify the type of study you are conducting. If it is intervention research focused on outcomes, perhaps testing for differences between or within groups will work best for you. If it is non-intervention research, then perhaps your best bet might be to examine relationships between variables.
3. Decide what you want to measure in your study and how you will do so.

WHAT NEXT?

Now that you know your options, consider some forms of analysis that might be suitable for you when it comes to analysing your data. Identify also what statistics or computer software you will need to undertake these.

CONCLUSION

Quantitative methods are a useful way of conducting research. Two very common ways of analysing quantitative data are by testing for relationships between variables and by testing for differences between groups. Within each method, there are a variety of design considerations and analysis options that you will have available to analyse your data. Before you even get to this step, however, you will need to identify scales or measures that are reliable and valid, which can be used to gauge your constructs of interest.

 Further reading and resources

The following resource provides an entry-level discussion to univariate statistics, which will help you to learn the foundations of statistical methodology in the behavioural sciences.

Gravetter, F. J., & Wallnau, L. B. (2016). *Statistics for the behavioral sciences.* Boston, MA: Cengage Learning.

(Continued)

(Continued)

The following texts cover more advanced topics.

Hayes, A. F. (2013). *Introduction to mediation, moderation, and conditional process analysis: a regression-based approach*. New York: The Guilford Press.

Kline, R. B. (2015). *Principles and practice of structural equation modeling*. New York: Guilford Publications.

Tabachnick, B. G., & Fidell, L. S. (2007). *Using multivariate statistics*. Boston, MA: Allyn & Bacon/Pearson Education.

DEVELOPING CONFIDENCE IN STATISTICS

19

HOW CAN I BECOME CONFIDENT IN STATISTICS?

LEARNING OUTCOMES

In completing this chapter and related activities, you will be able to:

1. describe how you can use coaching methods to successfully complete quantitative projects;
2. create a list of non-technical actions necessary to complete the quantitative component of your project;
3. identify how confident you are in each of these actions;
4. identify and commence ways to increase confidence in each of these actions.

WHAT IS THE CURRENT REALITY REGARDING STUDENT CONFIDENCE IN STATISTICS?

Many people are not confident with mathematics in general, and this is true also for applied statistical methods at higher education level. In fact, Hembree (1990) conducted a meta-analysis see Chapter 9, examining 151 studies concerning maths anxiety. It determined that maths anxiety is related to poor maths performance and negative attitudes concerning maths. Hembree further suggests that maths anxiety may often lead to avoiding maths. You may say to yourself, 'I don't have maths anxiety and that is good'. However, many people do lack confidence in this area and it can hinder their performance and their motivation. As per the main message of your book, let's use your coaching and mentoring skills to approach this. How can you develop your confidence for statistics? Who can help? Who do you know who has done it?

This is important. Well-known self-efficacy researcher Bandura (1993) states that students' beliefs in their efficacy to regulate their own learning and to master academic activities determine their aspirations, level of motivation and academic accomplishments. What is your belief in regulating your own learning? What is your belief in mastering statistics? According to this research, at a group level people's answers will influence what they aspire to, how motivated they are and what they achieve. We will then look at your beliefs about how you will learn and do statistics.

WHAT IS YOUR CURRENT REALITY? HOW CONFIDENT ARE YOU WITH STATISTICAL ANALYSIS?

If you are reading this chapter, it is likely that your research will involve some quantitative methods, and more specifically statistical methods such as Correlational Analysis, Analysis of Variance, Regression Analysis. Let's do an audit of where you are currently in terms of your knowledge and, importantly, your confidence in completing the actions required to learn and then do the statistical analysis in your project.

Consider the following story of Corinna.

Corinna was a 44-year-old woman, returning to formal study for the first time since her three-year commerce degree many years earlier. Corinna had had a successful career in human resources and maintained a rewarding family life. Corinna had been involved in implementing mentoring programmes for a long time and more recently specifically tailored coaching programmes. As her course tuition was sponsored by her employer, a global professional services organization, her research programme needed to be relevant to organizational improvement. Given that programmes are implemented on a large scale in multiple nations, demonstration of programme efficacy is a relevant issue, including quantitative data and quasi-experimental designs. When Corinna first heard this, she went into a mild panic and started wondering whether or not to continue with the idea of further study.

After reflecting and thinking through her well-honed project management skills, Corinna found out what was required to conduct such research. She also went to speak to several in-house researchers and an adviser at the university about the steps of doing quantitative research. Most importantly, she was able to identify which types of analyses were most relevant to the possible project, and were expected and relevant to her applied research. Also, as

Corinna had done some work with finance subjects, she told herself that numbers per se were not the problem.

As Corinna made things more certain, her anxiety declined. As she worked through the basics of correlations, then analysis of variance, she began to feel more confident. She worked closely with an adviser with strong quantitative skills and learned by doing what was needed for the task at hand, as opposed to trying to master the whole gamut of statistical methods. Corinna also had a few colleagues with similar challenges and they met regularly to share success.

 **Activity**

Actions audit for learning and doing my statistical analysis

The task

Create a list of non-technical actions necessary to complete the quantitative component of your project.

Your list may look something like this:

1. Enter the data into XYZ programme.
2. Screen for missing data.
3. Choose analysis to run.
4. Run descriptive analyses.
5. Interpret report.

Write your first list below. This may be repeated multiple times. For now, keep it simple with a maximum of five actions. The issue at hand is exploring your confidence, not planning the whole process. If you really don't know the steps yet, find out soon, as this will increase general confidence and reduce anxiety from uncertainty.

Key actions for your statistical analysis process

Action 1

0	10	20	30	40	50	60	70	80	90	100
Not at all confident										Fully confident

Figure 9.1 a

(Continued)

(Continued)

Action 2

0	10	20	30	40	50	60	70	80	90	100
Not at all confident										Fully confident

Figure 19.1 b

Action 3

0	10	20	30	40	50	60	70	80	90	100
Not at all confident										Fully confident

Figure 19.1 c

Action 4

0	10	20	30	40	50	60	70	80	90	100
Not at all confident										Fully confident

Figure 19.1 d

Action 5

0	10	20	30	40	50	60	70	80	90	100
Not at all confident										Fully confident

Figure 19.1 e

Now, let's assess your confidence in completing each task. From 0 to 100, rate each separate action above – i.e., *how confident are you that you can complete the action needed within the time frame of your project*? (This relates also to Chapter 12 on feasible timelines.) If it makes it more tangible, add a specific time point to each action before you rate. As a coach, you may be very familiar with scaling confidence or importance; if so, use it frequently for yourself during your research journey.

What are your options in terms of learning, using statistical methods?

Now let's reflect on your ratings. You have options on how you use your time. The more confident you are about the actions, the more motivated you will be and the more will get done.

With each action ask yourself the following questions.

- Why did you rate your confidence at that level? Why not lower; why not higher?
- Are any of your ratings below 70 per cent. If so, ask yourself what would make you more confident? Break it into smaller tasks and do the exercise again.
- Who could assist you with this particular action?
- What further knowledge or skill is needed to complete this action?
- Have you also explored online resources to assist your learning?
- What personal strengths do you have to approach this action in a slightly different way?

Your options emerge from answering these questions. Write your three key insights and what else you could do to approach the learning and doing of statistical methods. This is how you will go about the learning and doing of statistics. What new options or ideas have opened up here? They might look like this.

- Insight 1: I need to get more help with ANOVA.
- Insight 2: I really don't know how to set up the spreadsheet properly.
- Insight 3: Indrani and Stephen are really good at this – maybe we could meet up for an afternoon and I could help them with the writing piece.

Write your insights now.

WHAT NEXT?

There is only so much time to complete your project. Reflect on the options and insights above and make a commitment – that is, which overall action can you commit to that will be most likely to increase your confidence in completing other actions to learn and do statistical methodology?

To paraphrase Bandura (1993) again, we believe you can regulate your own learning about statistics. If you do this by consciously taking each action at a time and asking yourself 'What would make me more confident?' and then following through, your confidence and mastery will increase. Bring your coaching skills with you. Avoidance is not an option here.

To increase my confidence in statistics I am committing to …

CONCLUSION

Many practitioners commence research and feel overwhelmed by the technical aspects of statistics and research methodology. Using a coaching style of questions and vignettes, this chapter helps take the coaching skills set and apply it to the challenge of managing statistics and quantitative methods, with emphasis in breaking problems into smaller actions, committing and seeking support over time. It is important to address issues of confidence directly. It is also important to remember that you are part of a learning community and do not need to do it all on your own. Most new researchers have to manage a key area and improve skills just to be able to complete a project. For many students, this is writing; for some it is organization and time management; and for others it is technical skills, particularly quantitative methods. As research is project based, it is OK to just focus on your project needs as this stage, rather than to have a comprehensive understanding of all major statistical analyses. Use project-based learning. Remember, your work needs to be 'good enough' – you do not need to win the International Prize in Statistics.

 Further reading and resources

American Psychological Association resources on self-efficacy:

www.apa.org/pi/aids/resources/education/self-efficacy.aspx

SAGE resource on mastering statistics:

https://au.sagepub.com/en-gb/oce/mastering-statistics/book243532

Access to the General Self-Efficacy Scale:

http://userpage.fu-berlin.de/~health/engscal.htm

Online resource for learning and mastering statistics:

www.quora.com/Whats-the-best-way-to-learn-and-master-statistics

PART IV

QUALITATIVE AND MIXED METHODS FOR COACHING AND MENTORING RESEARCH

CHOOSING QUALITATIVE METHODS FOR DATA COLLECTION/ GENERATION

20

WHICH METHOD SHOULD I USE TO GENERATE DATA?

LEARNING OUTCOMES

In completing this chapter and related activities, you will be able to:

1. describe examples of common qualitative methods in coaching and mentoring research;
2. describe three types of sampling common to qualitative methodology, as well as their relevance to coaching and mentoring research;
3. understand your options in qualitative methods for data generation for your coaching or mentoring research project.

WHAT IS THE CURRENT REALITY IN TERMS OF COLLECTING OR GENERATING QUALITATIVE DATA FOR COACHING AND MENTORING RESEARCH?

This chapter in some ways complements Chapter 15 on choosing quantitative methods. As introduced in Chapter 6, there are many factors that should influence your choice of quantitative versus qualitative methodology, and consequent methods of data collection and analyses/interpretation. We encourage you to be methodologically innovative and spend some time exploring different methods to best suit your research question/s. These choices, importantly, are informed by the research question. However, they are also influenced by the feasibility of the project, including the time and resources available to you. See Agee (2009) for a more detailed exploration of qualitative research questions.

Both this chapter and the following one should be thought of as 'twin chapters' because the definitions in this chapter are relevant to both. Some qualitative researchers assert that data generation and data interpretation should not or cannot be separated. However, for introductory learning purposes we have chosen to separate them for clarity. As your understanding of the complex interrelations between epistemology, methodology, methods and interpretation grows, you will combine things as needed. Also, importantly these two chapters are unapologetically introductory, trying to help you choose a data-generation method and a data-interpretation approach. We have selected some common approaches that we believe are relevant for coaching and mentoring research, but in no way does this represent the complex array of approaches available, nor do we assert that those not described are less valid approaches for coaching and mentoring research. Moreover, we refer to collecting or generating data to recognize different epistemological and hence methodological approaches that have different views on language (Hugh-Jones, 2010).

Definitions relevant to qualitative coaching and mentoring research

Data saturation or information redundancy refers to when analysis and interpretation of data (e.g., from interviews, focus groups) yields no new information. This is the point that qualitative data collection may conclude. For example, after interviewing nine mentors it became clear that all new information was consistent with the seven themes identified through thematic analysis.

Methodology in general terms refers to the study of methods to generate knowledge. In the context of a specific project, it refers to the system of methods used (see Chapter 6). Hence, a qualitative methodology is a theory or justification of how the set of methods will be used to collect, analyse/interpret, evaluate and represent the information.

Methods are more specific techniques that one uses to carry out a methodology (see Chapter 6). It can refer to the way data is collected (e.g., interviews, focus group, diaries). Alternatively, it can refer to the way in which data (qualitative or quantitative) is analysed or interpreted. It is important to clarify which meaning of the term is being used and at which time. A formal method section, standard in quantitative research, incorporates all aspects of measurement tools, sampling, data analysis strategy and design.

Analysis, derived from Medieval Latin via Greek, meaning 'loosening', breaking something into its elements to understand its structure. Although the term is more commonly used in quantitative methodology consistent with positivist approaches, it is also used in qualitative approaches. A key issue is whether the analysis is deductive (theory driven, inferring from general theory to specific instances) or inductive (data driven, inferring from specific instances to a general theory). Qualitative approaches are more often inductive.

Interpretation has a special meaning in the context of qualitative research. Depending on one's epistemological assumptions (i.e., the theory of how you can know something), some assert that we cannot objectively describe reality, but only interpret it. This relates to 'interpretivist' approaches in general. More specifically, it relates to debates in phenomenology and hermeneutics. Hermeneutics, derived from Hermes, messenger to the gods, refers to how we interpret messages. Interpretive Phenomenological Analysis, for example, is derived from hermeneutic phenomenology, which asserts that it is not possible to access the essence of an experience, but it is possible to interpret it.

Representation in qualitative research most commonly refers to how complex data is summarized and communicated, usually visually in diagrammatic or tabular form. Unlike traditional quantitative methods where reporting and communicating of statistical data has accepted conventions (e.g., in graphs and tables), there is more variation in qualitative methods (e.g., concept maps, tables, spider diagrams, snake diagrams).

Reflexivity in general refers to self-examination, looking at one's own reasons for action. In qualitative research, it refers to the stance of a research, paying attention to one's own role in the context of constructing knowledge. This is done systematically in some qualitative methods to avoid claims of bias, particularly confirmation bias (see Chapter 4). The issue of bias is not simple though, due to different views of epistemology (see Chapter 5). Reflexivity has a different meaning in sociology.

Social Desirability Bias refers to how participants in studies may respond in ways they believe are socially desirable or acceptable. For example, when a participant is a parent and asked whether they love being a parent, there are strong social pressures to say 'yes'.

Purposive (purposeful) sampling, the most common sampling strategy for qualitative research stated simply, means choosing participants on purpose – that is, participants are prospected and recruited based on predetermined criteria, relevant to the research question. For example, if you were examining the experience of school children receiving mentoring, you may deliberately sample males and females from primary and secondary schools, across metropolitan, regional and rural schools. Different combinations of this mix may be sampled. In this

(Continued)

(Continued)

context, this approach is usually to gain diversity in viewpoints rather than to claim that it is representative of the population.

Quota sampling is a sampling approach where a quota of participant numbers is determined prior to sampling. This will typically involve ensuring sampling from a number of different participant demographics (e.g., age, gender, ethnicity, income level).

Snowball sampling is a method of sampling that asks participants to refer other possible participants to the researcher. This helps the researcher recruit more participants than they might not otherwise access. For qualitative studies where people have a common interest or experience, particularly which they would like to understood, this can be very effective. For example, those who have experienced a type of cancer, recruited alongside a group coaching programme, may refer to others who have suffered from cancer and who are willing to share their experience. This approach can also be used in sampling for quantitative studies.

While some positivist scholars in coaching and mentoring contexts are rightly calling for more experimental designs, particularly randomized controlled trials, there are many useful contributions that qualitative research methodology can make to this area. Moreover, for student research projects, large randomized controlled trials may not be feasible due to a lack of time and resources.

It is important to remember that coaching and mentoring are processes. Chapter 1 and the Appendix make the distinction between types of coaching and mentoring research: process, outcome, implementation/fidelity and non-intervention research. Qualitative research has significant untapped potential to inform process research in coaching and mentoring. If something works, why does it work? What is the process involved? What is the experience of the coachee or protégé? What is the experience of the coach or mentor? What change is reflected in the narrative of the coachee or protégé? These and many other important and relevant questions may be addressed using a qualitative methodology. Psychotherapy research has usefully explored client factors, relationship factors and therapist factors to frame its research endeavour. Coaching and mentoring research is well advised to do similar. Relationships factors are closely related to process – that is, what is going on in the process of interaction between the two or more people within the relationship? Qualitative approaches can be very informative for this purpose.

WHAT ARE SOME OF THE COMMON QUALITATIVE METHODS THAT MAY BE USED?

A range of methods can be used to collect, generate or capture data. We focus here on three types that are relevant to coaching and mentoring before addressing the practical issues of audio-visual recording.

INTERVIEW METHODS

The interview is the archetypal qualitative method for generating data. The data generated in interviews are only as good as a) the questions that are asked; b) the appropriate level of structure and sequence; and c) the quality of the relationship between interviewer and interviewee.

There are three types of interviews: 1) structured interviews; 2) semi-structured interviews; and 3) narrative interviews (Stuckey, 2013). In coaching and mentoring research, it is relevant first to consider who might be involved in an interview. The majority of interviews will be with a) a coachee/protégé; b) a coach/mentor; c) someone with a stake in a specific coaching or mentoring process or outcome (e.g., employer, family member, friend); d) someone who holds a view of coaching or mentoring in general. We will cover each of these in turn.

Structured interviews

Structured interviews are referred to as 'structured' because the research follows a set script – that is, a specific set of questions in a predetermined sequence, with a limited number of response categories. The interviewer controls the responses and hence the data tightly. The questions are asked in the same way, using the same language as much as possible, for consistency. The interviewer may record the responses according to a predetermined coding scheme, established and related to the research question. For this reason, larger numbers of participants are able to be involved in these interviews. Structured interviews in some ways occupy the methods space between self-report scales and semi-structured interviews, and thus can contain aspects of quantitative and qualitative methodology.

Semi-structured interviews

Semi-structured interviews commence with a set of predetermined questions that are relevant to the research question. The interview, however, is given freedom to unfold in a natural way. The interviewer aims to cover all questions if they do not arise in the narrative of the interviewee. There is, however, an established set of questions that are generated prior to the interview, which allows for a comparison of responses across participants. Before developing the questions for semi-structured interviews, a researcher is likely to have done previous qualitative work, such as observation or unstructured narrative interviews, which ensure the relevance and meaningfulness of the semi-structured questions. Semi-structured interviews can provide a useful balance between structure and flexibility for the researcher.

Narrative interviews

Narration is one of the oldest human activities – humans are natural-born story tellers. A narrative is a story of events, actions or experiences that have unfolded over time, from the perspective of the participant. A narrative interview is open-ended, unstructured and very useful if little is known about the phenomenon of interest. Hence, it is more inductive in nature.

OTHER THOUGHTS ON INTERVIEWS

A key strength of using interviews is that they allow a person to describe experiences, meanings and beliefs in their own language rather than that prescribed by the research, such as in self-report scales. Whether your interview method is structured, semi-structured or open-ended, the narrative should be guided by how much is known about the phenomenon being investigated. This is similar to the 'theory-driven' versus 'data-driven' distinction in analysing data, described in Chapter 21. If a significant amount is already known about a phenomenon and one is confirming rather than exploring, a structured interview may be more appropriate. Conversely, if a topic or experience is not well understood, then an open-ended narrative interview may be appropriate because it allows information to emerge in a relatively open-ended fashion.

Hugh-Jones (2010) makes the useful distinction between *interviews as excavation* and *interviews as co-constructed*. The excavation metaphor is based on the assumption that 'excavates' required information from a participant's head. This is consistent with the term 'data collection'. Hugh-Jones (2010) explains that a more contemporary understanding conceives the interview as a way of *formulating*, rather than *collecting* data. In this sense the data is hence generated in the interaction. If you are a coach and/or a mentor, it is useful to think about the coaching or mentoring process itself as excavating or as co-constructing. Our prediction is that most coach and mentor practitioners would identify with co-constructing more than excavating. Your approach to interviewing may be similar.

Similar to coaching and mentoring itself, interviews can be conducted using different communication media including, but not limited to the list below.

a.   Face-to-face
b.   Telephone
c.   Text-based via desktop device
d.   Text-based via mobile device
e.   Online audio only via desktop device
f.   Online audio only via mobile device
g.   Online audio and visual via desktop device
h.   Online audio and visual via mobile device

While this list may seem overly detailed, it is important to consider the medium and the context in which data are generated. For example, a mobile device allows an interviewee to comment on experiences *in* the relevant situation, such as at home, at work, or in whichever context a researcher is most interested. Some of the other mediums may rely on participants retrieving their narratives or stories by memory, which often isn't completely accurate.

FOCUS GROUP METHODS

Focus group methods have a slightly different purpose from interviews. Consider how you may communicate one-to-one compared to how you may communicate in a group. A focus group is usually a small but diverse group of people, having a discussion focused on a particular topic. The discussion produces data and insights that would likely be less accessible without the interaction. The act of listening to others' verbalized experiences and opinions stimulates memories, ideas, and one's own experiences and opinions. This is sometimes referred to as 'chaining' or 'cascading'.

Focus group methods have been used extensively in market research and political research to test views of new products or policies. In the context of coaching and mentoring, they may be used to generate data about common coachee/mentee/protégé experiences, or those of the coach/mentor. Alternatively, the focus group method may be used to elicit commonly held views of new programmes, or they may serve as devices in organizational needs analysis, prior to programme implementation.

A focus group facilitator may take notes during the session. They may also audio-record the session and later have it transcribed if themes and language are important. One reason for conducting focus groups is to understand the language and vernacular of particular groups, e.g., how 16-year-old males communicate about a topic. For this reason, in our view audio-recording followed by transcription is preferred. However, it requires more work after the focus group itself. This represents the speed-precision trade-off which is common in much applied research.

Like most methods, there are different variations of focus groups. One of the advantages of qualitative methods in general is that they can be adapted. As long as the method is described well, within ethical parameters, variations are accepted as fit for purpose. Variations of focus groups include the following.

a. Dual moderator focus groups, where one moderator ensures that the session goes smoothly, while the other moderator ensures that all the topics are covered.
b. Two-way focus groups, when one focus group watches another focus group and then discusses the interaction and what was observed.
c. Duelling (fencing) moderator, where two moderators deliberately take opposite sides of the discussion or debate.

The size and composition of focus groups can vary, ranging from as small as four up to 12. The selection of participants is quite important and will also depend on whether there is one or multiple focus groups to be used. Similar to issues of sampling more broadly, and purposive sampling in particular, the homo- or heterogeneity of participants will depend on your research questions, and also the intended type of analysis or interpretation. A key issue is whether you are deliberately seeking differences or commonalities in views, themes or experiences.

Like all methods, the focus group has limitations. The majority of the criticisms come from researchers who adopt a positivist epistemology (see Chapter 5). For example, one criticism is that the results are influenced by the researcher and their involvement in guiding the discussion (i.e., data that is generated). From this standpoint, it leads to problems of validity. Moreover, depending on the sampling, there will be questions of generalizability to other groups of people in other situations (referred to as external validity; see Chapter 15). These critiques are valid from the standpoint of positivism. From this standpoint, however, most of the qualitative research methods are critiqued. This is one further example of why the ways of knowing, discussed in Chapter 5, are so foundational to becoming a competent researcher. As per Chapter 6, epistemology leads to methodology, which leads to method – in this case, a focus group method.

Further challenges to using a focus group method include the following.

a. Possible intrusiveness of a recording device (similar to the interview method).
b. Loss of anonymity of the participants and concerns about confidentiality.
c. Social desirability or ingratiating responding, where participants say what they believe is socially acceptable or try to please the moderator.

DIARY METHOD

Diary method and diary studies collect qualitative (and sometimes quantitative) information by having participants record entries about their everyday life in a diary, log or journal at a time designated by the researcher. The diary will typically be about an activity or experience of interest. Instructions on how to do this may vary depending on the research question and theoretical approach of the study. An advantage of diary studies, unlike interviews or focus groups, is that this approach is longitudinal, meaning that the data are collected over a period of time. Diary studies can be used in outcome, implementation, process studies or non-intervention research outlined in Chapter 1 and the Appendix.

Another advantage of diary studies is that they enable the researcher to gain more information from people actually in, or recently in their context of interest. Experience sampling method (ESM) (Hektner, Schmidt & Csikszentmihalyi, 2007) or ecological momentary assessment (EMA) (Shiffman, Stone & Hufford, 2008) are examples of this method. The idea behind these methods is to repeatedly sample experiences from participants at different points in time so their thoughts, feelings and behaviours can be tracked over time. Such techniques have become more common with the advance of smartphone technology, as apps can be set up that beep several times a day, when the experiences are sampled. With the popularity and functionality of smartphone technology, we can now expand diary methods to the use of photos, video and text.

SUMMARY

As a researcher, it is up to you to work out how best to use such an approach to answer your research question. We recommend you read Chapter 21 before fully deciding on an interview, a focus group or diary method. Remember also that you may use all three methods, for different purposes, in the same study. Let's now turn to a common technique that you could use across all methods.

AUDIO-VISUAL RECORDING

In the last 30 years, technology has developed exponentially. A qualitative researcher is spoiled with an array of digital recording devices (both audio and visual), which facilitates easy transcription. Smartphones have created new possibilities in audio- and video-recording of qualitative research. In general, it is preferable to audio-record (and if relevant video-record) data-generation in qualitative research and later fully transcribe the data. This is because it is otherwise difficult to capture direct quotes that may be relevant to some types of language analysis. Moreover, rapport and remaining attentive in the moment is easier when you do not have to take notes furiously about what participants are saying. It is also possible to use audio- or video-recording of actual coaching or mentoring sessions if that is needed, assuming that all parties give consent.

Some research studies involve the use of smartphones or tablets as part of an intervention, which allows a researcher to generate and capture simultaneously. For example, a coaching/mentoring intervention may issue homework, to be completed via a tablet, which creates the possibility of capturing this data for experience sampling or reflective journaling.

SAMPLING APPROACHES

The three types of sampling approaches common in qualitative research are purposive sampling, quota sampling and snowball sampling. These are formally defined alongside other important definitions in this chapter. In combination with consideration of the sampling method, it is important to understand sample size discussions in qualitative research. Beginning researchers and sometimes the general public default to quantitative assumptions. For example, in quantitative research, a sample of 50 is necessarily better than a sample of 10 because it is more representative of the population. However, the purpose and epistemology of qualitative methodology is different. Seeking to understand experiences, gain rich descriptions, diverse views within specific contexts, or explore how language is used, all carry different assumptions that govern different sampling approaches. Hence, as outlined in Chapters 23 and 24, you may have a sample of one, using a one-person case study, especially for people with unique or rare experiences (e.g., a study of a person with a rare disease or a study about the first female prime minister of the UK).

In qualitative research, sample size is often not defined before the study, but sampling continues until data saturation or information redundancy occurs (saturation point). Note that this is in stark contrast to quantitative methodology, which requires sampling to be determined *a priori* to achieve the appropriate power (see Chapter 16). In qualitative research, an interviewer starts to feel 'I've heard this before; we are repeating information now'. For this reason, data collection/generation and analysis/interpretation should occur simultaneously. This is why Chapters 20 and 21 are sister chapters and need to be considered together.

 **Activity**

What is your reality in using qualitative methods of data generation for coaching/mentoring research?

To evaluate your current level of skills and awareness in qualitative research, let's start with your personal experience. Write some brief responses to the following questions.

1. Have you been interviewed before? If so, what did you like (or not like) about that interaction? What did the interviewer do well? What might they have done differently?
2. If you are a coach or mentor, what skills do you have that may help with interviewing? Think about sequencing and guiding in addition to listening, asking and summarizing.
3. Have you been in a focus group before, or participated in a small-group discussion of a key theme? Did you have your say? Did someone dominate too much? Did an idea from someone else trigger a new perspective for you?
4. Have you kept a journal, a diary or a log of activities in some way before (e.g., in hard copy or electronic format)? If so, why?
5. Have you been coached or mentored? Have you ever coached or mentored someone? In what way could you best communicate your experience? (Note, the question is not 'What was your experience?', but 'How can you communicate the experience?').

What are your options to collect/generate qualitative data for your coaching or mentoring research?

Consider your options in terms of sampling. Based on the options of qualitative sampling described in this chapter, use Table 20.1 to write down some advantages and disadvantages of each approach for your hypothetical, planned or current project.

Now consider your options in terms of methods to generate qualitative data, based on Table 20.2. Based on the descriptions of interviews, focus groups and diary methods in this chapter, jot down some advantages and disadvantages of each approach for your hypothetical, planned or current project. You might also extend interviews to both structured, semi-structured, and open-ended interviews.

Table 20.1   Advantages and disadvantages of different sampling approaches for your context

	Advantages	Disadvantages
Purposive sampling		
Quota sampling		
Snowball sampling		

Table 20.2   Advantages and disadvantages of different data generation methods

	Advantages	Disadvantages
Interviews		
Focus groups		
Diary methods		

Reflecting on your answers regarding both sampling and data-generation options, what is your preferred approach? Remember to consider all issues from previous chapters, including your epistemology, research question, timeline and feasibility, as well as the possible risks of data collection before deciding.

WHAT NEXT?

Given that many qualitative methods, particularly relating to data interpretation, assume different epistemologies from positivism, which for some researchers is the default, a further What next? may be to refresh yourself on epistemology by re-reading Chapter 5, before moving on to Chapter 21.

CONCLUSION

In this chapter we described examples of common qualitative methods in coaching and mentoring research, including interview methods, focus groups, diary methods, and the practical issue of audio-visual recording, as well as sampling. Whatever your chosen methods in qualitative research, linking these choices to your research question are essential, as each serves a different purpose. It will also be important to consider sampling methods that are appropriate for your context.

 Further reading and resources

Agee, G. (2009) Developing qualitative research questions: a reflective process, International *Journal of Qualitative Studies in Education*, 22(4), 431–47, DOI: 10.1080/09518390902736512

Forrester M. A. (Ed.). (2010). *Doing qualitative research in psychology: a practical guide*. London: SAGE.

Hektner J. M., Schmidt, J. A., Csikszentmihalyi, M. (2007). *Experience sampling method: measuring the quality of everyday life*. Thousand Oaks, CA: SAGE.

Hugh-Jones, S. (2010). The interview in qualitative research. In Forrester, M. A. (Ed.). (2010). *Doing qualitative research in psychology: a practical guide*, pp. 77–97. London: SAGE.

Krueger, R. & Casey, M. (2009). *Focus groups: A practical guide for applied research* (4th ed.). Thousand Oaks, CA: SAGE.

Robinson, O.C. (2014). *Sampling in interview-based qualitative research: a theoretical and practical guide, qualitative research in psychology*, 11(1), 25–41, DOI: 10.1080/14780887.2013.801543

CHOOSING QUALITATIVE METHODS FOR DATA ANALYSIS/ INTERPRETATION

21

WHICH METHOD SHOULD I USE TO MAKE SENSE OF MY DATA?

LEARNING OUTCOMES

In completing this chapter and related activities, you will be able to:

1. describe common qualitative analyses relevant to coaching and mentoring research, including thematic analysis, Interpretive Phenomenological Analysis and discourse analysis;

2. choose between theory-driven versus emergent approaches in analysing/interpreting data;

3. list several criteria to evaluate the quality of qualitative research and how they are different from quantitative criteria.

WHAT IS THE CURRENT SITUATION IN TERMS OF COMMON QUALITATIVE METHODS AND ANALYSES IN COACHING AND MENTORING RESEARCH?

Qualitative methodology and its related methods of data collection/construction and data analysis/interpretation have a very important role in furthering our understanding of the processes, experiences and practices of coaching and mentoring (Grant, 2016). In Chapter 1 and the Appendix we describe the important distinction between outcome and process research. Qualitative methods are very helpful with, but not limited to, understanding the processes of coaching and mentoring. *What are the experiences of being mentored? What are the themes that emerge in coaching interactions for young culturally and linguistically diverse males? What was the difference in experience between those who improved and those who did not?*

A key challenge with qualitative methods is that, compared to quantitative methods, they often require more discussion of theories of knowledge (epistemology) because they vary in their assumptions. For example, Interpretive Phenomenological Analysis (IPA), which is described later in this chapter, is derived from certain assumptions in phenomenology, whereas Discourse Analysis derives from assumptions about language and action. Hence, these approaches may not have the same 'click and go' feel and certainty that particular statistical analyses have once mastered. Moreover, even the words 'data collection' and 'analysis' are not always accepted in qualitative research. Based on some approaches, data is generated rather than collected and it is interpreted rather than analysed. While these may seem trivial or semantic issues, they are important assumptions reflected in language. We recommend that you refresh yourself on the issues covered in Chapter 5 and read the definitions provided here, to better appreciate this chapter.

---------------------   **Definitions relevant to qualitative**   ---------------------
data analysis and interpretation

Account. A description or report provided during a research interview by an interviewee. The description or report (account) represents the understanding, perception or experience that the interviewee has of the topic (i.e., issues) of the research interview.

Narrative. A narrative describes a story or tale, or it can also describe a form of writing or talk that tells a story incorporating a plot structure. The term 'narrative' is extensively used in social research and in social theory.

Story. A story conveys factual information and meaning by describing an event (or series of events). Stories can have multiple purposes, including instruction, the formation of a worldview or for pure entertainment. In the context of research, the researcher will want to consider the interviewee's story (or stories) in the light of the purpose and function the story serves for the interviewee, and the rationale or reason why the interviewee has provided the story in the particular way they have provided it.

Qualitative data. Qualitative data refers to non-numeric information such as text documents, interview transcripts, notes, video and audio recordings, and images.

Phenomenology. Phenomenology is the study of the structures of consciousness and experience. It is a philosophical movement founded in the early 20th century by Edmund Husserl, which later expanded and became popular at the German universities of Göttingen and Munich.

Idiographic. The term 'idiographic' means a study pertaining to individual cases or events, such as in psychology where idiographic means the study of an individual who is viewed as unique and composed of aspects that are dissimilar to other individuals. The term comes from the Greek word *idios*, meaning 'private' or 'own'. An autobiography is an example of an idiographic study, as it outlines the individual's unique aspects in narrative format, detailing the events that have contributed to the individual's life story.

Nomothetic. The term 'nomothetic' is the counter to 'idiographic', and means a study pertaining to a group of cases or classes (cohorts) of individuals, such as in psychology where nomothetic means the study of aspects that individuals share with each other. The term comes from the Greek word *nomos*, meaning 'law', referring to generalizations.

Both terms, 'nomothetic' and 'idiographic', were introduced by Gordon Allport in 1937.

Hermeneutics. Hermeneutic analysis deals with the interpretation of text and is a term that is used to cover a variety of methods. In this approach, the process of systematic interpretation provides an understanding, which is in contrast to research approaches that focus on the independence of interpretations in the formation of knowledge and objectivity.

Discourse. Discourse can be considered as a system of statements that constructs an object.

In this section, we focus on thematic analysis, Interpretive Phenomenological Analysis and discourse analysis, as three relatively popular qualitative approaches (methods and analyses) relevant for coaching and mentoring research. Many other approaches, such as grounded theory, narrative analysis, ethnographic analysis, constant comparative analysis and content analysis, may also be relevant depending on the situation and context, but are not covered here. Many of these additional approaches also have many variants and subtleties, depending on key authors' elucidation of such approaches.

ANALYSIS AND INTERPRETATION METHODS

1. THEMATIC ANALYSIS

In qualitative research, thematic analysis is a very common form of analysis. This approach accentuates investigating, exploring and recording themes (or 'patterns') within data. A theme is a pattern related to a research question that has been identified across data sets and is central to a phenomenon's description. Rather than a single method, thematic analysis encapsulates many different approaches, all of which have different procedures because different versions of thematic analysis are underpinned by differing conceptual and epistemological assumptions (Guest, MacQueen & Namey, 2012).

In qualitative research, thematic analysis allows the identification and examination of themes within data and highlights the rich description of the data set and its organization. Unlike quantitative research, which focuses on counting words and phrases, thematic analysis identifies explicit and implicit ideas within the data available. Themes are developed by coding, which is the main process for identifying themes with the data. Here, the researcher recognizes important moments within the data and encodes it prior to interpretation. In order to identify codes, a researcher can identify co-occurrence of themes, compare how frequently themes occur, or visually compare relationships between themes. Thematic analysis has been deemed a useful method for catching the particulars of meaning with a set of data (Boyatzis, 1998).

The text used as data can vary from a single-word response to lengthy, open-ended questions, to very lengthy or complete text comprising many pages and thousands of words. As such, and because the text utilized ranges so much, there is also a wide range of what a data set can be. Because of this variation, the strategy to analyse the data varies according to the length of the data available. As an approximation, it is not unusual for a qualitative researcher to analyse an in-depth interview of one to two hours in length, which can have around 30 to 40 pages of transcribed text for each interviewee. In addition, the level of complexity of a study should also be taken into consideration, as complexity can vary with regard to different data types.

The approach of thematic analysis supports the assertations made with direct reference to data and takes this approach directly from the qualitative approach of Grounded Theory (Strauss & Corbin, 1990). Grounded Theory is an approach that develops theories that are grounded from the data available. Such an approach is apparent in thematic analysis where the researcher reads the text (transcripts), identifies themes, contrasts and compares these themes, and then builds theoretical models from these findings.

Similar to phenomenology, which focuses on the human subjective experience, thematic analysis does likewise. Here the object of study is the person's experiences, perceptions and emotions, and these aspects are emphasized. Phenomenology has its roots in humanistic psychology, which considers a key aspect of qualitative research to be giving voice to the 'other'. Such an approach allows the interviewee to use their own words to discuss the topic, which is free from the limitations of fixed-response questions that are common in quantitative studies. We now describe a method derived from the phenomenology tradition.

2. INTERPRETIVE PHENOMENOLOGICAL ANALYSIS

Interpretative Phenomenological Analysis (IPA) has an idiographic focus and as such offers understandings into how individuals in various contexts make sense of the world and phenomena they are surrounded by. In many cases, the phenomena under question are personally relevant to the individuals, such as critical life events or aspects related to the individual's personal relationships. Interpretative Phenomenological Analysis has a combination of psychological, interpretative and idiographic components, which makes it distinct from other qualitative approaches. As an approach, IPA originated from hermeneutics and phenomenology, and theorists such as Edmund Husserl, Maurice Merleau-Ponty and Martin Heidegger are often referenced (Brocki & Wearden, 2006).

Many IPA studies draw on a small number of participants (many theorists suggest six participants as a good number, with between three and 15 being acceptable). Because of the small number of participants, the studies then involve a close and detailed examination of the experiences and meaning-making activities of the few participants. These participants in an IPA study are invited because they can offer a distinct and meaningful insight into the topic of the study – i.e., it is not randomized sampling, but rather purposive sampling (sometimes called homogeneous sampling). With a small sample, an IPA study illustrates how a phenomenon is understood in a given context and from a shared perspective. Some variants of an IPA study may bring together samples that offer different perspectives on a shared experience (e.g., practitioners and clients, wives and husbands), or they may collect accounts longitudinally from the same participants to develop a longitudinal analysis.

In IPA, data is gathered using approaches such as focus groups, interviews or access to written texts such as diaries. These data are gathered by a researcher taking an open-ended, flexible, curious and facilitative approach, rather than an interrogative or challenging stance. The emphasis is on capturing personal accounts that are rich and descriptively deep, so that the researcher can work with a thorough and precise transcript. With this data, a hypothesis is not tested, but rather the researcher self-reflects upon their preconceptions about the data, attempts to suspend these and focuses on investigating the experiential world of the research participant.

Transcripts are coded in substantial detail, with the researcher focusing on interpreting the meaning of the key claims the participant is making. This is because IPA has a hermeneutic stance of enquiry and meaning-making. This often leads to a double hermeneutic, with the researcher attempting to make sense of the person's attempt to make sense of their experiences. As such, IPA is a useful approach for determining what a given experience was like – i.e., its phenomenology – along with how the person made sense of their experience – i.e., their interpretation.

The approach of analysis in IPA is described as bottom-up. This is because the researcher creates codes from the data, rather than utilizing a pre-existing theory to identify codes that might then be applied to the given data. As mentioned above regarding hypothesis testing, IPA studies do not test questions or theories; however, the outcomes of an IPA analysis are often pertinent to existing theories. This is because the open-ended inquisitive approach between researcher and participant often leads to seeing phenomena in a new light. When the data is transcribed, the researcher studies the text intensively and carefully, coding closely the identified insights of their experience and perspective, and as the analysis and emerging codes develop, the researcher looks for patterns in the codes. These patterns are named themes, and so themes are recurring patterns of meaning that are identified in the text. Themes can identify an aspect that is personally significant to the participant – i.e., a topic of importance, an object – and also convey something of meaning related to the aspect that is personally significant. As the analysis continues and emerges, various themes will be grouped under broader themes often named 'superordinate themes'. When the analysis nears completion or conclusion, a final set of themes is generally summarized and placed into a table where evidence from the text (e.g., a quote) is provided to support the themes produced.

The overall aim of analysis with IPA is to balance insightful interpretation, which is located within participants' accounts, with phenomenological description. It is also to uphold an idiographic focus and emphasis on the meaning of the text. Crucial to the plausibility and transferability of an IPA study is the degree of transparency of the research process (i.e., clear account of process, detail of the sample, commentary on the data, verbatim quotes used to illustrate key points). Likewise, confidence is also increased with engagement with credibility issues (e.g., cooperative enquiry, cross-validation, independent audit, triangulation).

3. DISCOURSE ANALYSIS

The term 'discourse analysis' is an umbrella term that covers a variety of research practices and perspectives, with quite different aims, philosophical underpinnings and theoretical backgrounds. Even though discourse analysis is still a relatively evolving research approach, there are already many different 'species' of discourse analysis which vary in terms of what they are looking for in a piece of text and the specific ways by which the analyses are carried out. For example, some common yet different frameworks for studying texts include Potter and Wetherell's (1987) 'ten stages in the analysis of discourse', Billig's (1988) 'implicit theme' method, Hollway's (1989) 'intuitive feel' approach, and Parker's (1992) '20 step guide to conducting discourse analysis' accompanied by his 'seven criteria for identifying discourses'.

As an approach to research, discourse analysis takes discourse itself as the focus of research interest. One difference between a discursive approach and the traditional empiricist approach is that discourse analysts are interested in the content and organization of naturally occurring talk and texts themselves, rather than seeing talk and texts as a pathway to getting at some other reality that is assumed to lie behind or beyond the discourse (Potter & Wetherell, 1987). Instead, the research interest is with the actual detail of the passages of discourse, with what is said and written, and with the resources that are drawn upon to enable that talk and text (Potter & Wetherell, 1987). As Edwards and Potter (1992) explain, 'what we want to do as discourse analysts is study the flavour and texture of language, and the way in which discourse and talk are constitutive of social life and work as crucial practices or functioning elements in social action in their own right' (p. 4).

This focus on, and primacy of, discourse itself is a common feature of the various discursive approaches. They all share a rejection of the idea that talk and text are a neutral means of reflecting or describing the world, and instead maintain that talk and text play a central importance in constructing social life (Burr, 1995). This shifts the research approach into a post-positivist paradigm interested in the workings of language (Gergen, 1994).

Under a discursive approach, the aims of social enquiry are substantially different as compared to the traditional empiricist approach in psychology. Under the empiricist approach, the assumptions and practices are focused on internal psychic structures and processes, with the aim being to 'uncover' the 'truth' about such structures and processes (Burr, 1995). However, discourse analysis, at a broad level, aims to gain 'a better understanding of social life and social interaction' (Potter & Wetherell, 1987: 7). At a more specific level, 'the goal becomes a pragmatic and political one, a search not for truth but for any usefulness that the researcher's "reading" of a phenomenon might have in bringing about change for those who need it' (Burr, 1995: 162). In other words, the research is evaluated not with regard to its truth or potential truthfulness, but on the understandings produced and their actual usefulness. The aim, then, is to highlight plausible and helpful ways of seeing and understanding certain phenomena, rather than to highlight 'one true way' of understanding or seeing certain phenomena.

Across the social sciences and humanities, various disciplines have embraced discourse analysis, including sociology, education, social work, cultural studies, linguistics, anthropology, social and cognitive psychology, and biblical studies just to name a few, each of which incorporates its own methodologies and dimensions of analysis, and has its own assumptions. In addition, text linguistics is also closely related to discourse analysis. While discourse analysis aims at revealing the socio-psychological characteristics of a person, text linguistics aims at revealing the structure of text.

EVALUATING THE QUALITY OF QUALITATIVE RESEARCH

Quantitative research methods – measurement, more specifically – have a well-established set of standards by which to assess quality – namely, reliability and validity of measurement, with a range of indices to assess and report this (see Chapter 17). What evaluative criteria are relevant for qualitative research? Different qualitative researchers have provided different criteria, in the same way that quantitative researchers revise their statistical indices for reliability. Table 21.1 illustrates the evaluative criteria used by Lincoln and Guba (1985) and Yardley (2000). Further examples of evaluative criteria are in the Further reading and resources section at the end of the chapter. Qualitative research within coaching and mentoring contexts would benefit from more systematic and routine use of these or similar criteria.

Table 21.1   Evaluative criteria for qualitative research.

Lincoln & Guba (1985)	Yardley (2000)
Credibility	**Sensitivity to context**
Confidence in the 'truth' of the finding	
Techniques for establishing credibility	*Is the analysis and interpretation sensitive to the data, the social context, and the relationships (between researcher and participants) from which it emerged?*
1. Prolonged engagement	
2. Persistent observation	
3. Triangulation	
4. Peer debriefing	
5. Negative case analysis	
6. Referential adequacy	
7. Member-checking	
Transferability	*What was the nature of the researcher's involvement or prolonged engagement/ immersion in data?*
Showing that the findings have applicability in other contexts	*Does the researcher consider how he or she may have specifically influenced participants' actions (reflexivity)?*
Techniques for establishing transferability	*Does the researcher consider power balance/ imbalance a situation?*
1. Thick description	**Completeness of data collection, analysis and interpretation**
	Is the size and nature (comprehensiveness) of the sample adequate to address the research question?
	Is there transparency and sufficient detail in the author's account of methods used and analytical and interpretive choices (audit trail)?
	Is every aspect of the data-collection process, and the approach to coding and analysing data discussed?
	Does the author present excerpts from the data so that readers can discern for themselves the patterns identified?
	Is there coherence across the research question, philosophical perspective, method and analysis approach?
	(See Chapter 6.)

Lincoln & Guba (1985)	Yardley (2000)
Dependability	**Reflexivity**
Showing that the findings are consistent and could be repeated	*Does the researcher reflect on his or her own perspective and the motivations and interests that shaped the research process (from formulation of the research question, through method choices, analysis and interpretation)?*
Techniques for establishing dependability	
1. Inquiry audit	
Confirmability	**Importance**
A degree of neutrality or the extent to which the findings of a study are shaped by the respondents and not researcher bias, motivation or interest.	*Is the research important? Will it have practical and theoretical utility?*
	(See Chapter 2.)
Techniques for establishing confirmability	
1. Confirmability audit	
2. Audit trail	
3. Triangulation	
4. Reflexivity	

CHOOSING BETWEEN THEORY-DRIVEN QUALITATIVE ANALYSIS OR EMERGENT ANALYSIS IN QUALITATIVE METHODS

Research designs and analysis may *be deductive, theory driven, top-down, confirmatory* or *inductive, data driven, bottom-up, emergent, exploratory*. For example, Interpretive Phenomenological Analysis (IPA) is bottom-up in terms of interpreting the phenomenon at hand. Theory-based preconceptions are limited as much as possible. Grounded theory is an example of a popular inductive qualitative research approach. Alternatively, one may have a theory developed, and possibly evidence from quantitative research, and using a mixed-methods approach (see Chapter 24), may wish to confirm a theory with qualitative descriptions. MacFarlane and Brún (2012) assert that in addition to inductive approaches, tight qualitative research designs informed by social theory can be useful to sensitize researchers to concepts and processes that they might not necessarily identify through inductive processes. In a coaching or mentoring context, the intervention approach may be based on a particular theoretical approach – e.g., humanistic, solution-focused, etc. Deductive, but qualitative, research may be useful and insightful within such a framework. The decision between these two options is illustrated in Table 21.2 applied to both your overall research design and sequence, and more specifically to analysing data.

Table 21.2   Deductive and inductive approaches in qualitative research

Deductive inference: *general to specific*	Inductive inference: *specific to general*
Theory driven	Data driven
Top-down	Bottom-up/emergent
Confirmatory	Exploratory

 **Activity**

What is your current level of understanding of qualitative analysis and interpretation approaches? It is useful to reflect on our level of awareness and skills with qualitative methods. If you have not done any qualitative research before, consider how you would approach interpreting an interview transcript where the interviewer conducted a narrative open-ended interview to a mentee/protégé asking the question: 'Please describe your experience of mentoring.'

1.   Would you look for themes?
2.   Are you interested in how the person interprets their own experience?
3.   Are you interested in how the person uses language to position themselves in a broader discourse?

Your answers will hint at your preferences between the three methods/approaches described in this chapter.

WHAT NEXT?

Before finalizing your commitments to particular methods to generate and interpret qualitative data, you need to read on. The remaining chapters will further your understanding related to these issues. We remind you, as per Chapter 6, how important it is to align your epistemology, methodology and method with your research questions. Chapter 22 examines the approach of programme evaluation, which often uses a qualitative methodology. Chapter 23 examines the use of case study designs, which are quite relevant to approaches such as Interpretive Phenomenological Analysis (IPA). Chapter 24 concludes with bringing quantitative and qualitative methods together to get the right balance and sequence of inductive and deductive reasoning.

To further your understanding of qualitative methods, we recommend that you access and compare the following two articles: Honsová & Jarošová (2018) and Shaw & Glowacki-Dudka

(2018), and assess the qualitative methods using the evaluative criteria of either Lincoln & Guba (1985) or Yardley (2000) (see Further reading and resources at the end of the chapter). These are selected as examples of coaching research related to the topics of this chapter, with no evaluation of their quality made here.

CONCLUSION

In this chapter we reviewed the important contribution of qualitative methodology to coaching and mentoring research. A theme of this book is that there are a range of decisions to make when designing and conducting your research. Chapters 5 and 6 described the epistemological and methodological choices. In Chapter 20 we covered how to generate qualitative data and in this chapter we reminded you of the importance of your theory of knowledge (epistemology) in understanding and using qualitative methods to interpret qualitative data. The key distinction between using inductive data-driven approaches versus theory-driven deductive approaches was emphasized. Criteria to assess what constitutes good qualitative research was also discussed.

 Further reading and resources

Guest, G., MacQueen, K. M., & Namey, E. E. (2012). *Applied thematic analysis*. Thousand Oaks, CA: SAGE. DOI: http://dx.doi.org/10.4135/9781483384436

Honsová, P., & Jarošová, E. (2018). Peak coaching experiences, *Coaching: An International Journal of Theory, Research and Practice*, DOI: 10.1080/17521882.2018.1489867

Lincoln, Y. S., & Guba, E. G. (1985). *Naturalistic inquiry*. Newbury Park, CA: SAGE.

Miles, M. B., Huberman, M., & Saldana, J. (2014). *Qualitative data analysis: a sourcebook*. London: SAGE.

Shaw, L., & Glowacki-Dudka, M. (2018). The experience of critical self-reflection by life coaches: a phenomenological study, *Coaching: An International Journal of Theory, Research and Practice*, DOI: 10.1080/17521882.2018.1489869

Shaw, R. (2010). Interpretive Phenomenological Analysis. In Forrester, M. (Ed.). (2010). *Doing qualitative research in psychology: A practical guide*. 177–201. London: SAGE.

Wiggins, S. & Riley, S. (2010.). Discourse analysis. In Forrester, M. (Ed.). (2010). *Doing qualitative research in psychology: a practical guide*. 135–153. London: SAGE.

Yardley, L. (2000). Dilemmas in qualitative health research. *Psychology and Health*, 15, 215–228.

SAGE URL to explore research methods: http://methods.sagepub.com/methods-map

PROGRAMME EVALUATION AND ACTION RESEARCH

22

WHAT'S THE DIFFERENCE BETWEEN A RESEARCH PROJECT AND A PROGRAMME EVALUATION?

LEARNING OUTCOMES

In completing this chapter and related activities, you will be able to:

1. describe key similarities and differences between research versus programme evaluation in a coaching and mentoring context;

2. describe key concepts of programme logic as it relates to a coaching or mentoring programme;

3. describe the key difference between process versus outcome evaluations;

4. outline key aspects of action research and its relevance to coaching and mentoring contexts.

WHAT IS THE CURRENT REALITY IN TERMS OF COACHING, MENTORING AND PROGRAMME EVALUATION?

In organizational contexts, including schools, hospitals, offices – formal or informal – coaching and mentoring programmes are commonly implemented. Managers and practitioners often wish to 'evaluate' these programmes and may claim that they wish to do 'research', using the terms 'evaluation' and 'research' interchangeably. There are important differences that are relevant to coaching and mentoring practitioners, evaluators and researchers. It is also relevant to return to the distinction in Chapter 1, between outcome, process and fidelity/implementation. This distinction is relevant to understanding programme evaluation alongside research. Action research, with its emphasis on local involvement and change, further adds to the need to clarify terms. Once again, a revisiting of terms from Chapter 5, including 'pragmatism', is useful to gain a greater understanding.

Like many aspects in qualitative methodology, there are contested epistemologies, methods, models and language. This is true for programme evaluation. A useful starting point for understanding programme evaluation is Stufflebeam and Shinkfield's (2007) assertion that it 'improves rather than proves'. The word 'evaluation' implies that it is a valuation, examining the merit or worth of something. In terms of this book, it is likely a coaching programme or mentoring programme that is being evaluated. In Chapter 1 and the Appendix, there is a differentiation between process, outcome and implementation/fidelity for intervention studies. This is also relevant to programme evaluation, as there are outcome evaluations, process evaluations and many other evaluations, including an ongoing examination of implementation with active steps to improve things as they are happening. This is very different from an experimental study, which will run to completion as designed to see the outcome. Table 22.1 illustrates some common differences between programme evaluation approaches and positivist outcomes research (i.e., experimental studies). There are variations in programme evaluation, and hence aspects of this comparison will vary as you learn more about programme evaluation.

Researchers must stand back and wait for the experiment to play out. Researchers ask, 'Did the participants in the coaching group gain more than those in control?' Evaluation, on the other hand, is a *process* unfolding *'in real time'*. In addition to determining the amount the coaching participants gained, evaluators also enquire about related areas such as, 'How much assistance did participants need?' 'Are there reasons people are not turning up?' If evaluators realize that activities are not adequate, staff are free to adjust accordingly.

Table 22.1 Differences between programme evaluation and positivist quantitative outcomes research

Programme evaluation	Outcomes research
'Improve it'	'Prove it'
Assess value of programme against a standard	Aims to stay value-free

Programme evaluation	Outcomes research
Contextualized	Decontextualized
'Is it working?'	'Did it work?'
Real-time modifications	Modifications after completion
Improve a particular programme	Aim to generalize to larger population
Pragmatism as guiding epistemology	Positivism as guiding epistemology

Definitions relevant to programme evaluation and action research

Action research involves examining practice to improve it. It emphasizes collaboration and participation by all relevant parties, rather than researchers imported from outside contexts. It usually involves repeating cycles of collaborative plan–act–observe–reflect. **Action research** is an interactive enquiry process that balances problem-solving actions implemented in a collaborative context with data-driven collaborative analysis. The research also aims to enable future predictions about personal and organizational change (Reason & Bradbury, 2008).

Formative evaluation is a type of evaluation undertaken to gather evidence that will be used to inform programme improvement – for example, evaluating the beginning of a mentoring programme for young people.

Summative evaluation is a type of evaluation used to determine the merit or worth of a programme – for example, evaluating whether the mentoring programme for youth has been worthwhile once it has run.

Programme logic sets out the relationship between programme activities and the intended outcomes of a programme. It is usually referred to as a model and illustrated in a visual format (see Figure 22.1). The problem statement, inputs, activities, participation and short-, medium- and long-term outcomes of the problem are represented.

Needs assessment refers to proactive evaluation, used to establish the type and level of need within a target group, to assist planning and intervention. For example, the needs of staff in a large banking corporation are established prior to developing the coaching programme.

Process evaluation is an evaluation that seeks to identify programme processes to refine and improve the programme. It is often used to set up a programme for the later outcome evaluation. A process evaluation may include issues of participant satisfaction, participant attendance, programme implementation and fidelity. For example, in the large bank, while the coaching programme is being implemented, satisfaction, attendance, quality of coaching and whether it matches the coaching model are all evaluated.

(Continued)

(Continued)

Performance monitoring is often used to monitor programme implementation, over time. A limited number of performance indicators are often identified and monitored at time intervals – e.g., monthly, quarterly. For example, for a coaching programme within a large banking corporation, the number of coaching sessions, fidelity adherence and aggregate goal attainment are all tracked.

Outcome evaluation examines the outcomes of a programme for participants and organizations. There is often confusion between different terms such as outcome, output, impact and effect. Quantitative researchers reserve the term 'effect' in experimental and quasi-experimental designs for causal claims about the effect a programme or individual variable has on an outcome. For example, after 18 months of running a coaching programme in a large banking corporation, the outcomes of the programme are evaluated, comparing it to prior levels and sites that did not have the coaching programme.

Economic evaluation is a type of evaluation that addresses the cost benefit or cost-effectiveness of programmes. This form of evaluation usually comes later, after there is some evidence of programme effectiveness from outcome evaluations. This is related to other terms such as Return on Investment, Return on Expectations. For example, a large banking corporation implemented a comprehensive coaching programme for employees. The cost-effectiveness of the programme was evaluated as time and financial inputs were quantifiable, and the financial and other outcomes were also measurable.

ACTION RESEARCH AND COACHING AND MENTORING

Kurt Lewin first coined the term 'action research' in 1944. This has evolved over 60 years. Similar to the practical emphasis of some forms of programme evaluation, Torbert (1981) captures a key understanding of action research in his assertion that 'knowledge is always gained through action and for action. From this starting point, to question the validity of social knowledge is to question, not how to develop a reflective science about action, but how to develop genuinely well-informed action – how to conduct an action science'.

The balance that action research seeks to achieve is between the actions taken and research that results from the reflective understanding of the actions. This may involve tension between a researcher's view and a participant's view. In simple terms, it may be understood as collaborative action and reflection cycles. The reflection, however, informs further local actions. It is similar to programme evaluation in its emphasis on local improvement. As coaching and mentoring are practices (i.e., actions) that are often conducted collectively in organizations, action research approaches are very relevant.

WHAT IS YOUR REALITY IN TERMS OF PROGRAMME EVALUATION?

For research or evaluation endeavours for less than a year, depending on resources, it can be difficult to do outcome evaluations. This is similar to trying to do a controlled trial in less than one year. Hence, for you as a beginning coaching or mentoring researcher or evaluator, a process evaluation or even comprehensive needs assessment may be more feasible. This may or may not be acceptable for certain course requirements; however, it is worth considering. Similarly, an action research-oriented project may or may not be acceptable as part of course requirements. This is because different curricula have different assumptions about what constitutes research, as discussed in Chapter 5. Further investigation may be necessary on your part.

If you are not a university-based researcher, you may already be using programme evaluation and action research and will be well beyond this chapter.

WHAT ARE YOUR OPTIONS IN CONSIDERING A PROGRAMME EVALUATION?

An important component of contemporary programme evaluation is the development of a theory of change using programme logic. Programme logic sets out the relationship between programme activities and the intended outcomes of a programme. It is usually referred to as a model and illustrated in a visual format. An example of programme logic is illustrated in Figure 22.1. This is an example of a three-year programme, involving coaching and other programmes, to run a university college/dormitory based on the principles of positive psychology (Oades & Spence, 2017). Figure 22.1 illustrates the essential elements of programme logic, which include: 1) inputs; 2) outputs; 3) outcomes; 4) situation; 5) goal. Underlying the approach is a theory of change – that is, how the inputs will lead to the outcomes. A programme evaluation may vary in whether it is a process evaluation or an outcome evaluation. The majority of this evaluation was a process evaluation. Search the internet using 'Program Logic Template' and numerous resources are available. Gugiu and Rodriquez-Campos (2007) have developed a semi-structured interview protocol for constructing logic models.

WHAT NEXT?

This chapter is very introductory in terms of both programme evaluation and, particularly, action research. The main aim has been to include them so you are aware of them as relevant approaches alongside other research methodology. It is important to note that both

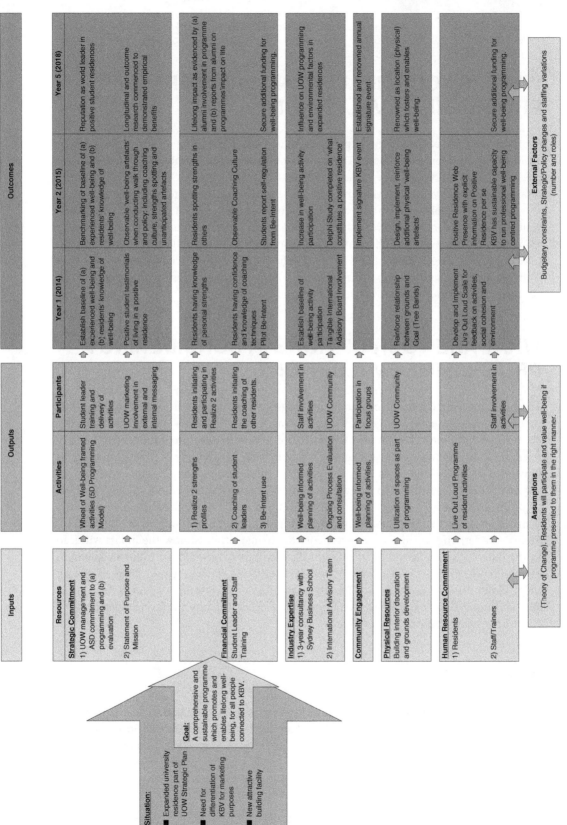

Figure 22.1 Example of program logic

programme evaluation and action research use many qualitative methods. The simple 'What next?' here is more reading on both programme evaluation and action research. A further 'What next?' is to find a person and talk with someone who has conducted a programme evaluation and/or action research. If you are a university-based student researcher, examine whether these approaches are viable options for course requirements.

CONCLUSION

Many coaching practitioners working as organizational consultants or mentors within organizations will develop programmes which they seek to evaluate. Many of the qualitative methods described in Chapter 21, alongside action research approaches, are common in programme evaluation. There are important similarities and differences between empirical research projects and programme evaluation which are useful for coaching researchers to understand. This chapter described those differences before providing a summary of programme logic for programme evaluation and developing evaluation strategies. The different types of programme evaluation were described, particularly the difference between process and outcome evaluations. Action research was described as an example of an approach seeking to make tangible within context changes, through iterations of action and reflection, involving the participants within that change.

 Further reading and resources

Ely, K., Boyce, L. A., Nelson, J. K., Zaccaro, S. J., Hernez-Broome, G., & Whyman, W. (2010). Evaluating leadership coaching: a review and integrated framework, *The Leadership Quarterly, 21*(4), 585–599.

Greenwood, D.J., & Levin, M. (2007). *Introduction to action research* (2nd ed.). Thousand Oaks, CA: SAGE.

Gugiu, P. C. & Rodriquez-Campos, L. (2007). Semi-structured interview protocol for constructing logic models. *Evaluation and Program Planning, 30*, 339–50.

Kanier, J., & Kramer, M. (2011). Collective impact. *Stanford Social Innovation Review*. Stanford, CA: Stanford University.

Mathison, S. (2005). *Encyclopedia of evaluation.* Thousand Oaks, CA: SAGE. DOI: 10.4135/9781412950558

Noffke, S., & Somekh, B. (Eds.) (2009). *The SAGE handbook of educational action research.* London: SAGE.

Owen, J. (2006). *Program evaluation: forms and approaches* (3rd ed.). Crows Nest, NSW: Allen & Unwin.

Patton, M. (2008). *Utilization-focused evaluation* (4th edn). Thousand Oaks, CA: SAGE.

(Continued)

(Continued)

Pine, G. J. (2008). *Teacher action research: building knowledge democracies*. SAGE.

Reason, P. and Bradbury, H. (2008) (Eds.) *The Sage handbook of action research: participative inquiry and practice*. Thousand Oaks, CA: SAGE.

Stringer, E. T. (1999). *Action research*. Thousand Oaks, CA: SAGE.

Stufflebeam, D. L., & Shinkfield, A. J. (2007). *Evaluation theory, models and applications*. San Francisco, CA: Jossey Bass.

Wyatt Knowlton, L. & Phillips, C. C. (2009). *The logic model guidebook: better strategies for great results*. Thousand Oaks, CA: SAGE.

Example URLs for programme evaluation and action research resources

https://aifs.gov.au/cfca/how-develop-program-logic-planning-and-evaluation

https://managementhelp.org/blogs/nonprofit-capacity-building/2012/01/08/four-differences-between-research-and-program-evaluation/

https://journals.sagepub.com/home/arj

https://journals.sagepub.com/home/evi

CASE STUDY DESIGNS

23

SHOULD I USE A CASE STUDY DESIGN?

LEARNING OUTCOMES

In completing this chapter and related activities, you will be able to:

1. describe the concept of a case study design as it applies to individuals, programmes or organizations relevant to coaching and mentoring;

2. list advantages and disadvantages of a case study design in your current situation;

3. identify examples of high standard published case study designs.

WHAT IS A CASE STUDY DESIGN AND HOW IS IT RELEVANT TO COACHING AND MENTORING RESEARCH?

A case study is an empirical inquiry that investigates a contemporary phenomenon in depth and within its real-life context (Yin 2018). Yin (1999: 1211) states that 'the all-encompassing feature of a case study is its intense focus on a single phenomenon within its real-life context'. He claims further that the number of variables of interest are much greater than the number of data-points.

Table 23.1 illustrates the key elements of a case study based on Yin (2018), with a coaching example.

Table 23.1   Key elements of a quality case study.

Element	Author
1. Clearly delineated boundaries	Punch (1998)
Restricts attention to areas relevant to research problem	Stake (1995)
E.g. *Examines changes over time of a single coach–coachee relationship.*	
2. Study of an enclosed system, with a focus on the integrity of that system	Stake (1994)
E.g. *The system is a coach–coachee relationship, particularly the bond, agreed goals and levels of directiveness, roles and responsibilities in that system.*	
3. It is a case of something	Punch (1998)
E.g. *Examines interactional and motivational changes over time of a single coach–coachee relationship.*	
4. Seeks to understand as much as possible of the case in question	Punch (1998)
E.g. *The individuals in the coaching dyad are described and explored to understand their interactions and motivations.*	
5. Likely use of multiple sources of data	Punch (1998)
E.g. *May include diary methods, interviews, video observations, goal attainment scales.*	
6. An empirical inquiry investigating a contemporary issue in its context.	Yin (1984).
E.g. *Data used to support the over case study, of coaching in a specific life coaching context, in a city within a culture, with two actual people.*	

Cavaye (1996) reminds researchers that case study research can be used in the positivist and interpretivist traditions. It may be used to test or build theory, using a single or multiple case study design, using qualitative or mixed methods. In this regard, it is a very adaptable approach and, due to its rich and illustrative nature, can be very influential as people understand narratives and contexts often more easily than research, which may feel decontextualized or requiring the technical skills of much of quantitative research.

In our view, while coaching and mentoring research will no doubt benefit from further experimental designs, particularly randomized controlled trials, case study designs (single or multiple) are underutilized. Gaining a large amount of data from a small sample – e.g., one person, one team or one organization, can be very useful. Moreover, it may reduce the risk of not getting data or a sufficient number of participants for beginning researchers who usually have short time frames to complete their research.

Activity

What is your current reality in understanding case study research? An effective and efficient way to learn about case study methods is to examine a published case study method. Also, it is useful to evaluate its quality. The term 'case study' is sometimes used very loosely, and some authors report illustrative case studies that are little more than brief vignettes. While there is nothing wrong with illustrative vignettes per se, they are not the comprehensive and rigorous case study method to which this chapter refers.

Stake's (1995) checklist for assessing the quality of a case study report is useful and listed below. Now run a search for a refereed journal article with either coaching and case study *or* mentoring and case study. Once you locate an article, read it and evaluate it using the criteria below.

Stake's (1995) checklist for assessing the quality of a case study.

1. Is this report easy to read?
2. Does it fit together, each sentence contributing to the whole?
3. Does this report have a conceptual structure (i.e., themes or issues)?
4. Are its issues developed in a serious and scholarly way?
5. Is the case adequately defined?
6. Is there a sense of story to the presentation?
7. Is the reader provided some vicarious experience?
8. Have quotations been used effectively?
9. Are headings, figures, artefacts, appendices, indexes effectively used?
10. Was it edited well, then again with a last-minute polish?
11. Has the writer made sound assertions, neither over- nor underinterpreting?
12. Has adequate attention been paid to various contexts?
13. Were sufficient raw data presented?
14. Were data sources well chosen and in sufficient number?
15. Do observations and interpretations appear to have been triangulated?
16. Is the role and point of view of the researcher nicely apparent?
17. Is the nature of the intended audience apparent?
18. Is empathy shown for all sides?
19. Are personal intentions examined?
20. Does it appear that individuals were put at risk?

WHAT ARE YOUR OPTIONS IN TERMS OF USING A CASE STUDY IN YOUR COACHING OR MENTORING RESEARCH?

Punch (1998) (as in Table 23.1) stresses the importance of clearly delineated boundaries to the case. In terms of your options within using a case study, you are served well by first delineating the boundaries of what you are aiming to explore. This is similar to the issue of scoping covered in Chapter 7. Are you looking at an individual, a dyad, a team, a family, a division, an organization, a region, etc.? A further option is to clarify (see Definitions, below) whether, based on Stake (1995), you are claiming that it is an intrinsic case study, will be used instrumentally (instrumental case study) or will be a collection of case studies (collective case study).

▬▬▬▬▬ Definitions relevant to case study research ▬▬▬▬▬

Intrinsic case study is typically undertaken to learn about a unique phenomenon. The researcher needs to explain how the phenomenon is unique, which distinguishes it from all others – for example, being the political mentor of a leader of a new nation.

Instrumental case studies use a particular case (some of which may be better than others) to gain a broader appreciation of an issue or phenomenon (Stake, 1995). The study may help develop new concepts to elucidate certain aspects of what has been studied or propositions that link concepts within the case. These, in turn, can be assessed for how they can be applied and transferred to other situations (Punch, 2009): for example, a whole organization case study implementing workplace coaching, while only one organization may be used as an instrument to inform other organizations for comparison and learning purposes. A quantitative researcher would see $n = 1$ as not generalizable. The purpose is different.

Collective case studies involve multiple cases simultaneously or sequentially in an attempt to generate a still broader appreciation of a particular issue (Stake, 1995). For example, similar to purposive sampling, one may complete a study with four coaches – older male, younger male, older female, younger female (see Stake, 2006).

WHAT NEXT?

Case studies are a type of design, similar to experimental designs (see Chapter 16) or survey designs (see Chapter 17). Within the design there will be a range of methods, often qualitative, sometimes quantitative. Hence, it is necessary to choose not only the case study design, but also the methods within. Go now to the chapters that include the methods and analyses that you will put in this type of design. For example, if you are doing an intrinsic case study, rich qualitative descriptions may be relevant and interviews using Interpretive Phenomenological Analysis may suit – hence, go to Chapters 21 and 22. However, you may also wish to profile the person's psychometrics using quantitative methods. Therefore, you need to understand reliability and validity (see Chapter 17) and how it is a mixed-methods approach (see Chapter 25). See the Further reading and resources section at the end of the chapter where there are numerous papers to illustrate a range of case study designs and how to use this approach.

CONCLUSION

Case studies can be very relevant to coaching and mentoring research. Case studies can be at individual, dyad, small group/team, programme or organizational level. In applied research, the requirements for an experimental design are often not achievable and hence a case study method might be a better and more feasible alternative. Case study designs can include both quantitative and qualitative data, and depend upon the research question posed.

 Further reading and resources

Burn, J., & Robins, G. (2003). Moving towards e-government: a case study of organisational change processes, *Logistics Information Management, 16*(1), 25–35, https://doi.org/10.1108/09576050 310453714

Crowe, S., Cresswell, K., Robertson, A., Huby, G., Avery, A. & Sheikh, A. (2011). The case study approach. *BMC Medical Research Methodology, 11,* 100.

Fouché, P., du Plessis, R., & van Niekerk, R. (2017). Levinsonian seasons in the life of Steve Jobs: a psychobiographical case study, *Indo-Pacific Journal of Phenomenology, 17*(1), 1–18.

George, A. L. & Bennett, A. (2005). *Case studies and theory development in the social sciences.* Cambridge, MA: MIT Press.

Hezlett, S. (2005). Protégés' learning in mentoring relationships: a review of the literature and an exploratory case study. *Advances in Developing Human Resources, 7*(4), 505–526, November. DOI: 10.1177/1523422305279686

Pan, S. L., & Tan, B. (2011). Demystifying case research: a structured–pragmatic–situational (SPS) approach to conducting case studies, *Information and Organization, 21*(3), 161–176.

Punch, K. (1998). *Introduction to social research. Quantitative and qualitative approaches.* London: SAGE.

Punch, K. F. & Oancea, A. (2014). *An introduction to research methods in education* (2nd ed.). London: SAGE.

Sheikh, A., Halani L., Bhopal, R., Netuveli, G., Partridge, M., Car. J., et al. (2009). Facilitating the recruitment of minority ethnic people into research: qualitative case study of South Asians and asthma. *PLoS Medicine, 6*(10), 1–11.

Simons, H. (2009). *Case study research in practice.* London: SAGE.

Stake R. E. (1995). *The art of case study research.* London: SAGE.

Stake, R. E. (2006). *Multiple case study analysis.* New York: Guilford Press.

van Harten, W. H., Casparie, T. F. & Fisscher, O. A. (2002). The evaluation of the introduction of a quality management system: a process-oriented case study in a large rehabilitation hospital. *Health Policy, 60*(1), 17–37.

Walsh, J. N. & O'Brien, J. (2018). Knowledge asymmetries and service management: three case studies, *Journal of Information & Knowledge Management, 17*(03).

Yin, R. K. (2018). *Case study research and applications: design and methods* (6th ed.). Thousand Oaks, CA: SAGE.

MIXED METHODS

24

COULD OR SHOULD I USE MIXED METHODS?

LEARNING OUTCOMES

In completing this chapter and related activities, you will be able to:

1. describe the concept of mixed-methods research, including the different purposes of mixed-methods approaches;
2. list the advantages and disadvantages of a case study design and why one might be used;
3. identify examples of published mixed-methods designs.

WHAT IS THE CURRENT STATE IN TERMS OF MIXED- METHODS RESEARCH?

In general, mixed-methods research is a type of research that involves collecting, analysing and interpreting both qualitative and quantitative data to answer a research question. Mixed-methods research is more of a recent phenomenon than mono-method approaches, and is growing in its use and reach (Leech & Onwuegbuzie, 2009). However, mixed-methods approaches are still less common than mono-methods research designs that focus solely on a quantitative or qualitative method. The essential premise of a mixed-methods approach is that combining both quantitative and qualitative approaches provides a better understanding of a research question than either approach used in isolation (Creswell & Creswell, 2017). Hence, through combining both quantitative and qualitative research components, the research conclusions and corresponding contribution to the published literature will be strengthened.

It is important to design mixed-methods research well, and while convergence between qualitative and quantitative approaches can lend more weight to research conclusions, mixed-methods approaches do not by themselves guarantee higher quality and more rigorous research. A criterion that a mixed-methods study must satisfy is 'multiple validities legitimation' (Onwuegbuzie, Johnson, & Collins, 2011; Schoonenboom & Johnson, 2017). This requires that the study meets the relevant combination set of qualitative, quantitative and mixed-methods validity protocols in research. In other words, the study will need to ensure appropriate rigour in each of the different methods (qualitative or quantitative) that make up the mixed-methods study. If the study falls short on any one of these areas, then the study will be flawed by this shortcoming and its conclusions will be weakened or potentially even invalidated.

So why, then, do a mixed-methods study? A classification for the purpose of mixed-methods research was introduced by Greene, Caracelli & Graham (1989: 259), who distinguish five essential purposes of mixed-methods research, which are shown in Table 24.1 below.

Table 24.1   Purposes of mixed-methods research (Greene, Caracelli, & Graham, 1989)

Triangulation	Triangulation seeks convergence and corroboration of results across different methods used.
Complementarity	Complementarity seeks elaboration, enhancement, illustration or clarification of results from one method with results from the other method.
Development	Development seeks to use the results from one method to help develop or inform the results obtained from the other method. Development here is broadly construed as sampling, implementation or measurement decisions. A common example of this is when qualitative research collected via interviews is used to then develop items in a self-report scale.
Initiation	Initiation seeks the discovery of paradox and contradiction, new perspectives of frameworks, or the recasting of the questions or results from one method from results obtained by the other method.
Expansion	Expansion seeks to expand the breadth and scope of enquiry by using different methods for different aspects of the research question.

Perhaps the most commonly referred to purpose of mixed-methods research is to obtain **triangulation**, the idea of which is to seek convergence and confirmation of findings across different methodological approaches. The core premise behind triangulation is that all designs have inherent biases and limitations, which may ultimately be overcome via the use of different methods that can offset the biases of mono-method approaches. This occurs when the results of these complementary methods converge and corroborate one another.

Complementarity is also a commonly employed objective in mixed-methods research, potentially because a combination of qualitative with quantitative data can help elaborate and clarify one line of findings with the other. An advantage of qualitative data is that it can be more sensitive to detecting changes from interventions, thus capturing information that is more difficult to detect with quantitative measures alone. Quantitative data are limited by the factors described previously (see Chapters 15–18), but – particularly when it comes to intervention research – they are also limited by what are referred to as 'ceiling' or 'floor' effects – which are tendencies for participants to respond towards the poles of scales (Allen, 2018). Both effects are common artefacts of self-report measures that use Likert-type rating statements (e.g., 1 = strongly disagree, to 5 = strongly agree) (Allen, 2018).

A ceiling effect is when most people endorse the top end of the scale (e.g., 90 per cent of a sample might endorse 5 = strongly agree), and a floor effect is when most people endorse the bottom end of the scale (e.g., 90 per cent of a sample might endorse 1 = strongly disagree). If either ceiling or floor effects are present, the variability of participant responses will be restricted, which has important consequences for quantitative research. In correlational research, reduced variability will make the observed correlations between variables smaller – that is, closer towards 0. In intervention research, it will limit how much change is possible to detect due to the intervention or programme you are implementing.

To illustrate this effect, let us consider an example. Imagine you have designed a six-week long 'state of the art' coaching-based intervention that you expect will improve employee well-being. You want to test whether your intervention is effective in obtaining the desired result, and thus you design a fully controlled randomized experiment to evaluate it (Chapter 16). You sample 100 people overall, 50 of whom are randomly allocated into your intervention group to receive your six-week intervention, and the other 50 of whom are assigned to receive a more conventional six-week coaching intervention.

LEARNING CHECK

Exercise question. The control group in this case will be as follows.

1. An active control group.
2. A no-intervention control group.
3. A wait-list control group.
4. An intervention control group.

You have picked two validated measures to operationalize employee well-being, which include measures of:

- job satisfaction;
- burnout.

These scales are self-report measures and respondents respond on a 5-point Likert scale (1 = strongly disagree, and 5 = strongly agree) against each item. You want to see whether your coaching group obtain higher job satisfaction and lower burnout after your intervention, relative to the control group. However, after you begin your experiment and obtain baseline (pre-test) data, you realize that the average score of your intervention sample is near the maximum (the ceiling) for job satisfaction, and near the bottom (the floor) for burnout. Thus, even if your intervention were very effective, there is still limited scope for improvements based on the self-report scales; participants are nearing the extremes already. And herein lies our dilemma with ceiling and floor effects: even if your programme were maximally effective, it may still be difficult to detect the full extent of this efficacy due to a limited scope for change on the quantitative-based measures. Hence, qualitative data can be a useful supplement to quantitative data in such cases. It is possible, for example, that participants will collectively identify that they now feel 'less tired and burned out' in the qualitative data, despite no reduction being recorded from pre- to post-intervention in the burnout measure. While such a finding would not be definitive, it may still provide valuable support for the intervention.

Expansion is also an important goal from mixed-methods research, which will involve expanding the breadth of scope for enquiry by combining both qualitative and quantitative data. For example, in some cases qualitative research can supplement quantitative findings to capture additional information and personal insights that may be missed in the self-report scales, which tend to include only a very limited number of questions (or items). Using the example above, it is also possible that participants might identify other areas where they changed as a result of the coaching/mentoring intervention, which may not have been captured with the measures that were used. For example, perhaps the sample will collectively identify that they were able to 'grow and develop' as a result of the intervention, or that it helped them 'set better goals at work', or that it helped them 'develop more adaptive strategies to build relationships with peers', or something else entirely. None of these possible outcomes were evaluated with the self-report measures listed above, and thus qualitative data might present a rich source of information for exploratory research.

Finally, another way in which mixed methods can be used for expansion is that qualitative data can yield useful information about why the intervention was (or was not) effective. Issues such as the scheduling, delivery style, facilitators, type of content, rapport, and so on might impact on how much participants benefit from the coaching programme. Such issues might emerge with qualitative data, but are rarely evaluated with self-report scales, which means they are often left unmeasured and unconsidered in mono-method quantitative studies. Incorporating qualitative methods into such designs will expand the breadth of enquiry.

WHAT IS MY CURRENT REALITY IN TERMS OF UNDERTAKING A MIXED-METHODS STUDY?

Take a moment to note some of your situation and consider some of your own reasons or motivations for a mixed-methods approach. In doing so, refer back to Table 1.1 in Chapter 1 of this book to identify the different types of intervention and non-intervention research. Note the following.

- Are you more interested in the process, outcome or implementation research?
- If you are interested in more than one type of research, can mixed-methods research help you answer different aspects of your research question? For example, a common approach in mixed-methods studies is to use qualitative data to determine the characteristics of the intervention that worked and did not, which might then explain why changes were observed (or were not observed) in your outcome variables of interest. Such a study would aim for *complementarity* between qualitative and quantitative data.

WHAT ARE MY OPTIONS IN TERMS OF MIXED-METHODS RESEARCH?

We have already reviewed the different purposes of mixed-methods research, which can be used in essentially all the different types of research in coaching or mentoring (Table 1.1 in Chapter 1). You have the option of using mixed methods to address different types of research in Table 1.1, within the same project.

Another option for you in this context is to opt for a case study research design. Yin (2003) defines a case study as a form of empirical enquiry that a) investigates a contemporary phenomenon in its real-life context, particularly when b) the boundaries between that phenomenon and the context are not clearly evident. Thus, what is of interest to most case studies is the context (e.g., where or with whom the coaching or mentoring actually occurs), which is highly important for our phenomenon of enquiry (coaching or mentoring itself). For this reason, case studies are often used to examine in-depth specialized examples in their real-world setting – typically, those that are difficult to capture in large numbers. Thus, case studies can be useful alternatives to survey or experimental forms of research.

An example of this would be if we wanted to study coaching or mentoring in a group of, say, astronauts. Astronauts are an elite and highly trained group of people who frequently work in extreme conditions – on a spacecraft in zero-gravity – for highly specialized missions. They are typically highly educated, skilled and trained, and are required to pass strict physical and psychological fitness criteria before being eligible to board a spacecraft. Conducting a randomized control RCT among a group of astronauts to test the efficacy of a coaching

programme will be an extremely resource-intensive and onerous exercise, and may ultimately be of limited value given how 'atypical' astronauts are as a population. For this
reason, the study would possess limited generalizability, unless your aim is to generalize to
other astronauts. A case study, on the other hand, may provide useful insight into how
coaching or mentoring research would work in groups of people who work in extreme conditions and require highly specialized training.

Activity

List three further examples of populations that could be explored in a case-study research design.

a.   Astronauts
b.   ...
c.   ...
d.   ...

Case-study research is focused primarily on the context, which will shed useful insight
on the phenomenon of enquiry. This differs dramatically from experimental research,
which 'deliberately divorces a phenomenon from its context, so that attention can be
focused on only a few variables' (Yin, 2003: 13). The experiment does so in order to ensure
a more highly 'controlled' study that is free from extraneous influences that might cloud
our conclusions (i.e., the pursuit of internal validity). It also does so in an attempt to ensure
more generalizability (i.e., external validity) in the research findings. Given the focus on
context in case-study research, both internal and external validity are less of a concern.

FURTHER READING IN MIXED METHODS

To consolidate your learning on mixed methods, we find it helpful to walk through some real
examples of mixed-methods studies, which we describe here.

Grant, Curtayne and Burton (2009) conducted a randomized controlled trial of a coaching
intervention with 41 public health executives, using a mixed-methods approach. The coaching programme included 360-degree feedback, half a day of leadership training, and four
individual coaching sessions over a ten-week period. Intervention participants were compared against a waitlist control group using measures of goal attainment, resilience,
workplace well-being, stress and depression.

In addition, the research team included two qualitative questions to gauge each participant's experience of the programme, including the following.

- What specific positive benefits (if any) did you gain from participating in this programme?
- What specific positive outcomes (if any) have flowed into your workplace?

The quantitative component of the study showed evidence that the coaching intervention enhanced goal attainment, resilience and workplace well-being, and reduced depression and stress in the intervention group. However, effect sizes with confidence intervals (CIs) were not reported, making it difficult to determine how 'strong' these effects were. As noted in Chapter 18, it is now strongly recommended that effect sizes and CIs are always reported for primary outcomes, as doing so is essential to allow for accurate interpretation of research studies (Wilkinson, 1999).

In addition to the quantitative evidence, the qualitative component of the study showed that the coaching helped increase participants' perceptions of self-confidence and personal insight. It also showed that the intervention helped participants deal with the stress associated with organizational change, as well as enhance their managerial skills. Thus, in this study the two methodological approaches provided *complementary* evidence that helped *expand* the scope for enquiry to demonstrate other possible areas of benefit from the coaching programme, some of which would have been missed if the quantitative or qualitative data had been used in isolation.

Vella, Crowe and Oades (2013) used a mixed-methods case study design to evaluate the perceived effectiveness of a sports coaching education programme in a sample of nine sports coaches. The authors asked how helpful different aspects of the education programme were, which rated on a Likert scale from 1 = not at all helpful, to 5 = extremely helpful. The authors also asked the participants (*n* = 9) four qualitative questions.

- What aspect of the training programme stood out to you?
- Why was this aspect important?
- What would you suggest is added to the training programme?
- What barriers do you anticipate in trying to be a transformational coach?

The limitation of the case-study approach is that the results are based on a small set of participant experiences, and generalizability (external validity) is limited. However, as noted, inference is not necessarily the goal of case-study research. Instead, case studies are often used to explore the depth of experience. In this case, Vella et al. (2013) are able to go into detail about individual changes that each participant experienced as a result of the coach education programme.

WHAT NEXT?

We invite you to find a further example of a mixed-methods study in the coaching or mentoring field, and, as above, address the following.

- What was the essential purpose of conducting the mixed-methods enquiry (e.g., triangulation, complementarity, etc.)?
- What were some limitations with the study?
- What did the mixed-method approach add to the study that would not have been possible with mono-methods approaches?

CONCLUSION

Mixed-methods research studies are growing in popularity and involve the combination of quantitative and qualitative data. Often these forms of data will converge or complement each other, and thus allow the researcher to strengthen their contribution to the literature. Mixed-methods approaches might also allow the researcher to design a more sensitive study than a mono-method study. Still, it is important to design mixed-methods studies well and they must satisfy the requirement of multiple validities legitimation.

 Further reading and resources

We recommend that you read the following text, which provides in-depth coverage of mixed-methods approaches in research.

Creswell, J. W. & Creswell, J. D. (2017). *Research design: qualitative, quantitative, and mixed methods approaches.* Thousand Oaks, CA: SAGE.

APPENDIX

EXAMPLES OF PROCESS, OUTCOME AND IMPLEMENTATION/ FIDELITY RESEARCH IN COACHING AND MENTORING

EXAMPLES OF PROCESS RESEARCH

Examining the process of coaching/mentoring may include the relationship between coach and coachee/mentor and mentee, or the personal experiences over time of the coach/mentor or coachee/mentee. An example of a process study may be to video the interaction of the relationship between coach and coachee and look for 'turning points' in coaching. Process research often, but not necessarily, adopts qualitative methodologies.

- Grant, A. M. (2014a). Autonomy support, relationship satisfaction and goal focus in the coach–coachee relationship: which best predicts coaching success? *Coaching: An International Journal of Theory, Research and Practice, 7*(1), 18–38.

The role of the coach–coachee relationship in influencing coaching outcomes has emerged as an area of interest in research into the mechanics of effective coaching. Although extensively researched in the psychotherapeutic domain, exploration of the working alliance represents a new phase in executive and life-coaching research. The paper by Grant (2014a) presents an exploratory empirical study that explores four aspects of the coach–coachee relationship to investigate, which is more related to specific measures of coaching success: 1) autonomy support; 2) the extent to which a coachee feels satisfied with the actual coach–coachee relationship; 3) the extent to which the coaching relationship was similar to an 'ideal' coach–coachee relationship; and 4) a goal-focused coach–coachee relationship. This is the first study to use multiple measures of the coach–coachee relationship in order to directly compare the relative efficacy of different aspects of the coach–coachee relationship. In a within-subject study, 49 coach–coachee dyads conducted four coaching sessions over a 10- to 12-week period. Results indicate that satisfaction with a coach–coachee relationship does not predict successful coaching outcomes, and while autonomy support and proximity to an 'ideal' relationship moderately predicted coaching success, a goal-focused coach–coachee relationship was a unique and significantly more powerful predictor of coaching success. The findings emphasize the importance of goals in the coaching process and highlight important differences between psychotherapeutic and coaching working alliances.

- Passmore, J. (2010). A grounded theory study of the coachee experience: the implications for training and practice in coaching psychology. *International Coaching Psychology Review, 5* (1), 48–62.

Passmore's study sought to identify the key behaviours used by executive coaches that were perceived by coachees to have the most favourable impact on their experience and progress. The study used a semi-structured interview design within a qualitative approach. Methods: grounded theory was employed to analyse the transcripts and to build a series of descriptive and conceptual codes. The results from this small-scale study suggest that coachees seek not only particular behaviours, but also certain personal attributes in a coach. Key behaviours and attributes identified were common-sense confidentiality, being collaborative, setting take-away tasks, balancing challenge and support, stimulating problem-solving, effective communication, staying focused, containing emotions, helping develop alternative perspectives, use of a variety of focusing tools and techniques, and use of self as a tool. The study makes some tentative practical recommendations for those involved in coaching practice and coach training.

EXAMPLES OF OUTCOME RESEARCH

Outcome research examines what outcomes are achieved by a coaching/mentoring intervention, or what predicts desired or undesired coaching/mentoring outcomes. An example of an outcome study is a randomized controlled trial which shows that a coaching or mentoring intervention has had an effect. Outcome research often, but not necessarily, adopts quantitative methodologies. Outcome research may be further classified in terms of whether it focuses on coach/mentor factors, relationship factors or coachee/mentee factors, each of which may predict better outcomes.

- Green, L. S., Oades, L. G., & Grant, A. M. (2006). Cognitive-behavioral, solution-focused life coaching: enhancing goal striving, well-being, and hope. *Journal of Positive Psychology, 1*(3), 142–9.

Research is in its infancy in the newly emerging field of coaching psychology. This study examined the effects of a 10-week cognitive-behavioural, solution-focused life-coaching group programme. Participants were randomly allocated to a life-coaching group programme (n = 28) or a waitlist control group (n = 28). Participation in the life-coaching group programme was associated with significant increases in goal-striving, well-being and hope, with gains maintained up to 30 weeks later on some variables. Hope theory may explain such positive outcomes. Life-coaching programmes that utilize evidence-based techniques may provide a framework for further research on psychological processes that occur in non-clinical populations who wish to make purposeful change and enhance their positive psychological functioning.

- Deane, F. P., Andresen, R., Crowe, T., Oades, L. G., Ciarrochi, C., & Williams, V. (2014). A comparison of two coaching approaches to enhance implementation of a recovery-oriented service mode, *Administration and Policy in Mental Health, 41*(5), 660–667.

Moving to recovery-oriented service provision in mental health may entail retraining existing staff, as well as training new staff. This represents a substantial burden on organizations, particularly since transfer of training into practice is often poor. Follow-up supervision and/or coaching have been found to improve the implementation and sustainment of new approaches. We compared the effect of two coaching conditions, skills-based and transformational coaching, on the implementation of a recovery-oriented model following training. Training followed by coaching led to significant sustained improvements in the quality of care planning in accordance with the new model over the 12-month study period. No interaction effect was observed between the two conditions. However, *post hoc* analyses suggest that transformational coaching warrants further exploration. The results support the provision of supervision in the form of coaching in the implementation of a recovery-oriented service model, and suggest the need to better elucidate the mechanisms within different coaching approaches that might contribute to improved care.

- Grant, A. (2013). The efficacy of coaching. In J. Passmore, D. Peterson, & T. Freire, T. (Eds.). *The Wiley-Blackwell handbook of the psychology of coaching and mentoring* (pp. 15–40). Chichester: John Wiley & Sons.
- Grant, A. M., & Cavanagh, M. J. (2007). Evidence-based coaching: flourishing or languishing? *Australian Psychologist, 42*(4), 239–254.

Coaching and coaching psychology offer a potential platform for an applied positive psychology and for facilitating individual, organizational and social change. Experts from around the world were invited to comment on the emerging discipline of coaching psychology and the commercial coaching industry. Several key themes emerged, including the potential of coaching to contribute to health promotion, social change and organizational development. There was unequivocal consensus for the need for an evidence-based approach to coaching. A review of the psychological coaching outcome literature found that there have been a total of 69 outcome studies between 1980 and July 2007: 23 case studies, 34 within-subject studies and 12 between-subject studies. Only eight randomized controlled studies have been conducted. This indicates that coaching psychology is still in the early stages of development, and can be understood as an emerging or protoscientific psychological discipline. A languishing–flourishing model of coaching is described. To flourish, coaching psychology needs to remain clearly differentiated from the frequently sensationalistic and pseudoscientific facets of the personal development industry, while at the same time engaging in the development of the wider coaching industry.

- Theeboom, T., Beersma, B., & van Vianen, A. E. (2014). Does coaching work? A meta-analysis on the effects of coaching on individual level outcomes in an organizational context. *The Journal of Positive Psychology, 9*(1), 1–18.

While coaching is often considered as a useful tool for individual and organizational development (Grant, Passmore, Cavanagh, & Parker, 2010), the lack of a quantitative review of research on the outcomes of coaching makes it prone to scepticism (Bono, Purvanova, Towler, & Peterson, 2009). With this in mind, we conducted a meta-analysis in order to answer the question whether coaching can be applied effectively in organizational contexts. In our review we focused on five dominant outcomes categories in the broader psychological literature: well-being, coping, work and career-related attitudes and goal-directed self-regulation.

EXAMPLES OF IMPLEMENTATION AND FIDELITY RESEARCH

This research examines how coaching or mentoring interventions or practices may be, have been or should be implemented by individuals, teams or organizations. Fidelity refers to how well/closely an intervention matches what is meant to be delivered. An example of an implementation study may examine the best way to implement coaching across a whole department.

- Stewart, L. J., Palmer, S., Wilkin, H. and Kerrin, M. (2008). Towards a model of coaching transfer: operationalising coaching success and the facilitators and barriers to transfer. *International Coaching Psychology Review, 3*(2), 87–109.

Executive coaching has become a respected learning and development strategy. Coaching outcomes and the conditions required for coachees to implement and sustain their development in the workplace have yet to be fully understood. These deficits impede coaching evaluation. The present study sought to operationalize a successful coaching outcome, and to propose and verify a model of coaching transfer. Although exploratory, this study provided some understanding of the influence of the factors that impact on coaching transfer. The findings indicate that there is value in coaching research, examining the complex interplay of factors beyond the coachee–coach relationship.

- Grant, A. M. (2011). The solution-focused inventory: a tripartite taxonomy for teaching, measuring and conceptualising solution-focused approaches to coaching. *The Coaching Psychologist*, 7(2), 98–106.

Solution-focused approaches to facilitating purposeful positive change through methodologies such as coaching have great potential to contribute to the broader human change enterprise. To date, there has been limited exposition of psychological theory within the solution-focused arena, and few attempts to articulate taxonomies specific to solution-focused research, teaching and practice, thus restricting the development and broader adoption of the solution-focused paradigm. Drawing on the established solution-focused literature, this paper seeks to address this issue by articulating a tripartite taxonomy for solution-focused coaching based on the framework underpinning the Solution-Focused Inventory. This model consists of three factors: a) goal-orientation; b) resource activation; and c) problem disengagement – subscales of the solution-focused inventory. Implications of this taxonomy for teaching, research and practice are discussed and a range of future directions for research explored.

- Uppal, S., Oades, L. G., Crowe, T. P. and Deane, F. P. (2010). Barriers to transfer of collaborative recovery training into Australian mental health services: implications for the development of evidence-based services. *Journal of Evaluation in Clinical Practice*, 16, 451–455. doi:10.1111/j.1365-2753.2009.01141.x

Transfer of Training (ToT) is defined as the application of competencies acquired during training into the workplace. Poor ToT to clinical practice in mental health settings has negative implications for evidence-based service provision.

This study aimed to explore the variables influencing differences in ToT across mental health settings. Variables of interest included organization type, caseload and several variables related to the opportunity to use training. A total of 173 mental health clinicians from community-based governmental and non-governmental mental health services in eastern Australia were trained in recovery-oriented interventions. Measures of ToT included time taken until the implementation of intervention protocols, assessed using a clinical audit and a questionnaire survey completed by clinicians to identify barriers to implementation six months after training. Approximately 37 per cent of the trained clinicians participating in the study were found to be implementing training protocols in clinical practice. In addition, the average time taken to implement the protocols was 5.6 months following training. The most frequently cited barriers were institutional constraints. Higher caseloads and more frequent client contact were related to a higher level of ToT, which can be difficult to achieve in clinical practice. Greater facilitation of ToT may be achieved through better integration of the new ideology and protocols, regular monitoring of progress, staff incentives and examination of external attributions by clinicians of their responsibility to transfer training.

REFERENCES

Adzeh, K. J. (2014). The challenges of conducting a quantitative business research: analysis of issues with survey design, sampling, validity and reliability. *Research Gate*, para. 11. Retrieved from: www.researchgate.net/publication/261562480

Agee, G. (2009) Developing qualitative research questions: a reflective process. *International Journal of Qualitative Studies in Education, 22*(4), 431–447. DOI: 10.1080/09518390902736512

Alexandrova, A. (2017). *A philosophy for the science of wellbeing.* New York: Oxford University Press.

Allen, M. (2018). Errors of measurement: ceiling and floor effects. In *The SAGE Encyclopedia of Communication Research Methods* (pp. 434–435). Thousand Oaks, CA: SAGE.

Allen, T. D., Eby, L. T., & Lentz, E. (2006). Mentorship behaviors and mentorship quality associated with formal mentoring programs: closing the gap between research and practice. *Journal of Applied Psychology, 91*(3), 567.

Allen, T. D., Eby, L. T., Poteet, M. L., Lentz, E., & Lima, L. (2004). Career benefits associated with mentoring for protégés: a meta-analysis. *Journal of Applied Psychology, 89*(1), 127.

Altheide, D. L., & Johnson, J. M. (1994). Criteria for assessing interpretive validity in qualitative research. In N. K. Denzin, and Y. S. Lincoln (Eds.) *Handbook of qualitative research* (pp. 485–499). Thousand Oaks, CA: SAGE.

Australian Research Council (ARC) 2017 Engagement and impact assessment pilot 2017: report. www.arc.gov.au/policies-strategies/strategy/research-impact-principles-framework

Babbie, E. R. (2015). *The practice of social research.* New York: Cengage Learning.

Bandura, A. (1993). Perceived self-efficacy in cognitive development and functioning. *Educational Psychologist, 28*(2), 117–148. DOI: 10.1207/s15326985ep2802_3

Barbour, R. S. (2001). Checklists for improving rigour in qualitative research: a case of the tail wagging the dog? *British Medical Journal, 322*, 1115–1117.

Barker, C., Pistrang, N., & Elliot, R. (1994). *Research methods in clinical and counselling psychology.* Chichester: John Wiley & Sons.

Barker, C., Pistrang, N., & Elliott, R. (2002). *Research methods in clinical psychology: an introduction for students and practitioners* (2nd ed.). Chichester: John Wiley & Sons.

Baumeister, R. F., & Leary, M. R. (1997). Writing narrative literature reviews. *Review of General Psychology, 1*(3), 311.

Billig, M. (1988). Rhetorical and historical aspect of attitudes: the case of the British monarchy. *Philosophical Psychology, 1*, 83–103.

Black, T. R. (1999). *Doing quantitative research in the social sciences: an integrated approach to research design, measurement and statistics.* London: SAGE.

Bless, C., Higson-Smith, C., & Kagee, A. (2006). *Fundamentals of social research methods: an African perspective.* Cape Town: Juta.

Bolger N., & Laurenceau J-P. (2013). *Intensive longitudinal methods: an introduction to diary and experience sampling research.* New York: Guilford Press.

Bono, J. E., Purvanova, R. K., Towler, A. J., & Peterson, D. B. (2009). A survey of executive coaching practices. *Personnel Psychology, 62*(2), 361–404.

Borenstein, M., Hedges, L. V., Higgins, J. P., & Rothstein, H. R. (2009). *Introduction to meta-analysis.* Chichester: John Wiley & Sons.

Bosco, F. A., Aguinis, H., Singh, K., Field, J. G., & Pierce, C. A. (2015). Correlational effect size benchmarks. *Journal of Applied Psychology, 100*(2), 431.

Boyatzis, R. (1998). *Transforming qualitative information: thematic analysis and code development.* Thousand Oaks, CA: SAGE.

Bozeman, B., Feeney, M. K. (2007). Toward a useful theory of mentoring: a conceptual analysis and critique. *Administration & Society, 39*(6): 719–739. DOI:10.1177/0095399707304119

Braun, V., & Clarke, V. (2006). Using thematic analysis in psychology. *Qualitative research, 3*(2), 102–103.

Breen, R. L. (2006). A practical guide to focus-group research. *Journal of Geography in Higher Education, 30*(3), 463–475, DOI: 10.1080/03098260600927575

Brickman, L., & Rog, D. J. (Eds.). (2008). *The SAGE handbook of applied social research methods.* London: SAGE.

Brocki, J. J. M., & Wearden, A. J. (2006). A critical evaluation of the use of interpretative phenomenological analysis (IPA) in health psychology. *Psychology and Health, 21*(1), 87–108.

Burke, C. S., Stagl, K. C., Klein, C., Goodwin, G. F., Salas, E., & Halpin, S. M. (2006). What type of leadership behaviors are functional in teams? A meta-analysis. *The Leadership Quarterly, 17*(3), 288–307.

Burn, J., & Robins, G. (2003). Moving towards e-government: a case study of organisational change processes. *Logistics Information Management, 16*(1), 25–35, https://doi.org/10.1108/09576050310453714

Burns, D. (2007). *Systemic action research: a strategy for whole system change.* Bristol: Policy Press.

Burns, D. (2015). *Navigating complexity in international development: facilitating sustainable change at scale.* Rugby: Practical Action.

Burr, V. (1995). *An introduction to social constructionism.* London: Routledge.

Campbell, D. T., & Stanley, J. C. (2015). *Experimental and quasi-experimental designs for research.* Ravenio Books.

Campion, M. A., Campion, J. E., & Hudson, J. P., Jr. (1994). Structured interviewing: a note on incremental validity and alternative question types. *Journal of Applied Psychology, 79*, 998–1002.

Carr, L. T. (1994). The strengths and weaknesses of quantitative and qualitative research: what method for nursing? *Journal of Advanced Nursing, 20*(4), 716–721.

Carter, A., & Peterson, D. B. (2015). Evaluating coaching programs. In J. Passmore (Ed.), *Excellence in coaching: the industry guide* (pp. 273–286). London: Kogan Page.

Cavaye, A. L. M. (1996). Case study research: a multi-faceted research approach for IS, https://doi.org/10.1111/j.1365-2575.1996.tb00015.x

Cipriani, A., & Geddes, J. (2003). Comparison of systematic and narrative reviews: the example of the atypical antipsychotics. *Epidemiology and Psychiatric Sciences, 12*(3), 146–153.

Clark, L. A., & Watson, D. (1995). Constructing validity: basic issues in objective scale development. *Psychological Assessment, 7*(3), 309.

Clark, T., Wright, M., & Ketchen, D. J. (Eds.). (2016). *How to get published in the best management journals*. Cheltenham: Edward Elgar Publishing.

Cohen, J. (1988). *Statistical power analysis for the behavioral sciences* (2nd ed.). Hillsdale, NJ: Erlbaum.

Cohen, J. (1994). The Earth is round (p < .05). *American Psychologist, 49*, 997–1003.

Cohen, M. (2011). *Critical thinking skills for dummies*. New York: Wiley.

Cooksey, R. W., & McDonald, G. M. (2011). *Surviving and thriving in postgraduate research*. Prahran, Victoria: Tilde University Press.

Creswell, J. W. (1998). *Qualitative inquiry and research design: choosing among five traditions*. Thousand Oaks, CA: SAGE.

Creswell, J. W., & Creswell, J. D. (2017). *Research design: qualitative, quantitative, and mixed methods approaches*. Thousand Oaks, CA: SAGE.

Crowe, S., Cresswell, K., Robertson, A., Huby, G., Avery, A., & Sheikh, A. (2011). The case study approach. *BMC Medical Research Methodology, 11*, 100.

Cumming, G. (2014). The new statistics: why and how. *Psychological Science, 25*(1), 7–29.

Davies, M. B., & Hughes, N. (2014). *Doing a successful research project: using qualitative or quantitative methods*. London: Macmillan International Higher Education.

Davison, R., Martinsons, M., & Kock, N. (2004). Principles of canonical action research. *Information Systems Journal, 14*(1), 65–86.

Dearnley, C. (2005). A reflection on the use of semi-structured interviews. *Nurse Researcher, 13*(1), 19–28.

De Meuse, K. P., Dai, G., & Lee, R. J. (2009). Evaluating the effectiveness of executive coaching: Beyond ROI? *Coaching: An International Journal of Theory, Research and Practice, 2*(2), 117–134.

Denscombe, M. (2010). *The good research guide: for small-scale social research*. Maidenhead: McGraw-Hill.

Denzin N. K., & Lincoln, Y. S. (Eds.) (2008). *Collecting and interpreting qualitative materials*. Thousand Oaks, CA: SAGE.

Dickson-Swift, V., James, E. L., Kippen, S., & Liamputtong, P. (2007). Doing sensitive research: what challenges do qualitative researchers face? *Qualitative Research, 7*, 327–353.

Downs, S. H., & Black, N. (1998). The feasibility of creating a checklist for the assessment of the methodological quality both of randomized and non-randomized studies of health care interventions. *Journal of Epidemiology and Community Health, 52*(6), 377–384.

Dreyfus, J. L., & Rainbow, P. (1983). *Beyond structuralism and hermeneutics* (2nd edn). Chicago, IL: University of Chicago Press.

Drost, E. A. (2011). Validity and reliability in social science research. *Education Research and Perspectives, 38*(1), 105.

Easton, K. L., McComish, J. F., & Greenberg, R. (2000). Avoiding common pitfalls in qualitative data collection and transcription. *Qualitative Health Research, 10*, 703–707.

Eby, L. T., Allen, T. D., Evans, S. C., Ng, T., & DuBois, D. L. (2008). Does mentoring matter? A multidisciplinary meta-analysis comparing mentored and non-mentored individuals. *Journal of Vocational Behavior, 72*(2), 254–267.

Eby, L. T., Allen, T. D., Hoffman, B. J., Baranik, L. E., Sauer, J. B., Baldwin, S., ... & Evans, S. C. (2013). An interdisciplinary meta-analysis of the potential antecedents, correlates, and consequences of protégé perceptions of mentoring. *Psychological Bulletin, 139*(2), 441.

Edwards, D., & Potter, J. (1992). *Discursive psychology.* London: SAGE.

Faul, F., Erdfelder, E., Lang, A. G., & Buchner, A. (2007). G* Power 3: A flexible statistical power analysis program for the social, behavioral, and biomedical sciences. *Behavior Research Methods, 39*(2), 175–191.

Feldman, D. C., & Lankau, M. J. (2005). Executive coaching: A review and agenda for future research. *Journal of Management, 31*(6), 829–848.

Ferry, N. M., & Ross-Gordon, J. V. (1998). An inquiry into Schön's epistemology of practice: exploring links between experience and reflective practice. *Adult Education Quarterly, 48*(2), 98–112.

Field, A. (2009). *Discovering statistics using SPSS.* London: SAGE.

Field, A. P., & Gillett, R. (2010). How to do a meta-analysis. *British Journal of Mathematical and Statistical Psychology, 63*(3), 665–694.

Field, A., Miles, J., & Field, Z. (2012). *Discovering statistics using R.* London: SAGE.

Forrester, M. (Ed.). (2010). *Doing qualitative research in psychology: a practical guide.* London: SAGE.

Fouché, P., du Plessis, R., & van Niekerk, R. (2017). Levinsonian seasons in the life of Steve Jobs: a psychobiographical case study. *Indo-Pacific Journal of Phenomenology, 17*(1), 1–18.

Fraenkel, J. R., Wallen, N. E., & Hyun, H. H. (1993). *How to design and evaluate research in education* (Vol. 7). New York: McGraw-Hill.

Geddes, J., & Carney, S. (2002). Systematic reviews and meta-analyses. *Evidence in Mental Health Care.* London: Routledge, 73–80.

George, A. L., & Bennett. A. (2005). *Case studies and theory development in the social sciences.* Cambridge, MA: MIT Press.

Gergen, K. J. (1994). *Realities and relationships: soundings in social construction.* Cambridge, MA: Harvard University Press.

Gill, M. J. (2014). The possibilities of phenomenology for organizational research. *Organizational Research Methods, 17*(2), 118–137.

Gill, P., Stewart, K., Treasure, E., & Chadwick, B. (2008). Methods of data collection in qualitative research: interviews and focus groups. *British Dental Journal, 204*(6), 291–295.

Gough, D., Oliver, S., & Thomas, J. (Eds.). (2017). An introduction to systematic reviews. London: SAGE.

Grant, A. M. (2003). The impact of life coaching on goal attainment, metacognition and mental health. *Social Behavior and Personality: An International Journal, 31*(3), 253–263.

Grant, A. M. (2013). The efficacy of coaching. In J. Passmore, D. Peterson, D. & T. Freire (Eds.). *The Wiley-Blackwell handbook of the psychology of coaching and mentoring* (pp. 15–40). Chichester: John Wiley & Sons.

Grant, A. M. (2014a). Autonomy support, relationship satisfaction and goal focus in the coach–coachee relationship: which best predicts coaching success? *Coaching: An International Journal of Theory, Research and Practice, 7*(1), 18–38.

Grant, A. M. (2014b). The efficacy of executive coaching in times of organisational change. *Journal of Change Management, 14*(2), 258–280.

Grant, A. M. (2016). The contribution of qualitative research to coaching psychology: counting numbers is not enough, qualitative counts too. *The Journal of Positive Psychology*, DOI: 10.1080/17439760.2016.1262616

Grant, A. M., Curtayne, L., & Burton, G. (2009). Executive coaching enhances goal attainment, resilience and workplace well-being: a randomised controlled study. *The Journal of Positive Psychology, 4*(5), 396–407.

Grant, A. M., Passmore, J., Cavanagh, M. J., & Parker, H. M. (2010). The state of play in coaching today: a comprehensive review of the field. *International Review of Industrial and Organizational Psychology, 25*(1), 125–167.

Grant, M. A., Rohr, L. N., & Grant, J. T. (2012). How informants answer questions?: implications for reflexivity. *Field Methods, 24*(2), 230–246.

Gravetter, F. J., & Wallnau, L. B. (2016). *Statistics for the behavioral sciences.* Cengage Learning.

Green J. T. (2009). *Qualitative methods for health research* (2nd ed.) London: SAGE.

Green, L. S., Oades, L. G., & Grant, A. M. (2006). Cognitive-behavioral, solution-focused life coaching: enhancing goal striving, well-being, and hope. *The Journal of Positive Psychology, 1*(3), 142–149.

Greene, J. C., Caracelli, V. J., & Graham, W. F. (1989). Toward a conceptual framework for mixed-method evaluation designs. *Educational Evaluation and Policy Analysis, 11*(3), 255–274.

Gugiu, P. C., & Rodriquez-Campos, L. (2007). Semi-structured interview protocol for constructing logic models. *Evaluation and Program Planning, 30*, 339–350.

Guest, G., MacQueen, K. M., & Namey, E. E. (2012). *Applied thematic analysis.* Thousand Oaks, CA: SAGE. doi: 10.4135/9781483384436

Hayes, A. F. (2013). *Introduction to mediation, moderation, and conditional process analysis: a regression-based approach.* New York: The Guilford Press.

Hektner, J. M., Schmidt, J. A., & Csikszentmihalyi, M. (2007). *Experience sampling method: measuring the quality of everyday life.* Thousand Oaks, CA: SAGE.

Hembree, R. (1990). The nature, effects, and relief of mathematics anxiety. *Journal for Research in Mathematics Education, 21*, 33–46, DOI: 10.2307/749455

Hezlett, S. (2005). Protégés' learning in mentoring relationships: a review of the literature and an exploratory case study. *Advances in Developing Human Resources, 7*(4), November, 505–526, DOI: 10.1177/1523422305279686

Hollway, W. (1989). *Subjectivity and method in psychology: gender, meaning and science*. London: SAGE.

Hugh-Jones, S. (2010). The interview in qualitative research. In M. A. Forrester (Ed.). *Doing qualitative research in psychology: a practical guide*, pp. 77–97. London: SAGE.

Jadad, A. R., Moore, R. A., Carroll, D., Jenkinson, C., Reynolds, D. J. M., Gavaghan, D. J., et al. (1996). Assessing the quality of reports of randomized clinical trials: is blinding necessary? *Controlled Clinical Trials, 17*(1), 1–12.

Johnson, P., & Duberley, J. (2000). *Understanding management research*. London: SAGE.

Jones, R. J., Woods, S. A., & Guillaume, Y. R. (2016). The effectiveness of workplace coaching: A meta-analysis of learning and performance outcomes from coaching. *Journal of Occupational and Organizational Psychology, 89*(2), 249–277.

Kahneman, D. (2011). *Thinking, fast and slow* (p. 14). London: Penguin Books.

Kline, R. B. (2015). *Principles and practice of structural equation modeling*. New York: Guilford Publications.

Kvale, S. (1996). *Interviews: an introduction to qualitative research interviewing*. London: SAGE.

Larkin, M., Watts, S., & Clifton, E. (2006). Giving voice and making sense in interpretative phenomenological analysis. *Qualitative Research in Psychology, 3*(2), 102–120.

Lawn, R. B., Slemp, G. R., & Vella-Brodrick, D. A. (2018). Quiet flourishing: the authenticity and well-being of trait introverts living in the West depends on extraversion-deficit beliefs. *Journal of Happiness Studies*, 1–21.

Leech, N. L., & Onwuegbuzie, A. J. (2009). A typology of mixed methods research designs. *Quality & Quantity, 43*(2), 265–275.

Legard, R., Keegan, J., & Ward, K. (2003). In-depth interviews. In R. Ritchie, & J. Lewis (Eds.). *Qualitative research practice: a guide for social research students and researchers*. London: SAGE.

Lenth, R. V. (2001). Some practical guidelines for effective sample size determination. *The American Statistician, 55*(3), 187–193.

Lincoln, Y. S., & Guba, E. G. (1985). *Naturalistic inquiry*. Newbury Park, CA: SAGE.

Linley, P. A., Nielsen, K. M., Gillett, R., & Biswas-Diener, R. (2010). Using signature strengths in pursuit of goals: effects on goal progress, need satisfaction, and well-being, and implications for coaching psychologists. *International Coaching Psychology Review, 5*(1), 6–15.

Lipsey, M. W., & Wilson, D. B. (2001). *Practical meta-analysis*. Sage Publications, Inc.

MacFarlane, A., & Brún, M. O. (2012). Using a theory-driven conceptual framework in qualitative health research. *Qualitative Health Research, 22*(5), 607–618. https://doi.org/10.1177/1049732311431898

MacKenzie, S. B., Podsakoff, P. M., & Podsakoff, N. P. (2011). Construct measurement and validation procedures in MIS and behavioral research: integrating new and existing techniques. *MIS Quarterly, 35*(2), 293–334.

Malterud, K. (2001). Qualitative research: standards, challenges, and guidelines. *The Lancet, 358*(9280), 483–488.

Maxwell, J. A. (2009). Designing a qualitative study. In L. Bickman, & D. J. Rog (Eds.), *The SAGE Handbook of Applied Social Research Methods* (pp. 214–253), Thousand Oaks, CA: SAGE.

Mays, N., & Pope, C. (2000). Qualitative research in health care: assessing quality in qualitative research. *British Medical Journal, 320*(21), 50–52.

Moosa, I. A. (2018). *Publish or perish: perceived benefits versus unintended consequences.* Cheltenham: Edward Elgar Publishing.

Moriarty, M. F. (1997). *Writing science through critical thinking.* Burlington, MA: Jones & Bartlett Learning.

National Collaborating Centre for Methods and Tools. (2008). Quality assessment tool for quantitative studies (QATQS). Hamilton, ON: McMaster University.

NHMRC (2007, updated May 2015). National statement on ethical conduct in human research. The National Health and Medical Research Council, the Australian Research Council and the Australian Vice-Chancellors' Committee. Commonwealth of Australia, Canberra.

Nicholl, H. (2010). Diaries as a method of data collection in research. *Pediatric Nursing, 22*(7), 16–20.

Nijhawan, L. P., Janodia, M. D., Muddukrishna, B. S., Bhat, K. M., Bairy, K. L., Udupa, N., & Musmade, P. B. (2013). Informed consent: issues and challenges. *Journal of Advanced Pharmaceutical Technology & Research, 4*(3), 134–140.

Oades, L. G. & Spence, G. (2017). Positive tertiary education in a residential setting. Kooloobong Village. In M. Slade, L. Oades, & A. Jarden (Eds.). *Wellbeing, recovery and mental health* (pp. 265–276). Cambridge: Cambridge University Press.

Onwuegbuzie, A. J., & Johnson, R. B. (2006). The validity issue in mixed research. *Research in the Schools, 13*(1), 48–63.

Onwuegbuzie, A. J., Johnson, R. B., & Collins, K. M. (2011). Assessing legitimation in mixed research: a new framework. *Quality & Quantity, 45*(6), 1253–1271.

Orvik, A., Larun, L., Berland, A., & Ringsberg, K. C. (2013). Situational factors in focus group studies: a systematic review. *International Journal of Qualitative Methods, 12*(8), 338–358.

Pan, S. L., & Tan, B. (2011). Demystifying case research: a structured–pragmatic–situational (SPS) approach to conducting case studies. *Information and Organization, 21*(3), 161–176.

Parker, I. (1992). *Discourse dynamics: critical analysis for social and individual psychology.* New York: Routledge.

Parker, A., & Tritter, J. (2006) Focus group method and methodology: current practice and recent debate. *International Journal of Research & Method in Education, 29*(1), 23–37, DOI: 10.1080/01406720500537304

Passmore, J., & Theeboom, T. (2016). Coaching psychology research: a journey of development in research. In L. E. van Zyl, et al. (Eds.). *Meta-theoretical perspectives and applications for multi-cultural contexts of coaching and psychology.* Switzerland: Springer.

Patton, M. Q. (2008). Utilization-focused evaluation (3rd ed.). Thousand Oaks, CA. SAGE.

Persch, A. C., & Page, S. J. (2013). Protocol development, treatment fidelity, adherence to treatment, and quality control. *American Journal of Occupational Therapy, 67*(2), 146–153.

Podsakoff, P. M., & Organ, D. W. (1986). Self-reports in organizational research: problems and prospects. *Journal of Management, 12*(4), 531–544.

Podsakoff, P. M., MacKenzie, S. B., Lee, J. Y., & Podsakoff, N. P. (2003). Common method biases in behavioral research: a critical review of the literature and recommended remedies. *Journal of Applied Psychology, 88*(5), 879.

Pollack, J. M., Vanepps, E. M., & Hayes, A. F. (2012). The moderating role of social ties on entrepreneurs' depressed affect and withdrawal intentions in response to economic stress. *Journal of Organizational Behavior, 33*(6), 789–810.

Pope, C., Ziebland, S., & Mays, N. (2000). Analysing qualitative data: qualitative research in health care. *British Medical Journal, 320,* 114–116.

Potter, J., & Wetherell, M. (1987). *Discourse and social psychology: beyond attitudes and behaviour.* London: SAGE.

Punch, K. (1998). *Introduction to social research: quantitative and qualitative approaches.* London: SAGE.

Punch, K. F. (2009). *Introduction to research methods in education.* London: SAGE.

Punch, K. (2013). *Introduction to social research: quantitative and qualitative approaches* (3rd ed.). London: SAGE.

Punch, K. & Oancea, A. (2014). *An introduction to research methods in education* (2nd ed.). London: SAGE.

Reason, P. and Bradbury, H. (2008) (Eds.) *The SAGE handbook of action research: participative inquiry and practice.* Thousand Oaks, CA: SAGE.

Reid, K., Flowers, P., & Larkin, M. (2005) Exploring lived experience: an introduction to interpretative phenomenological analysis. *The Psychologist, 18*(1), 20–23.

Rimando, M., Brace, A. M., Namageyo-Funa, A., Parr, T. L., Sealy, D., Davis, T. L., Martinez, L. M., & Christiana, R. W. (2015). Data collection challenges and recommendations for early career researchers. *The Qualitative Report, 20*(12), 2025–2036. Retrieved from: https://nsuworks.nova.edu/tqr/vol20/iss12/8

Robson, C., & McCartan, K. (2016). *Real world research.* Chichester: John Wiley & Sons.

Schmidt, F. L. (1996). Statistical significance testing and cumulative knowledge in psychology: implications for training of researchers. *Psychological Methods, 1,* 115–129.

Schmidt, F. L. (2010). Detecting and correcting the lies that data tell. *Perspectives on Psychological Science, 5*(3), 233–242.

Schmidt, F. L. (2017). Beyond questionable research methods: the role of omitted relevant research in the credibility of research. *Archives of Scientific Psychology, 5*(1), 32.

Schmidt, F. L., & Hunter, J. E. (2015). *Methods of meta-analysis: correcting error and bias in research findings.* London: SAGE.

Schmidt, F. L., & Oh, I. S. (2016). The crisis of confidence in research findings in psychology: Is lack of replication the real problem? Or is it something else? *Archives of Scientific Psychology, 4*(1), 32.

Schoonenboom, J., & Johnson, R. B. (2017). How to construct a mixed methods research design: Wie man ein Mixed Methods-Forschungs-Design konstruiert. *KZfSS Kölner Zeitschrift für Soziologie und Sozialpsychologie, 69*(2), 107–131.

Sheikh, A., Halani, L., Bhopal, R., Netuveli, G., Partridge, M., Car, J., et al. (2009). Facilitating the recruitment of minority ethnic people into research: qualitative case study of South Asians and asthma. *PLoS Medicine, 6*(10), 1–11.

Shiffman, S., Stone, A. A., & Hufford, M. R. (2008). Ecological momentary assessment. *Annual Review of Clinical Psychology*, *4*(1), 32. DOI: 10.1146/annurev.clinpsy.3.022806.091415

Shotter, J. (1993). *Cultural politics of everyday life: social constructionism, rhetoric and knowing of the third kind*. Toronto: University of Toronto Press.

Siegfried, G. (2013). Conducting organizational-based evaluations of coaching and mentoring programs. In J. Passmore, D. Peterson, & T. Freire (Eds.). *The Wiley-Blackwell handbook of the psychology of coaching and mentoring* (pp. 445–470). Chichester: John Wiley & Sons.

Silvia, P. J. (2007). *How to write a lot: a practical guide to productive academic writing*. Washington, DC: American Psychological Association.

Simons, H. (2009) *Case study research in practice*. London: SAGE.

Slemp, G. R., Jach, H. K., Chia, A., Loton, D. L., & Kern, M. L. (2019). Contemplative interventions and employee distress: a meta-analysis. *Stress and Health*. Published online first. doi: https://doi.org/10.1002/smi.2857

Slemp, G. R., Kern, M. L., Patrick, K. J., & Ryan, R. M. (2018). Leader autonomy support in the workplace: a meta-analytic review. *Motivation and Emotion*, *42*(5), 706–724.

Smith, J. A. (Ed.). (2003). *Qualitative psychology: a practical guide to research methods*. London: SAGE.

Smith, J. A. (2007). Hermeneutics, human sciences and health: linking theory and practice. *International Journal of Qualitative Studies on Health and Well-Being*, *2*, 3–11.

Smith, J. A. (2011). Evaluating the contribution of interpretative phenomenological analysis. *Health Psychology Review*, *5*(1), 9–27.

Smith, J. A., & Osborn, M. (2003). Interpretative phenomenological analysis. In J. A. Smith (Ed.). *Qualitative psychology: a practical guide to research methods* (pp. 51–80). London: SAGE.

Spence, G. B., Armour, M. R., Driessen, D., Lea, R. P., & North, J. (2016). Contributing to coaching knowledge whilst learning how to research: a review and discussion of four student-coaching studies. *Coaching: an international journal of theory, research and practice*, *9*(2), 169–184.

Spence, G. B., & Grant, A. M. (2007). Professional and peer life coaching and the enhancement of goal striving and well-being: an exploratory study. *The Journal of Positive Psychology*, *2*(3), 185–194.

Spence, G. B. & Grant, A. M. (2012). Coaching and well-being: a brief review of existing evidence, relevant theory and implications for practitioners. In S. David, I. Boniwell, & A. Conley Ayers (Eds.). *The Oxford handbook of happiness* (pp. 1009–1025). Oxford: Oxford University Press.

Stake R. E. (1995). *The art of case study research*. London: SAGE.

Stake, R. E. (2006). *Multiple case study analysis*. New York: Guilford Press.

Stone, A., Shiffman, S., Atienza, A., et al. (2007). *The science of real-time data capture: self-reports in health research*. New York: Oxford University Press.

Strauss, A., & Corbin, J. M. (1990). *Basics of qualitative research: grounded theory procedures and techniques*. Thousand Oaks, CA: SAGE.

Stuckey, H. L. (2013). Three types of interviews: qualitative research methods in social health. *Journal of Social Health and Diabetes*, *1*, 56–9.

Stufflebeam, D. L., & Shinkfield, A. J. (2007). *Evaluation theory, models and applications*. San Francisco, CA: Jossey Bass.

Tabachnick, B. G., & Fidell, L. S. (2007). *Using multivariate statistics*. Boston, MA: Allyn & Bacon/Pearson Education.

Theeboom, T., Beersma, B., & van Vianen, A. E. (2014). Does coaching work? A meta-analysis on the effects of coaching on individual level outcomes in an organizational context. *The Journal of Positive Psychology, 9*(1), 1–18.

Torbert, W. R. (1981). Why educational research has been so uneducational: the case for a new model of social science based on collaborative inquiry. In P. Reason, & J. Rowan, *Human Inquiry* (pp. 141–151). Chichester: John Wiley & Sons.

Tversky, A., & Kahneman, D. (1971). Belief in the law of small numbers. *Psychological Bulletin, 76*(2), 105.

Tversky, A., & Kahneman, D. (1974). Judgments under uncertainty: heuristics and biases. *Science, 185*(4157), 1124–1131, DOI:10.1126/science.185.4157.1124, PMID 17835457, reprinted in D. Kahneman, P. Slovic, & A. Tversky (Eds.) (1982). *Judgment under uncertainty: heuristics and biases* (pp. 3–20). Cambridge: Cambridge University Press.

UNESCO *Statistical Yearbook* (2001). 68 and 65, Ch. 5. Paris: UNESCO.

Vella, S. A., Crowe, T. P., & Oades, L. G. (2013). Increasing the effectiveness of formal coach education: evidence of a parallel process. *International Journal of Sports Science & Coaching, 8*(2), 417–430.

Verhagen, S. J., Hasmi, L., Drukker, M., van Os, J., & Delespaul, P. A. (2016). Use of the experience sampling method in the context of clinical trials. *Evidence-Based Mental Health, 19*(3), 86–89.

Vogt, W. P., Gardner, D. C., & Haeffele, L. M. (2012). *When to use what research design*. New York: Guilford Press.

Whitmore, J. (2010). *Coaching for performance: growing human potential and purpose: the principles and practice of coaching and leadership*. London: Nicholas Brealey Publishing.

Wilkinson, L. (1999). Statistical methods in psychology journals: guidelines and explanations. *American Psychologist, 54*, 594–604. http://dx.doi.org/10.1037/0003-066X.54.8.594

Woods, P. (1999). *Successful writing for qualitative researchers*. New York: Routledge.

Yardley, L. (2000). Dilemmas in qualitative health research. *Psychology and Health, 15*, 215–28.

Yin, R. (1999). Enhancing the quality of case studies in health services research. *Health Services Research, 34*(29), 1209–1224.

Yin, R. K. (2003). *Case study research design and methods* (3rd ed.). London: SAGE.

Yin, R. K. (2018). *Case study research and applications: design and methods* (6th ed.). Thousand Oaks, CA: SAGE.

INDEX

NOTE: page numbers in *italic type* refer to tables and figures.